MUDSLINGERS

Mudslingers

THE TOP 25 NEGATIVE POLITICAL CAMPAIGNS OF ALL TIME

Countdown from No. 25 to No. 1

KERWIN C. SWINT

PRAEGER

Westport, Connecticut
London

Library of Congress Cataloging-in-Publication Data

Swint, Kerwin C.
　Mudslingers : the top 25 negative political campaigns of all time : countdown from no. 25 to no. 1 / Kerwin C. Swint.
　　p. cm.
　Includes bibliographical references and index.
　ISBN 0–275–98510–5 (alk. paper)
　1. Political campaigns—United States—History. 2. Advertising, Political—United States—History. 3. Negativism. I. Title: Top 25 negative political campaigns of all time. II. Title.
　JK2281.S883　2006
　324.7'0973—dc22　　　2005020948

British Library Cataloguing in Publication Data is available.

Library of Congress Catalog Card Number: 2005020948
ISBN: 0–275–98510–5

First published in 2006

Praeger Publishers, 88 Post Road West, Westport, CT 06881
An imprint of Greenwood Publishing Group, Inc.
www.praeger.com

Printed in the United States of America

The paper used in this book complies with the
Permanent Paper Standard issued by the National
Information Standards Organization (Z39.48–1984).

10 9 8 7 6 5 4 3 2 1

38.21　　　324.709
　　　　　　Swi

Dedicated to my wife, Sandy; and my three boys,
Jake, Zach, and Matt

CONTENTS

Contents

ACKNOWLEDGMENTS

First, I'd like to acknowledge the groundbreaking work of authors such as Paul Boller, Greg Mitchell, Dan Carter, Shelley Ross, Larry Sabato, and Kathleen Hall-Jamieson. They help to blaze a trail for the rest of us and inspire us to look at politics and history in new ways.

I'd also like to thank the many librarians, archivists, and others who helped me obtain the images in the book. Specifically, John Anderson of the Texas State Library and Archives Commission, Ken Tilley of the Alabama State Archives, Heather Moore of the U.S. Senate Historical Office, Bert Altman of the Claude Pepper Museum, and Joanne Nestor of the New Jersey State Archives were a tremendous help. I should also thank the archivists at the Library of Congress for maintaining and making available their national treasures of historic photographs and images.

A big thank you to Hilary Claggett of Praeger Publishers, who believed in this project and helped bring it to fruition.

Finally, I'd like to thank several of my students who were instrumental in helping me locate and obtain photos, including Christy Allen, Brad Klaus, Liz Pierson, and Courtney Henderson.

PROLOGUE

Don't let them fool you—people love negative campaigns. In survey after survey, registered voters say they don't like the negativity and the mudslinging in politics. But if that is true, then why is there so much mudslinging in campaigns? One reason is that the consultants who run most campaigns these days insist that they work. Maybe they are right; people love soap operas and they love gossip—and political campaigns have plenty of both.

There is another reason negative campaigns may be effective—people remember them. In this regard, this book is a sort of "greatest hits" compilation. There have been some very effective, very memorable, and very nasty political campaigns in the last couple hundred years, and the "top 25" are chronicled here.

This book covers more than two hundred years of American politics, beginning in 1800 with the bitter feud between Thomas Jefferson and John Adams, and ending with the 2004 blowout between George W. Bush and John Kerry. In between, there are rascals, patriots, robber barons, soldiers, and TV stars. And that's just among the presidential candidates.

The list of the most negative campaigns of all time also includes U.S. congressional races, races for governor, and even some for mayor. It was very difficult to choose just twenty-five campaigns because when looking at the vast landscape of American political history, there is a lot of material to choose from. It might be tempting to focus only on presidential races because they are the best known, and certainly they are usually extremely nasty affairs. But there are some, actually quite a few, campaigns below the level of president that deserved to make the list.

After all, was the 1984 race between Ronald Reagan and Walter Mondale particularly dirty, or was the 1996 campaign between Bill Clinton and Bob

Dole one for the ages? Absolutely not. But look at the 1983 mayoral campaign in Chicago between Harold Washington and Bernard Epton—it almost tore the city to shreds. And look at the 1934 campaign of the novelist Upton Sinclair to defeat California governor Frank Merriam—it almost caused a civil war.

So any ranking and analysis of the dirtiest campaigns ever has to look at all levels of office, not just president. But if there are so many to choose from, how does one do the choosing? Unfortunately, there is no easy answer or easy method. You could quantify the number of attacks per candidate per campaign, or measure the volume and depth of media advertising campaigns. You could employ some statistical maneuvers and weight various factors involved in the selection process. You could also rely on press clippings and interview historians about the most negative campaigns ever.

But none of these methods will provide a reliable solution. Some of the measures will be misleading, some of the statistics will turn out to be useless, and some of the factors will be weighted incorrectly. You would probably end up with the most negative campaign of all time being the 1966 campaign for mayor of Ottumwa, Iowa—not very exciting and totally useless.

When compiling a list, some are no-brainers—for example, the 1884 campaign between Grover Cleveland and James G. Blaine, remembered for the sarcastic chants of the Cleveland-haters: "Ma, Ma, Where's My Pa?" Voters had to decide between a candidate accused of fathering a child out of wedlock and a candidate who was the 1880s equivalent of Richard Nixon. Another is the 1828 rematch between Andrew Jackson and John Quincy Adams—a campaign so vile that it was blamed for the death of Jackson's wife, who succumbed to illness before her husband's inauguration.

And there are numerous 20th-century campaigns just as notorious, such as the 1950 U.S. Senate campaign of Richard Nixon, who ran against "the Pink Lady." There is the 1988 presidential campaign of George Herbert Walker Bush, which introduced the country to one of the most famous political names ever—Willie Horton. And there is the 1998 U.S. Senate campaign between New Yorkers Al D'Amato and Charles Schumer, who did everything but spit in each other's faces.

So, some are automatic. Few would disagree with including George Wallace's race-baiting campaign for Alabama governor in 1970, or the match between Abe Lincoln and his former commanding general, George McClellan, in 1864.

Beyond those ten or twelve that most people agree with, there is room for debate. The campaigns that round out the list of the top 25 were chosen because, in addition to being negative and nasty, they were significant in other ways. For example, the 1964 presidential campaign between Lyndon Johnson and Arizona senator Barry Goldwater was the first to highlight television advertising as a tool of political attack and mudslinging.

Another example is the vicious 1991 campaign for Louisiana governor. As far as anyone could remember, it was the first time voters had a choice between a corrupt, indicted former governor and the imperial wizard of the Ku Klux Klan.

And historians love the 1876 presidential campaign of Rutherford Hayes and Samuel Tilden. It involved a constitutional crisis lasting several months, which was not settled until literally days before the scheduled inauguration of the new president in March 1877. The "post-campaign" campaign was in some ways worse than anything the supporters of Hayes and Tilden had to say about each other leading up to election day the previous November.

So read on, take it all in, and see if you agree with the presence and rank of the campaigns included here.

MUDSLINGERS

FROM VIETNAM TO IRAQ

George W. Bush v. John Kerry, President, 2004

I can't believe I'm losing to this idiot.[1]

—John Kerry

Yes, the 2004 presidential election between George W. Bush and John Kerry was negative. Very negative. Intensely negative. But so are most, if not all, presidential elections in the modern era, you might say. That might be true, but this one was special.

Most observers agree: the negativity and mudslinging in 2004 were very bad—historically bad. Political scientist Kathleen Hall-Jamieson said it was "as dirty as I can remember." The 2004 campaign set a new modern standard for hostility and campaign warfare.

As *Los Angeles Times* reporter Janet Hook reports, "It has evolved into one of the most relentlessly negative political campaigns in memory, as attacks on a candidate's character, patriotism, and fitness for office, which once seemed out of bounds, have become routine. More ads than ever focused on discrediting an opponent rather than promoting a candidate, and independent political analysts warned the presidential campaign was breaking new ground in a candidate's willingness to bend the truth."[2]

So, what set this one apart from the 1992 election between Bush's father and Bill Clinton, or the 2000 race between George W. and Al Gore? Unlike 2004, for much of the 1992 election year, George H. W. Bush and his campaign ignored Clinton. The Bush team started its reelection campaign very late, preferring to focus on the president's duties, much like Jimmy Carter

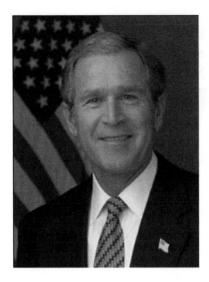

George W. Bush. White House photo by Eric Draper. Courtesy White House Photo Office.

had in 1980. It dismissed Clinton as a liberal, Democratic governor of "a small southern state."

In 2000, it did get very rough and at times personal. George W.'s supporters mocked Al Gore for his exaggerations, such as "inventing the Internet" and being the basis for the lead character in the movie *Love Story*. And Vice President Gore's team derided Bush as "not intelligent" enough to be president and a failure in private business. But much of this was an interesting sideshow to most Americans, an amusing circus, compared to the raw emotions and open wounds of the 2004 contest between Bush and Kerry.

Why was 2004 so different? One word: Iraq. The war in Iraq and the American response to the "War on Terror" drove the politics of 2004. It is the main reason that John Kerry got the Democratic nomination in the first place. Many Democratic leaders and primary voters believed Senator Kerry brought to the ticket a candidate with solid foreign-policy credentials; two decades of experience in national politics; and, most important, a distinguished record of military service in Vietnam.

Why was his military background so important? It gave him the legitimacy to criticize the war in Iraq and President Bush in a way that other Democratic candidates at the time—Howard Dean, Dick Gephardt, and the others—did not have. And since Kerry was solidly opposed to the war, as most Democratic leaders were, Kerry was the candidate best positioned to provide a credible voice of opposition to President Bush.

Kerry's team made his military background and his opposition to the Iraq war the centerpiece of its effort to oust George W. Bush from office. The dominant image from the Democratic National Convention in Boston was Senator Kerry, in his acceptance speech, saluting and "reporting for duty."

Of course, this played right into the Bush campaign's hands. Bush and his aides viewed a strong public focus on the terror war and efforts to secure Iraq as a "good" thing, provided events in Iraq didn't spin too far out of control. Their challenge was to paint Kerry as "not" credible, as someone who said

Senator Kerry was an "establishment" Democrat who could carry the party's antiwar message. AP/Wide World Photos.

things only for political gain, and as a president who would irresponsibly cede American power to "foreign" control, such as the United Nations. In this, they largely accomplished their goals.

The seeds of the nastiness of the 2004 campaign also grew from the ruins of the 2000 election and its aftermath. The Supreme Court decision that sealed the election for Bush over Gore was a bitter pill for many Americans, especially Democrats. And the fact that Gore won more overall popular votes than Bush led to an impression among many Americans that Bush had "backed into" the presidency.

The Democrats were livid. Many viewed Bush as an illegitimate president and held it against him throughout his first term. A significant number of Democrats saw it as their mission to defeat Bush in 2004 at all costs. It was similar to how many Republicans felt toward President Bill Clinton in the 1990s—pure, unbridled hatred.

Thus, when Democratic primary voters surveyed the field of candidates running in 2004, John Kerry seemed the most "electable"—a phrase that turned up routinely in media exit polls throughout the early Democratic presidential primaries. Though many Democrats were drawn to the strong antiwar views of former Vermont governor Howard Dean, Kerry was seen as less controversial and more mainstream. So, "electability" and "beating Bush" became the focus of the Democratic campaign.

Republicans were just as determined to reelect Bush. They—and Bush himself—badly wanted a second term to legitimize his claim to the presidency. And it was the War on Terror, and what they saw as Bush's success in rallying the country and defending its interests, that Republicans also wanted to vindicate in 2004.

VERY NEGATIVE, VERY EARLY

Former governor Howard Dean of Vermont was the early front-runner among Democrats for the presidential nomination. Part of the reason was that he was the most critical of President Bush on the Iraq war, and he staked out a very strong antiwar position when other Democratic candidates thought it was too risky to do so.

That earned him the admiration and loyalty of a number of Democratic Party activists around the country. This, in turn, led other Democratic candidates—including Kerry and Missouri's Richard Gephardt—to try and catch up to Dean on the issue. Thus, during the Democratic primaries and caucuses, the public heard candidate after candidate pummel George W. Bush on Iraq and his handling of the War on Terror.

During this time, the job-approval rating of President Bush dipped down into the forties, as many voters questioned his judgment and his handling of foreign affairs. The Bush administration, while very much aware of the barrage of criticism of the president and the damage it was causing him politically, held back from returning fire until it was certain which Democrat would emerge with the nomination.

Then, in early March, after the Super Tuesday primaries made it clear that Kerry would win the nomination, the Bush campaign pounced. In campaign appearances and in TV ads, the Bush team labeled Kerry not only as too liberal for the presidency but as someone who did not have the character and integrity required of the job.

Bush called him a flip-flopper for saying different things at different times about Iraq, the terror war, and economic policies as well. Of course, Senator Kerry did hand the Bush team some of the best material it could have hoped for to drive home its point.

For example, in responding to criticism that he did not support the $87 billion spending bill for the war in Iraq and therefore did not support the troops, he told an audience, "I actually did vote for the $87 billion before I voted against it." In his effort to appear moderate and reasonable on the issue, he only reinforced Bush's message that he wanted to have everything both ways and did not have an ethical core.

It was one of the biggest gaffes of the campaign and one that Bush used time and again throughout the election season. From that point until election day in November, the campaign from both sides was mean-spirited and vicious. Usually in a presidential election, the two candidates zero in on each other after the party conventions; in 2004, however, it was a nine-month marathon of mud.

From the standpoint of some observers, it was the earliest start to negative campaigning at the presidential level in quite some time. Because the Bush campaign spent "an unprecedented sum" on advertising so early in the campaign, "the average voter is getting a much more negative impression," said Ken Goldstein, who tracks political advertising at the University of Wisconsin at Madison.[3]

> No American has gone directly from service in the U.S. Congress to the presidency since John F. Kennedy in 1960. John Kerry joins Bob Dole, Walter Mondale, George McGovern, and Barry Goldwater as those U.S. senators who were nominated by their party but lost the election. Hubert Humphrey and Al Gore were sitting vice presidents when they were nominated, but both of them lost.

Dana Milbank and Jim Vande Hei of the *Washington Post* reported, "from the president and (Vice President) Cheney down to media aides stationed in every battleground state and volunteers who dress up like Flipper the flip-flopping dolphin at rallies, the Bush campaign relentlessly portrays Kerry as elitist, untrustworthy, liberal, and a flip-flopper on major issues."

But Milbank and Vande Hei, along with political observers interviewed by them, also accused President Bush of making false or misleading statements about Senator Kerry. "Scholars and political strategists say the ferocious Bush assault on Kerry this spring has been extraordinary, both for the volume of attacks and for liberties the President and his campaign have taken with the facts. Though stretching the truth is hardly new in a political campaign, they say the volume of negative charges is unprecedented—both in speeches and in advertising."[4]

RISE OF THE 527S

One of the reasons that the 2004 campaign was so memorably nasty was the role played by the 527s—independent political organizations named for the section of the Internal Revenue Service code that governs such groups.

As the other campaigns described in this book will show, much of the nastiness and vitriol have always come from groups and supporters outside a candidate's campaign organization. Unlike the campaign itself, these organizations and individuals are free to be as hard-hitting and dirty as they wanna be. But in 1884, Grover Cleveland's supporters did not have a multimillion dollar budget, television advertising, and the Internet.

After the McCain-Feingold campaign-finance reforms were passed, eliminating soft money, the national parties could no longer spend unregulated amounts to influence voters. But the money simply found another way into the campaign. Individuals began organizing their own political groups to collect money and spend it on independent political advertising. These 527s were one of the dominant features of the 2004 race.

The ads created by these groups were overwhelmingly negative. According to William Benoit, a professor of communication at the University of Missouri, approximately 80 percent of the television ads run by sources other than the candidates were attack ads.[5]

"Run by political pros and accountable largely to themselves, the groups are loud, mean, and devastatingly effective. They are also loaded, in part from lavish donations from billionaires like George Soros and T. Boone Pickens, who are blunt about their desire to influence the vote. . . . Soros pledged to spend as much of his fortune as necessary to beat Bush. He even boasted he'd spend it all if it would guarantee a Kerry win."[6]

The one rule that 527s are supposed to follow is a prohibition on any form of coordination with a candidate's campaign. But this was a laugh, as the groups on both sides hired partisan fund-raisers and staff, many of whom had worked in previous presidential campaigns.

The most egregious example was Benjamin Ginsberg, a Bush campaign attorney who also advised two Republican-leaning but supposedly independent 527 organizations. He resigned when the link became known. Another Bush campaign consultant, Tom Synhorst, was the founder of one pro-Bush 527, Progress for America.

On the Kerry side, one of the largest 527s, the Media Fund, was founded and directed by former Clinton White House official and later a top official

John Kerry's post–Vietnam War activities were exploited by pro-Bush groups, such as the Swift Boat Veterans. AP/Wide World Photos.

with the Democratic National Committee, Harold Ickes. Jim Jordan, who had been Kerry's campaign manager until being replaced early in the campaign, also went to work for the Media Fund. And Joe Sandler, a legal adviser to the DNC, also advised a Democratic 527 group, MoveOn.org.

MoveOn v. the Swift Boats

Early in 2004, it was Democratic 527s that were getting all the attention and impacting the race. One of the big names in 527s was a pro-Democrat, anti-Bush group called MoveOn.org. Billionaire businessman George Soros contributed millions of dollars to this one group alone. MoveOn developed a very aggressive presence on the Internet and on television in some of the key battleground states. One of their early TV ads compared George W. Bush to Adolf Hitler, creating quite a stir and producing denunciations from the White House.

But the eight hundred-pound gorilla turned out to be a start-up group, with very little money at first, called Swift Boat Veterans for Truth. This was a group of Vietnam veterans who had served on or near swift boats in the Mekong Delta of Vietnam, as had Kerry. The members of this group all had one thing in common: They hated John Kerry.

They viewed Kerry as a traitor and a liar. Kerry's antiwar activities upon returning from Vietnam might have been enough to produce resentment from these men, but what stoked their white-hot anger was Kerry's testimony to Congress that soldiers in Vietnam "routinely" committed war crimes and atrocities "reminiscent of Ghengis Khan."

Kerry's role as one of the leaders of Vietnam Veterans Against the War, and his notoriety for throwing his medals over the fence at the White House and leading antiwar speeches and marches motivated this group of veterans to take action. They ran ads in key battleground states questioning the senator's statements about his service in the war.

Based on his reports and statements by his crew, Senator Kerry had been awarded four Purple Hearts for injuries sustained in combat. But veterans who had served on other boats in the area refuted his story. In its TV ads, the Swift Boat Veterans group claimed he had inflated his role in combat and was not deserving of the medals he was awarded.

The group also ran ads that featured the senator's role as a Vietnam protester. It featured photos, well known by now, of Kerry speaking to Congress, while voice-overs talked of how offensive it was for John Kerry to besmirch the memory of the fallen and to tarnish their service to their country with his self-serving and "false" testimony.

The Kerry campaign, and most of the national media, took little notice at first. But when tracking polls began to show Kerry's support slipping in the states where these ads were running, political reporters focused on the role of the "Swifties," as they were called. Meanwhile, in the Kerry camp, aides were divided over how to respond and what to do.

Congressional Democrats and party officials urged the Kerry campaign to strongly denounce the ads and counterattack as a means of returning fire and deflecting attention. But senior Kerry advisers, such as campaign manager Mary Beth Cahill, urged restraint, arguing that the Swift Boat attacks would not cause significant damage and might even backfire on the pro-Bush forces.[7]

It is hard to overestimate the significance of the Swift Boat Veterans' attacks on Kerry. He had been running his campaign and basing his intense criticism of Bush's Iraq policy on his experience, and his Vietnam service was a large part of that. When it was called into question by veterans themselves, it removed a chunk of Kerry's rationale in seeking the presidency, at least to many voters.

CBS NEWS AND DAN RATHER

For a while, it looked as if President Bush was going to have his own "Vietnam" problem, as CBS News's *60 Minutes* once again looked into gaps in his service in the Texas and Alabama National Guard. But the segment used documents that were later proven to be forgeries, which made the story collapse, and Bush escaped any more scrutiny.

The Kerry campaign was apparently uninvolved in the episode, but had fervently hoped it would prove as costly to Bush as the Swift Boat ads had been to Kerry. As soon as the story aired, Internet posters on Web logs, or bloggers, questioned the authenticity of the documents. Then the "experts" CBS had used to authenticate the documents let their own doubts about them become public.

At first defensive and combative, CBS and Dan Rather had no choice but to back off the story. After an investigation, four CBS producers and staffers were fired, and Rather's own credibility took another hit. If anything, the whole thing boomeranged around to hurt Kerry. To many in the public, it looked as if the media, specifically CBS, had joined the Kerry campaign, but in their overeagerness had botched the job.

UP CLOSE AND PERSONAL

Certainly, one of the distinguishing characteristics that made campaign 2004 one of the most negative in modern times was the personal nature of many of the statements and criticisms. Modern campaigns are full of such name calling and personal attacks, but they usually do not come from the actual campaign organization, from official party sources, or from the candidates themselves. In 2004 they did, or at least they seemed to.

And it started early. In March 2004, for example, Kerry responded to reporters' questions about President Bush this way: "Let me tell you, we've just begun to fight. We're going to keep pounding. These guys are the most crooked, you know, the most lying group I've ever seen."[8] When the White House cried foul and asked Senator Kerry to apologize for the strong words, he refused.

The tone and the language used from official Kerry campaign sources and from party sources was unusually blunt and tough. Terry McAuliffe, the chairman of the Democratic National Committee, routinely called Bush a liar and a "deserter"—a reference to questions over the president's service in the National Guard during the Vietnam War.

But the Bush team could dish it out pretty well too. The president himself called Senator Kerry's honesty and integrity into question multiple times on the campaign trail. And when asked to condemn the harsh tone and words of the Swift Boat ads, he refused, preferring to question the role "of all such groups in the political process."

So, was 2004 the worst ever? Not by historical standards. But by modern standards, it has to rank in the top three or four. Ken Goldstein, director of the University of Wisconsin Advertising Project, says, "It's always tempting to say the campaign you're in is the worst ever, but this time it might actually be true. . . . you always had wacky things said by fringe groups. Now you're seeing it by mainstream groups and the candidates themselves."[9]

IT'S A JUNGLE OUT THERE

Upton Sinclair v. Frank Merriam, Governor, California, 1934

This is the question that's thinning my hair,
What'll I do about Upton Sinclair?

If I embrace him the slams will be hot,
And I'll be roasted if I do not.

Choosing a course is not such a snap,
Why did they put that guy in my lap?
　　　　　　　—a ditty by humor columnist H. I. Phillips, poking
　　　　　　　　　　　　fun at Franklin Roosevelt's dilemma

The casual observer of politics might be surprised to learn that the muck-raking columnist and author Upton Sinclair once ran for governor of California. Although it might be one of America's "forgotten" elections, it shouldn't be, because coming at the height of the Great Depression and the early stages of the New Deal, it almost caused a civil war in California.

Sinclair's 1934 campaign also earned a place in political lore as one of the most savage and brutal election campaigns in American history. He had a legion of enemies—including Hollywood moguls; California business associations; the real estate industry; and, of course, the state Republican Party—that threw everything at him, including the kitchen sink.

Sinclair is best known for his 1906 novel *The Jungle,* which exposed the horrible working conditions and sanitary procedures in meatpacking houses and food distribution centers in Chicago. The book became a sensation,

Sinclair was known as "The Old Muckraker" to many. San Francisco History Center, San Francisco Public Library.

spurring reform of U.S. meat-inspection laws and promoting passage of the Pure Food and Drug Act.

His groundbreaking book became known as the "Uncle Tom's Cabin of wage slavery."[1] President Theodore Roosevelt invited him to the White House and launched an investigation into the appalling conditions described in the book. It was Teddy Roosevelt that first applied the term "muckrakers" to social reformers like Sinclair.

Sinclair was an avowed Socialist, and in the early 20th century became a one-man crusade against corruption, big business, poverty, and organized religion. Other well-known Sinclair novels include *The Brass Check*, about the "prostitution" of the press, and *Boston*, a critical look at what he saw as the unfairness of the Sacco-Vanzetti trial.

In 1915 he founded a commune in Englewood, New Jersey, called Helicon Home Colony. He called it his utopia, and it was supposed to be a cooperative living experiment based on Socialist principles; however, it was destroyed by fire less than a year after it opened. Sinclair and his wife then moved to California to pursue writing and other creative projects.

In Southern California, the Sinclairs became active members of the literary and social scene, and Upton continued his passion for social reform and public policy. He hobnobbed and traded political talk with friends such as Albert Einstein, Charlie Chaplin, Henry Ford, King C. Gillette (the inventor of the safety razor), and fellow writer Sinclair Lewis, with whom he shared one name and many amusing anecdotes about people confusing the two of them.

His political beliefs and agenda for social reform came to a zenith with the coming of the Great Depression. He believed he had an answer for the economic and social problems gripping the nation and thought that California was an ideal place to put his ideas into action.

EPIC

In 1934 he abandoned the Socialist Party and then entered the Democratic Party primary for governor. He reasoned that a Socialist could not get elected and that he had to win an election before he could enact a single policy.

He based his campaign on a utopian novel he had just written, called *I, Governor of California, and How I Ended Poverty: A True Story of the Future.* In it, he outlined EPIC—his program to "End Poverty in California." The crux of the program was a concept he called "production for use."

"There are a half million persons in our state out of work," he said. "These persons can never again find work while the present system endures. . . . There is no solution to this problem except to put these unemployed at productive labor, to make them self sustaining, to let them produce what they are going to consume and so take them off the backs of the taxpayers."[2]

Frank Merriam was not the first choice of many for governor. San Francisco History Center, San Francisco Public Library.

He explained how it would work to a radio audience in August 1934:

There are a couple of thousand factories in our state standing entirely idle. Many of these are running into debt, and to keep them the state of California will say, "We offer to rent your factories. Keep your organization going, call in your workers, and run your machinery under the supervision of the state." The workers will turn out goods and they will own what they have produced.

The farmers of California, meanwhile, are producing huge quantities of foodstuffs for which they cannot find a market. To these farmers the state will say, "Bring your foodstuffs to our warehouses and you will receive in return receipts which will be good for your taxes. The farmers will eagerly comply and the food will be shipped to the cities and made available to the factory workers in exchange for the products of their labor. . . . So we will get going, by the credit power of the state, a new system of production in which Wall Street will have no share."[3]

In other words, he was proposing bringing socialism to California. He believed the credit power of the state could finance these huge public-works projects. But where would the state get the money—higher taxes? Selling bonds? And who would buy them? Naturally, business and industry interests both in and outside of California—not to mention the farmers and agricultural interests in the state—were absolutely horrified at what Sinclair was proposing.

But a legion of unemployed an underemployed Californians liked what they heard. Surprisingly to many, Sinclair won the Democratic nomination and set about to win over the state. He and his political organization esta-

EPIC was a significant political movement. Courtesy, The Lilly Library, Indiana University, Bloomington, Indiana.

blished EPIC clubs all over California but mainly in the southern part of the state. These organizations would be his field troops in the coming battle.

What Would FDR Do? (WWFD?)

Sinclair was an advocate of the New Deal and then some. He shared with Franklin Roosevelt a belief that the government could be the engine of economic enterprise, strengthening the society and protecting its less well-off citizens. But what Sinclair was advocating went beyond Roosevelt's New Deal policies. And Sinclair's well-known history as a Socialist, and the thought that he could be California's next governor was unsettling to many.

Sinclair believed that FDR's support would propel him to victory. He eagerly sought a meeting with the president. Roosevelt was in a pickle. After all, Sinclair was the gubernatorial nominee of the Democratic Party and a supporter of Roosevelt's policies. But Roosevelt knew that embracing Sinclair was dangerous—not only for California but for the success of the New Deal.

He was under pressure from many Democrats to disavow Sinclair and expose him as a Socialist in the cloak of a New Dealer. But FDR did not want to offend the many thousands who believed in Sinclair's message and who were working for social change. He decided to do nothing. He would not get involved in the race at all, either for Sinclair or against him.

Sinclair had bragged to reporters that FDR would endorse his EPIC program, thus giving him a huge boost in the election. But when that did not happen, it cost him dearly, both in public support and in lost credibility.

The incumbent governor at the time was a Republican, Frank Finley Merriam. He had taken office in June that year after the death of Governor James "Sunny Jim" Rolph. Merriam was an old-school politician, colorless and odorless, who made Calvin Coolidge look hyperactive by comparison.

But what Merriam had on his side was a Republican-leaning press, a very active network of Republican business interests, and a Hollywood movie industry that was afraid of a Sinclair administration in California.

Republican Hollywood?

Yep. Although most actors and writers were Democrats or Socialists or even Communists, most of the studio heads, the financiers, and many of the producers were Republicans, or at least had Republican sympathies on certain issues. And Upton Sinclair brought them together in a unified cause.

Sinclair proclaimed that the motion-picture industry—perhaps the most profitable business in California—had to contribute a fair share of the state's tax revenues. And movie moguls themselves would be taxed as individuals at a higher rate. But then he threatened to put the state of California in the movie-making business. "We will make our own pictures," he said, "and show them in our own theaters with our own orchestras."[4]

> Sinclair's circle of friends included many well-known authors of the day, including H. L. Mencken and Sinclair Lewis. He was also chummy with famed actor and director Charlie Chaplin.

The response of much of the Hollywood movie industry was to threaten to pack up the movie studios and move them to New York if Sinclair was elected. United Artists, Paramount, Universal, and Columbia Pictures made a show of looking for space in New York. MGM and RKO indicated they would follow suit. The entertainment newspaper *Variety* warned its readers that a Sinclair administration would mean the outright loss of the movie industry for California.

The Hollywood studios also became fund-raising machines for Governor Frank Merriam, virtually overnight. The movie mogul Louis B. Mayer predicted "chaos for California" if Sinclair was elected. And Harry Cohn of Columbia said his studio would "close in a minute" if Sinclair was elected.

ANTI-SINCLAIRISM

The California business community went all out to defeat Sinclair. It did not care that much for Merriam, but it hated what Sinclair stood for. For example, the California Real Estate Association—though not a political organization—did not feel it could stand idly by while a grave danger to property rights and American values was this close to the governor's mansion. Its slogan was, "It's Merriam or Moscow!"[5]

Brokers and property owners were organized in key cities to produce an anti-Sinclair panic. Realtors warned thousands of Californians attempting to sell their homes that no one would even look at their property until after the election. And if Sinclair won, their holdings would be worthless. Those in the market for real estate were told that virtually everything was off the market until November. It was the world's first self-induced real estate crash.

But that was amateur hour compared to what the real big guns had in store. Agribusiness magnate C. C. Teague organized a multimillion dollar ap-

We Appeal to the Exploited Masses!

"Help Us Save the State"

UPTÓN SINCLAIR

Emblem of Freedom

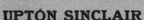

UPTON SINCLAIR | X

for GOVERNOR

SPONSORED BY THE

Young People's Communist League

VLADIMIR KOSLOFE, Secy., 234 N. Chicago St., Los Angeles

Handbills like these made Sinclair seem like Joseph Stalin's stooge. Courtesy, The Lilly Library, Indiana University, Bloomington, Indiana.

paratus with one goal—to destroy the candidacy of Upton Sinclair. Called United for California, the group included some of the biggest names in the state's business community.

One of the goals of the group was to use Sinclair's many quotes as campaign propaganda. Leaders of the group solicited mailing lists from the Knights of Columbus, the Boy Scouts, the American Legion, and numerous other organizations with the idea of creating pamphlets and flyers that would smear Sinclair. It was one of the first large-scale direct-mail efforts in American politics.

United for California became a household name by the end of the campaign. Anti-Sinclair bulletins and pamphlets turned up by the millions in mailboxes, in storefronts, on sidewalk tables, in churches, and on factory floors. The typical leaflet was four oblong pages with large, attention-getting type saying something like, "Out of His Own Mouth Shall He Be Judged."

The leaflets carried titles such as "Upton Sinclair on the Catholic Church"; "Upton Sinclair on the American Legion, the Boy Scouts, and the R.O.T.C."; "Upton Sinclair on Doctors and Dentists"; and "The Proof That Upton Sinclair Preaches Revolution and Communism."

In northern California, a separate front was created by Teague and his business allies called the California League Against Sinclairism. This group matched United for California pamphlet for pamphlet, and distributed thousands of leaflets across the northern part of the state, almost identical to the ones being spread across the south.

FAIR AND BALANCED?

One of the things Governor Merriam had going for him was the media. That may sound like a fantasy to many modern-day Republicans, but the newspapers supported California's business interests, and often boosted Republican candidates. The California Newspaper Publishers Association launched a coordinated campaign to smear Sinclair. The *Los Angeles Times* in particular went after Sinclair with a vengeance.

At first, the *Times* emphasized Sinclair's wealth and his bourgeois lifestyle with the headline, "Ex-Socialist Leaves Palatial Residence for Ballot Battle." The *Times* published photos of his three homes in Southern California—one in Pasadena, one in Hollywood, and one in Beverly Hills.

The *Times* also went after Sinclair with a time-honored political tradition: political cartoons. One pictured him with a big, ugly bear, which was labeled, "Extreme Left Doctrines." In the cartoon, the gate to California was barred by an elephant and a donkey, with the caption, "They Must Get Together to Keep Him Out."

According to one estimate, 92 percent of California's 700 newspapers supported Merriam over Sinclair. The anti-Sinclair press had a stranglehold on virtually every major city; few papers even acknowledged EPIC activities.[6] Along with the *LA Times,* the *San Francisco Chronicle* went on an anti-Sinclair tirade. Upton Sinclair is a "master of political propaganda," said its star reporter Earl Behrens. "He has hypnotized himself into a fanatical sincerity for the cause." He referred to Sinclair's victory in the Democratic primary for governor as the "rape of the Democratic party."

And William Randolph Hearst's newspapers could be counted on to slam Sinclair, as well. His *San Francisco Examiner, Los Angeles Herald-Express*, and *Call-Bulletin* joined forces to paint him as a dangerous extremist. The *Oakland Tribune* also joined the anti-Sinclair act, even going so far as to consult with its attorneys about how much it could lie about EPIC and get away with it.

But it was the *Los Angeles Times*, right in Sinclair's backyard, that was the journalistic point man in the anti-Sinclair crusade. Its main tactic was to take Sinclair's quotes and make them sound as threatening and un-American as possible. Sinclair on the American Legion: "They would like to take your schools and make 100,000 little West Points"; Sinclair on Christianity: "The shield and arrow of predatory economic might"; Sinclair on marriage: "I have had such a belief . . . I have it no longer."

According to Greg Mitchell, author of *Campaign of the Century,* the *Times* often dropped the opening or closing words of the excerpt, twisting its meaning. "Devoid of context, the barbs appeared to be the product of a deranged mind. Often the quoted words came from one of his novels; the *Times* deftly used this prodigious storyteller's own fictional characters against him."

Near the end of the campaign, the *Times* seemed to drop any pretense of objectivity. Its political editor, when asked by a *New York Times* reporter if Sinclair was really as bad as all that, replied, "We don't go in for that kind of crap that you have back in New York—of being obliged to print both sides. We're going to beat this son of a bitch Sinclair any way we can. . . . We're going to kill him."

CALIFORNIA HERE WE COME!

At least some of the political damage against Sinclair was self-inflicted. He enjoyed the banter with reporters, as did Roosevelt, but he did not have Roosevelt's gift for staying out of trouble. One day in late September he made a huge blunder. A reporter asked him what would happen if EPIC actually went into effect: "Wouldn't a great number of unemployed scurry to California from other states," he asked.[7]

Sinclair smiled and said, "I told them in Washington that if I am elected half of the unemployed of the United States will come to California, and they will have to make plans to take care of them." There was silence, as the furious scribbling on reporters' notepads could be heard. He had just supplied one of the nails for his own coffin.

The next morning, the *Los Angeles Times* jumped all over it. "Heavy Rush of Idle Seen by Sinclair," roared the headline. The *Times* calculated that about five million unemployed would swamp California if Sinclair were elected. "In other words," said the editorial, "Sinclair expects to end poverty in California by bringing in fifteen times as many poverty-stricken, jobless indigents as we have already. . . . the state would be thrown into chaos, at the mercy of riotous, Red-incited mobs."

United for California seized the opportunity. White cards with blue type were distributed across the state with the following inevitable song parody:

> *California here we come! Every beggar, every bum*
> *From New York and New Jersey—down to Purdue*
> *By millions—we're coming—so that we can live on you*
> *We hear that Sinclair's got your state*
> *That's why we can hardly wait*
> *Open up your Golden Gate*
> *California, here we come!*

Moviegoers across the state were also treated to state-of-the-art political propaganda. MGM studios distributed to its theaters a five-minute short called "California Election News." To the tune of "California, Here We Come," a cameraman interviewed "typical citizens" about who they were going to vote for in the upcoming election.

But it was clearly a hatchet job on Sinclair. Among those being interviewed, the respectable-looking people were supporting Merriam, while those down on their luck, or who looked a little goofy, were voting for Sinclair. One young, shifty-eyed Hispanic man endorsed "Uptown Saint-Clair" because the system needed to be shaken up. Another voter declared that Sinclair should be elected "because of his socialistic views."

The newsreel was particularly effective as an anti-Sinclair propaganda tool because it helped viewers associate certain faces and characteristics with Sinclair and with EPIC. Most voters wanted to be normal and have normal lives, like those people in the newsreel who were Merriam supporters. Those characters with little to be desired were supporting Sinclair.

A few weeks later, in late October, the second edition of "California Election News" hit theaters. It was even more biased than the first. In the newsreel, one Sinclair voter said he was supporting "Upton St. Clair . . . because he is the author of the Russian government. . . . It worked out very well there and I think it will here." Another man, speaking with a heavy eastern European accent, said, "I have always been a Socialist and I believe Sinclair will do best for working people."

Voter Intimidation

United for California and its sister organizations also organized a statewide campaign of voter intimidation. Mainly, this took the form of lawsuits and other formal means of challenging the voting status of certain California voters. At least, it was meant to appear that way. Group members knew that many of Sinclair's supporters were transient workers, and a number of them were recent arrivals to the state. These types of voters were likely to be susceptible to intimidation.

Lawyers for United for California drew up two separate lists of "illegal" registrants. One list identified individuals who would be ordered to appear in court to prove their right to vote. The other list, by far the most important, was filed with the local prosecutor's office and "sealed." In the newspapers it was reported as a "secret indictment," which sounds legal and scary. It might include tens of thousands of names or only a few dozen. The point of it was to give the impression that any Democrat's name "could" be on it, and so if they attempted to vote, they might be arrested.

A few voters did show up in court and, in almost every case, successfully defended their voter registration. But the real effect was to intimidate a mass of citizens who had intended to vote for Sinclair into staying home. The anti-Sinclair groups were fairly certain they were able to scare quite a few voters away from the polls on election day.

Meanwhile, Governor Merriam was almost invisible from the campaign, though it did not really matter. The campaign was not about him; it was about stopping Sinclair. In fact, at one point, Merriam thought there was too much focus on Sinclair and not enough on him—he wanted a more positive campaign.

To this, one of the founders of the United for California movement told him, "You're a tough guy to sell . . . and we're going to do it our way. We're going to continue to say that Upton Sinclair is a no-good son of a bitch, and we're going to spend a lot of money for that. In the last ten days we'll promote you with billboards with your name all over the place. That's what we have planned, and that's that."

BRAZEN CASE OF FRAUD?

Sinclair lost to Merriam by about 300,000 votes. His candidacy had been torpedoed by an alliance that included Hollywood, big business, the news media, realtors, and farmers. Commenting on the dismantling of the Sinclair campaign, Scripps-Howard columnist Heywood Broun observed, "Many American campaigns have been distinguished by dirty tactics, but I can think of none in which willful fraud has been so brazenly practiced. . . . Frank Merriam, if elected, will be the first out-and-out fascist governor the United States has known. The tactics he is pursuing in his campaign follow very closely the formula used by Hitler in smashing the German Republic."

After the election, Sinclair retreated to his home and continued his writing career. His first new book? It was called *I, Candidate for Governor, and How I Got Licked.*

23

SENATOR POTHOLE VERSUS "PUTZHEAD"

Alphonse D'Amato v. Charles Schumer, U.S. Senate, New York, 1998

Incumbent Republican Senator Alphonse D'Amato and his Democratic challenger, Representative Charles Schumer, had pet names for each other. D'Amato called Schumer a *putzhead*—a Yiddish word whose literal meaning cannot be printed here because this book is meant for all ages. But its common usage means "fool" or "idiot."

For his part, Schumer repeatedly labeled D'Amato an untrustworthy liar. Here we have a couple of politicians who have no problem saying what is on their minds. But it is actually kind of mild for the fireworks that this race caused in New York in 1998. It has been described as a South Bronx brawl and the dirtiest campaign New York has seen in decades.

"This is probably the meanest campaign in the country," said Peter Jennings of ABC News, late in 1998. Over at CBS, Dan Rather called the race "down and dirty, negative and nasty." And not to be left out, Tom Brokaw of NBC said, "One of the closest and nastiest races of all is going on in the state of New York."[1]

It was also the most expensive race in the senate in 1998. Approximately $40 million was spent ($25 million by D'Amato and Republican groups and $15 million by Schumer and Democratic groups), most of it on blisteringly negative TV ads.

The two men were polar opposites politically. Schumer was a liberal with a strong record on gun control, abortion rights, and environmental protection. D'Amato was a conservative Republican, though moderate on some so-

Alphonse D'Amato. U.S. Senate Archives.

cial issues, who was proudest of his record of constituent service.

D'Amato took a backseat to no one in the U.S. Congress when it came to answering constituent letters, phone calls, e-mails, and so on, and in making sure that his home state got its fair share of federal spending. For this, he came to be known as Senator Pothole—a derisive nickname at first, but one he came to wear as a badge of honor. It helped him reinforce to New York voters that he was there for them first.

D'Amato had been in the senate for eighteen years and was accustomed to fighting for every scrap of support he could get, whether it was votes from New Yorkers for his reelection campaigns, votes on the floor of the U.S. Senate, or media coverage for his pet causes and issues. In all of these traits, however, he met his match in Democrat Charles Schumer, who had represented the Brooklyn area of New York in the U.S. House of Representatives for sixteen years.

In fact, one of the things the two had in common was their shameless, unrelenting campaign style. D'Amato was the master of local politics and ethnic pandering. He showed up at Jewish gatherings wearing a yarmulke with "Alphonse" stitched on it. Schumer worked the local angle like a master, though, taking credit for popular programs whether he had anything to do with them or not. His House colleagues had learned that Schumer has very sharp elbows, which come in handy when you're running against Al D'Amato.

As David Plotz of the Internet magazine *Slate.com* noted, "In Schumer, D'Amato finally faces an opponent who's as hardheaded, shameless, and effective as he is."[2] D'Amato, the incumbent, of course had no opposition in the Republican primary. Schumer, on the other hand, had to overcome two well-known and popular New Yorkers to become the Democratic nominee: former congresswoman and 1984 vice presidential nominee Geraldine Ferraro and consumer advocate Mark Green. In fact, Ferraro led in some of the early polls. She was a sentimental favorite with many New Yorkers due to her place in history as the first female to run on a presidential ticket in either party.

Schumer bided his time, though. He ran on his record and his support of traditional, New York Democratic causes. His campaign made a point not to attack the popular Ferraro. As it turns out, the Ferraro campaign never really got out of the starting gate. Short on money and not really associated with any substantive issues in the primary campaign, Ferraro came in a distant second to Schumer. Mark Green was a very distant third.

The moment that Schumer won his party's nomination, he was attacked by D'Amato. D'Amato bought TV ads dismissing Schumer as a tax-and-spend liberal. But the Schumer camp was ready. They aired response ads the next day accusing D'Amato of putting national Republican Party politics ahead of the needs of New York.

D'Amato's top political strategist was a Republican political consultant named Arthur Finkelstein, well known to New York politicos as a slash-and-burn attacker, particularly against liberals and liberal causes. Schumer's TV ads were just as tough—in fact, many thought too tough.

One of the tag lines from some of Schumer's ads was "Al D'Amato: Too many lies for too long." Some New York Democrats feared it was too negative and would provoke a backlash, but Schumer's strategists believed they needed to match D'Amato blow for blow, or risk the perception of being shoved around by D'Amato and Finklestein.[3]

Charles Schumer. AP/Wide World Photos.

There was also a question about the direction that some of D'Amato's attacks took. Under Finkelstein's playbook, the D'Amato campaign attacked Schumer for being too liberal. But New York is a fairly liberal state, especially its urban areas. D'Amato himself took an accommodating perspective toward homosexual rights, earning him some criticism from the right. And Schumer took care not to swerve too far to the left, advocating strong national defense, for example, and listening to New York business interests on occasion.[4]

D'Amato also attacked Schumer on the number of votes he missed in the House while out campaigning for the Senate. "Full-time pay, part-time work!" the ads shouted. But this is rarely a significant issue with voters. It may have led to some doubts about Schumer, but it also raised D'Amato's own negatives, as he reinforced the image many had of him as combative and negative. It did not help matters when it came out that as a first-time candidate for the Senate in 1980, D'Amato himself had missed almost 1,000 votes as a member of the county board of supervisors.

JEWS AND GAYS

Part of the war between D'Amato and Schumer was fought over the support of two groups very important to New York politics: Jewish voters and gay voters. D'Amato went after the Jewish vote particularly hard. No small feat, since Schumer himself is Jewish and D'Amato is Italian. But he had been a steadfast supporter of issues dear to the hearts of Jewish voters, and in previous elections had won as much as 40 percent of the Jewish vote—very high for a Republican.

D'Amato played up his ties to the Israeli lobby, portraying himself as a staunch defender of Israel and a critic of Arab foreign policy. He also sought to wrap himself in the support of Holocaust survivors, which infuriated Schumer.

D'Amato even strong-armed a Jewish group organizing a rally calling for the Palestinian Authority to extradite a pair of terrorists. His price for speaking at the event was that the group had to leave Schumer's name off the list of invitees. Schumer wasn't invited and D'Amato had the event all to himself.[5]

At another rally a few weeks before the election, D'Amato, flanked by two Holocaust survivors and a rabbi, criticized Schumer for missing House votes of importance to the Jewish community. It was vintage D'Amato. "He [Schumer] doesn't care," D'Amato said. "He's not there on the battlefields because he is too busy pursuing his political career."

The main problem for D'Amato in this line of attack was that Schumer had a sterling reputation as a supporter of Israel, and had authored numerous pro-Israel pieces of legislation in the House. D'Amato may have miscalculated. Certainly, a number of Jewish community leaders thought he had gone too far. Responding to D'Amato's scathing attacks at the rally, Schumer said, "I think it's a shame that Al D'Amato would stoop to using the Holocaust for political purposes. . . . My record on the Holocaust, on Jewish issues, is second to none."

Whatever the rationale from the D'Amato campaign, the use of Holocaust survivors and the attacks on Schumer's commitment to Jews and Israeli causes struck many as crossing the line.

New York's gay and lesbian community was split over the D'Amato-Schumer contest. The nation's largest gay and lesbian lobbying organization, the Human Rights Campaign (HRC), endorsed D'Amato over the objections of numerous gay rights activists and Democratic political leaders in New York State.

The leadership of the HRC believed that they had to reward public officials who had helped them. And even though most gay activists believed Schumer to have a far better legislative record of support on gay issues, the fact was that D'Amato had made an extraordinary transformation in the early to mid-1990s. Former New York City mayor Ed Koch, a D'Amato friend, attributed the change to the loss of one of his senior staff members to AIDS.

One of the big symbolic issues of importance to the gay community in the early 1990s was gays in the military. Surprisingly to many, D'Amato was front and center in the movement to allow gays to serve openly, earning him the thanks of gay political leaders all over the country. This was seen as courageous by many because few Republicans were stepping forward on this issue, particularly because President Bill Clinton was its champion.

The problem for the HRC, and for D'Amato, was that even though he was a hero to a number of gay rights advocates in Washington, D.C., he remained a dubious figure to some of their counterparts in New York. The HRC endorsement was heavily criticized by many in the gay community.

Jeffrey Tooke, chair of the New York State Federation of Gay and Lesbian Democratic Clubs, said the D'Amato endorsement was "a call to arms for gays and lesbians throughout New York state to assure the election of our next U.S. Senator Chuck Schumer. . . . The HRC endorsement ignores that D'Amato, as head of the Republican Party in New York State, has repeatedly struck down our efforts for equal rights and non-discrimination."[6]

Obviously, the issue was an emotional one for many in the gay community. "Once again," continued Tooke, "the HRC has proven themselves to be nothing more than a bunch of narrow-focused, self-anointed, inside-the-beltway hacks."

The chair of the New York State Democratic Party, Judith Hope, jumped on the issue in an effort to rouse the anti-D'Amato forces. "There's nothing Al D'Amato would not do for a vote," she said. "He would have a carnival at a Holocaust memorial if he thought it would get him another vote."

Needless to say, Schumer went ballistic about the endorsement. He said that D'Amato "has a better scorecard from the Christian Coalition than he does from the HRC—and that the Christian Coalition is right now bashing gays and lesbians."

Indeed, D'Amato had a 92 rating from the Christian Coalition, while Schumer had a rating of zero. The main difference was over their votes on abortion legislation. For D'Amato, being a Catholic drove most of his sentiment over the abortion issue. But this stark difference made the choice between the two men an easy one for abortion rights advocates in New York unlike the split in the gay and lesbian community.

The Westchester (New York) Coalition for Legal Abortion released a statement critical of D'Amato: "Al D'Amato is so extreme that he even voted twenty times to restrict the use of critical family planning programs both here and abroad. Schumer, on the other hand, knows that access to safe, effective family planning is the best way to reduce the number of abortions."

Turning Point?

Then came the "putzhead" remark. About two weeks before the election, D'Amato met privately with top Jewish leaders in New York. During that meeting, he referred to Schumer as a *putzhead*, a Yiddish vulgarism.[7]

Those at the meeting created a buzz over the next few days about D'Amato's comments. It was offensive to many, who felt D'Amato had not understood the full meaning of the word. When asked about it in public, D'Amato at first denied saying it. "I just have no knowledge of ever doing it," he said. "I just don't. . . . I think it's ridiculous." When others at the meeting confirmed that he had in fact used the word, D'Amato apologized for any offense.

Schumer jumped. He called the comment a "cheap slur." And his Democratic colleague Representative Jerry Nadler—whom D'Amato had referred to as a "waddler" at that same meeting—said, "It shows a pattern of contempt for people generally, or perhaps, for Jews in particular." Overnight, it seemed, all of D'Amato's efforts at cultivating support in the Jewish community crumbled like a day-old cookie. Of course, the incident dominated media coverage of the campaign at a crucial time, and reinforced D'Amato's image of mean-spiritedness.

Another turning point may have been the murder of an abortion doctor in Buffalo in late October. This shocking news story helped draw attention to the abortion issue and to the anti-abortion protesters, some of whom had used increasingly violent tactics in the mid- and late 1990s. This made it possible for the abortion rights advocacy groups in New York to demonize the pro-life movement, which was bad for D'Amato because of his close ties to pro-lifers.

The National Abortion Rights Action League (NARAL) released a TV ad the week before the election, linking anti-abortion violence to D'Amato's opposition to legislation designed to protect abortion clinics. As ABC's John Cochran reported, "Abortion rights activists believe the doctor's murder can mobilize opposition to anti-abortion candidates, such as New York Senator Al D'Amato. D'Amato voted against a 1994 law making it a federal crime to interfere with abortions. It gave federal agents the authority to investigate in such cases . . . D'Amato has deplored anti-abortion violence, but advisers to his opponent, Chuck Schumer, believe the ads and news coverage of the murder help emphasize their differences on abortion."

CLINTON AND IMPEACHMENT

And then there was the Clinton factor. The year 1998 was the year of Monica Lewinsky, special prosecutor Kenneth Starr, and the impeachment scandal of Bill Clinton. New York voters, though, never wavered in their support of President Clinton. And many think the Republican fervor to impeach Clinton may have hurt several of their congressional candidates in 1998. National polls showed that impeachment of the president was not popular, and this was particularly the case in New York.

In fact, Bill and Hillary Clinton actively campaigned for Schumer in New York. D'Amato's close association with the national Republican Party and its leadership's efforts to oust Clinton probably hurt his chances for beating back the challenge from Schumer and holding on to his senate seat.

On election day, Schumer won surprisingly easily. The polls had indicated a very close race, and most experts, including those in New York, had called the race a toss-up. But Schumer ran very well with key demographic groups, such as women, minorities, urban voters, and blue-collar voters.

Schumer won the Jewish vote over D'Amato by a ratio of 75 to 25, trouncing D'Amato in some of New York City's largest precincts. D'Amato did well in upstate New York, but not by large enough margins to offset Schumer's strength elsewhere.[8]

The war was over, but no one was sure if the most negative candidate lost. D'Amato and Schumer traded many rough blows, but it may have been D'Amato and his consultant Finkelstein's judgment about how to go after Schumer that made the difference. That, and D'Amato's relative lack of knowledge about the power of certain Yiddish insults.

ELECTRONIC MUDSLINGING

Lyndon Johnson v. Barry Goldwater, President, 1964

Extremism in the defense of liberty is no vice.

—Barry Goldwater

One of the most significant things about the 1964 presidential race between Johnson and Goldwater is that it marks the moment when the negative TV ad was born. In fact, you could say that Johnson's campaign invented the negative TV spot—or at least perfected it and brought it into the big time.

Barry Goldwater had an image problem. He had a talent for saying things that sounded, well, looney. The Johnson campaign took Goldwater's public comments and used them against him, reinforcing and encouraging the doubts that many Americans had about his candidacy.

Johnson's TV spots were created by political advertising guru Tony Schwartz of the Doyle Dane Bernbach advertising agency. They are considered classics. The best known, and perhaps the most famous political TV ad of all time, is the "Daisy Girl" spot. As I have said before, this ad is "the Mother of all televised attack ads."

Tony Schwartz was a pioneer in the use of images and sound in the early days of television. In his book *The Responsive Chord*, he explains that political ads do not have to change fixed beliefs or political philosophies to be effective, but merely "touch" certain feelings or emotions in the voter that will affect his or her voting behavior.[1]

According to Schwartz, the real question in political advertising is how to surround the voter with the proper images and sounds to evoke the reaction

Lyndon Johnson. Library of Congress.

you want, which is a vote for your candidate. TV is the perfect medium to bring to the surface feelings voters already have, and mobilize them in the direction you want them to go.

Goldwater's talent for making controversial statements was a godsend for Johnson and his advertising team. All they had to do was create advertising that would emphasize the implications of Goldwater's comments, thereby stimulating the fear and apprehension that already existed about the possibility of a Goldwater presidency.

For example, one of the concerns people had about Goldwater was that he was a trigger-happy warmonger and seemed entirely too eager to consider the use of nuclear weapons. People had developed this belief out of statements Goldwater himself had made. At his nominating convention, which was rocked by internal fighting and turmoil, he made his famous statement about extremism: "I would remind you that extremism in the defense of liberty is no vice; and I would also remind you that moderation in the pursuit of justice is no virtue."

In interviews over the previous year, Goldwater had voiced support for NATO commanders to use nuclear weapons in the field, and had suggested that low-grade nuclear devices might be used as a defoliant in Vietnam. So, there was a background to the fears that people had about him—a background that was exploited, and sometimes twisted, by the Johnson campaign.

With regard to the Cold War and the American relationship with the Soviet Union, he was widely quoted as saying he would like to "lob a few missiles in the men's room of the Kremlin," although the quote was taken out of context. Comments like these made him seem intemperate and reactionary. The country was beginning to get tangled in Vietnam and was only a few years removed from the Cuban missile crisis. Goldwater seemed out of the mainstream and potentially dangerous.

BARRY GOLDWATER, NUCLEAR WAR, AND YOU

But for the Johnson campaign, it was manna from heaven. The "Daisy Girl" spot was intended to play on the fears and anxieties about Goldwater that he himself had created. The ad opens with a young girl sitting in a field of flowers, picking daisies as she counts them.

She's an adorable little girl, and it's even cuter how she miscounts them, "1, 2, 3, 4, 5, 7, 6, 6, 8, 9." It seemed authentic because she counts the way children do, with numbers out of the proper order. When the little girl gets to 9, an announcer begins a countdown, just like the ones at the NASA Space Center—10, 9, 8 . . . —as the camera slowly zooms in to her face.

At zero, the camera zooms in to the girl's eyes and we see a nuclear explosion, with a billowing mushroom cloud. Then, Lyndon Johnson's voice is heard, with a warning: "These are the stakes—to make a world in which all of God's children can live, or to go into the dark. We must either love each other, or we must die." An announcer then says, "Vote for President Johnson on November 3. The stakes are too high for you to stay home."

Barry Goldwater's views were portrayed as extreme by the Johnson forces but laid the seeds for the modern conservative movement. U.S. Senate Archives.

The ad never mentioned Goldwater by name. It did not have to; viewers knew exactly what the ad was trying to communicate. Said Schwartz, "It was comparable to a person going to a psychiatrist and seeing dirty pictures in a Rorschach pattern. The Daisy commercial evoked Goldwater's pro-bomb statements. They were like dirty pictures in the audience's mind."[2]

The ad aired only once, on the CBS *Monday Night at the Movies*, on September 7, 1964. The reaction to the spot was immediate and intense. The spot contained images that were pretty harsh by 1964 standards. The CBS switchboard lit up, as did the one at the White House. The Johnson campaign pulled the spot, but it had already accomplished its mission.

The ad created such a sensation that the next day all three networks showed it in its entirety on their evening news programs, enabling many more people to see the ad and so magnifying its effects. The Goldwater campaign reacted with fury, loudly criticizing the Johnson campaign and filing a formal complaint with the Fair Campaign Practices Committee.[3] In the end, all the fuss the Republicans raised about the ad only ensured that it would get more attention.

The Johnson campaign struck again a few days later with a different little girl. This ad also aired only once, on *Saturday Night at the Movies.* The girl is licking an ice cream cone. No nuclear explosions this time, but a female announcer warns us that Strontium 90, present in nuclear fallout, could be poisoning her and she wouldn't even know it. But the announcer informs us that thanks to the nuclear test ban treaty, which Goldwater opposed, the child is safe. The ad says that by voting against the test ban treaty, Senator Goldwater was actually endorsing Strontium 90 in the air and food.

Johnson's press secretary, Bill Moyers, believes the ad was effective because Strontium 90 was a big issue in the early 1960s. And when Goldwater rejected the test ban and called for more nuclear testing, it "played right into [the Johnson campaign's] hands."

The "Daisy Girl" ad was very controversial for its day, but it was a harbinger of things to come for American politics. Courtesy, Julian P. Kanter Archive/University of Oklahoma.

President Johnson's campaign produced a third ad in this series on Barry Goldwater and nuclear weapons, but this one was never aired. A female announcer discusses the need for nuclear restraint as a pregnant woman and her daughter walk through a lush, green park. As the announcer discusses the hazards posed by nuclear fallout to unborn fetuses, the image of the woman blends into the image of the girl, making her disappear.

But this ad led to disputes within the Johnson campaign. There was no evidence that fallout harmed fetuses, and the whole issue of unborn children was too sensitive, so the ad was scrapped.

It was left to radio to finish the job on the question of nuclear weapons. One radio ad asked, "Is Mr. Goldwater bored with peace?" The announcer then seemed to answer his own question by reading a series of quotes attributed to Goldwater, among them, the ones on lobbing missiles in the Kremlin, opposing a test ban treaty, and others, including, "I'd drop a low yield atomic bomb on the Chinese supply lines in North Vietnam," and the atomic bomb is "merely another weapon."

By election day, most voters were convinced, through Johnson's attack ads, that Barry Goldwater was a dangerous extremist who could not be trusted with the nation's military forces, particularly its nuclear arsenal.

REPUBLICAN V. REPUBLICAN

The Johnson team also raked Goldwater over the coals using the words of some of his fellow Republicans. The Republican campaign for the nomination created intense ill will and divisions in the party. The conservative wing led by Senator Goldwater was in open revolt against the moderate, establishment wing led by New York governor Nelson Rockefeller.

The Republican convention was a disaster. When Governor Rockefeller strolled to the podium to address the convention, he was booed and heckled by the delegates, most of whom were Goldwater loyalists. Responding to chants of "We Want Barry, We Want Barry," Rockefeller shook his head and scowled.

Rockefeller stoked the flames. As he was booed, he spoke of the unfair campaign tactics that had been used against him by the Goldwater campaign. "These things have no place in America," he shouted. "But I can personally testify to their existence. . . . And so can countless others who have also experienced anonymous midnight and early morning telephone calls, unsigned threatening letters, smear and hate literature, strong arm and goon tactics, bomb threats and bombings."[4]

This incident was an ugly dramatization of the real split within the party and the passions and intolerance of some of the participants. To make matters worse, the whole thing was broadcast on national TV, and as the nation watched, the Republican Party shot itself in the foot.

No one was surprised, then, when an anti-Goldwater ad by the Johnson team used the words of Rockefeller and other Republicans, such as Pennsylvania governor Bill Scranton. "Back in July in San Francisco the Republicans held a convention," the ad said, as the camera showed a heap of campaign signs dumped on the floor with the likenesses of Rockefeller and Scranton.

"Remember him?" A Rockefeller sign was raised from the confetti-strewn floor. "He was there. Governor Rockefeller. Before the convention, he said, 'Barry Goldwater's positions can'—and I quote—'spell disaster for the party and for the country.' Or him?" the announcer asks, as a sign with Scranton's picture is picked up. "The day before the convention, Governor Scranton called Goldwaterism a 'crazy quilt collection of absurd and dangerous positions.' So even if you're a Republican with serious doubts about Barry Goldwater, you're in good company."[5]

HE'LL DESTROY SOCIAL SECURITY!

Some of the worst mudslinging occurred over the sensitive topic of Social Security. The Johnson campaign spun Goldwater's comments about his concern over how Social Security was structured to make it sound as if he wanted to eliminate it altogether.

One of the more notable Johnson ads on the topic of Social Security used Goldwater's own running mate against him. The ad features a man walking down the street and taking his wallet out of his pocket. He sorts through its contents as the announcer speaks.

"On at least seven occasions," says the announcer, "Senator Barry Goldwater said he would change the present Social Security system." Now the man takes his Social Security card out and looks at it. The ad continues, "But even his running mate William Miller admits that Senator Goldwater's voluntary plan would destroy your Social Security." Now the ad shows the man taking the Social Security card and tearing it in two, dropping it onto the street. So, in a very provocative ad, the Johnson campaign makes the stretch that going to a voluntary system of Social Security is the same thing as destroying it—and it uses his running mate's words to make the case.

President Johnson shocked the world when a televised speech about the Vietnam conflict in 1968 had this surprise ending: "I will not seek, nor will I accept, the nomination of my party for another term as president." The Vietnam War had claimed another victim.

Another TV ad quoted Goldwater as saying that he would "drastically change" Social Security. In fact, he had said no such thing. In radio ads, the Johnson campaign told listeners that Goldwater "wants to pick your pocket, and he's asking you to help him do it" when it comes to Social Security.

What Goldwater actually said was that he wanted to make Social Security solvent and to improve it. He thought the system had accounting problems, that it promised more benefits to more people than it could provide. The Goldwater campaign ran ads documenting his votes in the Senate in favor of Social Security. But the Johnson ads sought to portray him as an ardent opponent of the Social Security program. And to a large degree, they were successful. This stand was consistent with the image most voters had of Goldwater as an antigovernment extremist.

BARRY THE MEAN

While the Johnson advertising team was systematically tearing Goldwater apart, the senator went after President Johnson on the issue of ethics and corruption in a series of campaign appearances and advertisements that appeared strident and vindictive.

According to presidential historian Paul Boller, Goldwater's attacks were unusually harsh for a man normally thought to be polite and amiable.[6] And one thing that made them noteworthy was that he attacked his opponent by name, which was unusual for presidential candidates at the time.

Goldwater called Johnson a "scheming wire puller," who had amassed a fortune in the U.S. Senate and associated with questionable figures who had come under fire for dishonest business dealings.

In 1963 a former Johnson staff assistant in the senate, Bobby Baker, was forced to resign his position after a Senate investigation revealed questionable financial and accounting practices. On a salary of $32,000 a year, Baker had attained a net worth of over $2 million. As a young staffer for Johnson in the late 1950s, Baker had once given him a $500 stereo system.

During the 1964 campaign, Goldwater and other Republicans also chastised Johnson over his link with Billy Sol Estes. Estes was an acquaintance of Johnson from Texas who was implicated in a scam to bilk the Department of Agriculture out of several million dollars in a complicated con game.

"To Lyndon Johnson," said Goldwater, "running a country means buying and bludgeoning votes. It means building a private fortune. It means surrounding himself with companions like Billy Baker, Billy Sol Estes, and other interesting men. It means craving and grasping for power—more and more, without end."

But Johnson was never directly implicated in any of the financial schemes the Republicans were criticizing him about. Johnson made public an audit of his financial holdings that satisfied many voters, and he called Goldwater's charges the "ravings of a demagogue." In any case, questions about a $500 stereo system just were not as important to most voters as questions concerning nuclear weapons and Social Security.

The outcome of the 1964 election was never in serious doubt. Johnson was a relatively popular incumbent, fulfilling the vision of the wildly popular President Kennedy, slain only a year before. And his opponent was a right-wing Republican who could not even get the support of all Republicans, and who left a legacy of controversial quotes and claims that doomed any chance he had of overtaking President Johnson.

But Johnson wanted more than just a win; he wanted a mandate—a landslide. The TV and radio ads his campaign ran against Goldwater achieved that for him. The anti-Goldwater spots were very effective in reinforcing Goldwater's negatives among the public, and set a new standard for political communication. Johnson won forty-four states, while Goldwater carried only his home state of Arizona and five southern states. Johnson's advertising campaign had given him one of the largest Electoral College landslides in American history, up to that time.

THE ART OF WAR

Jesse Helms v. Harvey Gantt, U.S. Senate, North Carolina, 1990

*North Carolinians are the most experienced and sophisticated view-
ers of negative ads in the country. They've seen more of them than
anyone else.*

—Democratic strategist Gary Pearce

There are plumbers who take special exams to become master plumbers.
Building contractors can earn a special designation as a master builder. Jesse
Helms of North Carolina will likely be known to future historians as a master politician. But his negative campaign tactics and aggressive posturing in
the Senate also earned him the nicknames Senator Mean and Dr. No.

Helms served in the U.S. Senate for thirty years (1972–2003), earning a
reputation as a tough, conservative opponent of liberal political causes, big
government, and "internationalist" foreign policy. But it is in the realm of
political campaigns that he honed his political skills and practiced the art of
political warfare.

Some observers would be less kind to the senator. They would emphasize his
penchant for race baiting, demagoguery, and dirty politics. And they are cor-
rect. But even his most ardent opponents would acknowledge his skill in modern political communication and tactical decision making in the heat of battle.

The journalist Howard Troxler notes his role as one of the leaders in the
conservative renaissance in American politics as well as his role in the development of modern attack politics and strategy. Troxler observes that Helms
"was one of the first and most effective Republican politicians to tap into deep

Jesse Helms. U.S. Senate Archives.

middle class and blue collar resentment over civil rights, Vietnam protesters, hippies, drugs, liberals, and what many thought was a decline in traditional American values."[1] In this way, Helms represents a historical bridge between Barry Goldwater and Ronald Reagan.

Helms was also a student of history. He had read and internalized much of the ancient Chinese general Sun Tzu's classic guide to conflict and warfare, *The Art of War*. He applied many of these lessons to his political campaigns. From the 1970s through the 1990s, he either invented or perfected many of the current trademarks of American political campaigns, such as direct-mail fund-raising and attack television ads.

He mastered the use of the organizational rules of the U.S. Senate to delay or block legislation and government appointees he found objectionable. He forced his colleagues to take positions on unpopular or controversial issues, then later used their votes against them. And he was a trailblazer in the development of some of the infrastructure and tools of the modern conservative political movement, such as think tanks, political action committees, and training opportunities for a new generation of leaders.

And along the way he "mocked and outraged government-funded artists, advocates for gay rights (homersexuals, he pronounced it), UN supporters, civil libertarians, atheists, and the general universe of what he called 'pointy-headed liberals.' They loved to hate him in return, and at times he seemed to relish it. He covered his office walls with hostile editorial cartoons."[2]

He was also reviled by his opponents for stands they believed to be racist and homophobic. David Broder of the *Washington Post* called Helms "the last prominent unabashed white racist politician in this country. . . . What is unique about Helms—and from my viewpoint, unforgivable—is his willingness to pick at the scab of the great wound of American history, the legacy of slavery and segregation, and to inflame racial resentment against African Americans."[3]

PUBLIC CRUSADE

Helms became known to North Carolinians back in the 1960s when he was a TV commentator. He was a one-man crusade against the 1960s counterculture of war protests, civil rights, and drug use. On the air, he gave fiery diatribes against "Negro agitators," "moral degenerates," and "student mobs."

In 1972 he entered his first political campaign. There was an open U.S. Senate seat, and Helms upset a better-known, better-funded liberal Democratic candidate by appealing to traditional values and railing against the "forces of social unrest." He also based much of his campaign on drawing stark contrasts between his values and beliefs and those of the opposition.

To Helms, politics and ideology were simple, black and white. He saw it as right versus wrong, good versus evil. His slogan for the 1972 Senate campaign was "He's one of us." It appeared in television ads and in flyers distributed around the state. The "He's one of us" theme was a way to communicate to voters that Helms understood their frustrations with modern society and that he was there to fight for them and their beliefs.[4]

But it also implied that the opponent was not "one of us." It was criticized by many newspaper editorials and by the Democratic Party as an open appeal to racism. His opponent accused Helms of trying to divide North Carolinians. "He's using an 'us versus them' mentality," one local Democrat said. Who did he mean by "them?" Blacks? Liberals? War protesters? Probably all of the above.

THE CONGRESSIONAL CLUB

One of the weapons that Helms used in his campaigns throughout the 1970s and 1980s was the fund-raising and political advocacy organization he and some allies founded, the Congressional Club. This group aggressively raised money, first in the Carolinas, then throughout the South and the rest of the country. Its forte was conservative ideological causes, and Helms was their champion.

The Congressional Club became a reliable source of money, communications assistance, and manpower with which Helms and his handpicked congressional candidates fought liberalism and the Democratic Party.

One of North Carolina's best-known and closely watched statewide campaigns was a heavyweight showdown in 1984, when that state's popular governor, Jim Hunt, challenged Helms for his U.S. Senate seat. The Congressional Club, as well as other conservative political groups, helped Helms wage war on the governor.

Not that he needed much help. The following exchange illustrates how Helms typically picked apart an opponent by forcing him into a corner. In a televised debate, he turned one of Hunt's criticisms back around in an act of political jujitsu. Hunt was criticizing Helms for voting to cut veterans' benefits. "Now I've got every single one of your votes right here, Senator. You can't fool me, and I don't think you're going to fool the people of North Carolina," Hunt crowed. Hunt seemed to have him. But Helms response was to quickly ask him a question: "Which war did you serve in?

> Hunt: "I did not serve in a war."
>
> Helms: "OK."
>
> Hunt: "Senator Helms, now wait just a minute. Since you asked that question . . ."
>
> Helms: "No, Mr. President, I was . . ."
>
> Hunt: "I was in college, Mr. Moderator, during the time of the Korean War, and I was too old with two children when Vietnam came along. And I don't like you challenging my patriotism, Senator."
>
> Helms: "I haven't challenged your patriotism."
>
> Hunt: "Yes, you have. You know exactly what that question was calculated to do."
>
> Helms: "Well, I just wondered . . ."[5]

HELMS V. GANTT

But it was Helms's 1990 reelection battle with Harvey Gantt that put both Helms and Gantt into the negative campaigning hall of fame—or rather, hall of shame. Gantt, an African American and the former mayor of Charlotte, North Carolina's largest city, represented a new style of Democrat: business friendly and open to opposing points of view. His challenge to Helms was largely seen as a contest between the politics of the future (Gantt) and the politics of the past (Helms).

Gantt criticized Helms for "representing the past, instead of representing North Carolina." Gantt's campaign tried to move beyond the polarizing issue of race and emphasize what North Carolina needed from a U.S. senator—jobs, support for education, and better health care. But in North Carolina, as in most southern states, race is never very far beneath the surface—a fact that Helms used to his advantage.

Campaign polls on both sides in September showed that Gantt's approach was working. Survey respondents leaned toward Gantt, and they emphasized issues that Gantt had pushed in his campaign—education, the environment, and job growth. But the Helms campaign started a TV ad blitz in mid-October that reversed Helms's slide in the polls.

Helms's TV ads were designed to paint Gantt as unacceptably liberal and to reintroduce race into the campaign but in a subtle way, not in a hammer-

Harvey Gantt. AP/Wide World Photos.

over-the-head way. One of the ads ostensibly dealt with abortion, always a controversial issue, and especially so in a culturally conservative state like North Carolina. It was no secret that Gantt favored *Roe v. Wade* and Helms opposed it, but the ad portrayed Gantt as an extremist on the issue and out of the cultural mainstream.

The ad shows a young woman wearing a red dress and looking earnestly into the camera. "Harvey Gantt is asking you and me to approve of some pretty awful things," she says. "Aborting a child in the final weeks of pregnancy. Aborting a child because it is a girl instead of a boy." When Gantt complained loudly about the intent of the ad and denied ever supporting abortion for sex selection, the Helms campaign aired a second ad on the issue.

This time, Gantt himself is featured in the ad, taken from a television interview. "Let's set the record straight," says the announcer. "Harvey Gantt denied he would allow abortion for sex selection, when parents want a boy and not a girl. But he told the press he would allow abortions, whether for sex selection or for whatever reason." As Gantt is speaking, the camera zooms in for a close-up.

As the tape rewinds, an incredulous voice asks, "Did he say even for sex selection?" Then he is shown again saying "for sex selection or for whatever reason." The tape rewinds again, and the announcer asks the viewer to "read his lips." The tape is then played in slow motion, and Gantt's voice becomes slurred, almost growling the words "abortion for sex selection." The text on the screen reads, "Harvey Gantt: Extremely Liberal with the FACTS."

According to political communication expert Kathleen Hall-Jamieson, the ad is manipulated to highlight personal features of Gantt that play in to racial stereotypes. As the tape rewinds in each instance, she believes, the image of Gantt is intentionally transformed from color to black and white.

The shadows created by the rapid rewinding image of Gantt's face alternatively lighten and darken his face. In rewinding the image, Gantt looks, according to Jamieson, "out of control, his head bobbing from side to side. First-time viewers who are asked to characterize the sound of his slowed voice most often use the words 'stupid,' 'definitely black,' and one even said 'the kind of really dumb black you used to see in the movies.' "[6]

Helms also ran ads tying Gantt to gay rights. Gantt did have moderate views on gay rights, but Helms took it a step further. One of the spots accused Gantt of running a "secret campaign" to rally gay support and collect campaign contributions. The ad said Gantt had "run ads in gay newspapers, had fund-raising drives in gay bars in New York and San Francisco," and had promised to back mandatory gay rights laws, including requiring local schools to hire gay teachers. An announcer then says, "Harvey Gantt is dangerously liberal. Too liberal for North Carolina." Of course, there was no proof to back up any of the charges.

Yet another ad further attempted to highlight race in the campaign. Gantt's campaign manager, Mel Watt, an African American, is shown in the ad denying Helms's charges, saying they are an "out and out lie." According to Jamieson, the audio is edited to make Watt's voice sound higher and "tinnier" than it actually is, to project weakness and indecisiveness.

WHITE HANDS

The best-known TV ad from that campaign has become one for the ages. It is often used as a case study of how to play to the emotions of the viewing audience by hitting on key fears and anxieties. Gantt's support for extending civil rights protections was used by Helms as evidence that Gantt favored racial quotas.

Helms and his media consultant, Alex Castellanos, created the ad that has come to be known as the "White Hands" spot. The ad—which very likely sewed up the race for Helms—showed the arms and hands of a white male opening, then crumpling up, a rejection letter. An announcer says, "You needed that job, and you were the best qualified. But they had to give it to a minority because of a racial quota. Is that really fair? Harvey Gantt says it is. Gantt supports Ted Kennedy's racial quota law that makes the color of your skin more important than your qualifications. You'll vote on this issue next Tuesday. For racial quotas, Harvey Gantt. Against racial quotas, Jesse Helms."[7]

This ad really struck a chord with North Carolina voters, as Helms began moving up in the polls immediately after it started airing. Gantt's campaign manager credits the ad with winning the campaign for Helms. Everyone agrees it was effective, but it is also the subject of intense criticism for playing on racial fears.

Alex Castellanos, who created the ad, defends it. "The message in that spot's very clear, and that is nobody should get a job, or be denied a job because of the color of their skin. The vast majority of Americans believe that. And if it's wrong for us to discriminate that way, then it's wrong for our government to discriminate that way."[8]

Helms and his Congressional Club were also accused of trying to discourage blacks from voting. Someone sent over 100,000 postcards to North Carolina voters warning that if they were not eligible to vote and they tried to vote anyway, they could be prosecuted and jailed for fraud. What makes the mailing suspicious is that the vast majority of the recipients of the voter mailing were black. A Justice Department investigation of the mailing after the election traced it to four direct-mail and marketing firms that worked for the Helms campaign.[9]

The Helms attacks on Gantt seemed to work, as there was a surge of support for Helms in tracking polls during the last two weeks of the campaign. Helms defeated Gantt 52 percent to 48 percent. Of course, Gantt won the black vote overwhelmingly, but blacks made up only about 20 percent of the population of North Carolina. In order to win, Gantt would have had to win at least 40 to 45 percent of the white vote; he won 38 percent, while Helms took over 60 percent of the white vote.

In 1996 Helms was once again challenged by Gantt. In some ways, the 1996 campaign was a replay of 1990, with the focus once again on race, gays, and liberals. Gantt and some Democratic Party advocacy groups emphasized Helms's attack tactics and controversial stands, but the power of incumbency once again proved too much to overcome; Gantt lost again.

In the 1990s, with Republicans firmly in control of the senate, Helms represented a very powerful voice in the legislature. As chairman of the Senate Foreign Relations Committee, he exerted enormous influence, and he used this power both to further his beliefs and to stick it to what he perceived to be the liberal, internationalist establishment.

In the Senate, he held up ambassadorial appointments in the Clinton administration, stalled payment of U.S. dues to the United Nations, vehemently criticized American foreign policy, and generally made life as miserable as he could for President Bill Clinton.

In his last years in the Senate, some saw what might have been a slight mellowing of Helms, as evidenced by his frequent meetings and cooperation with Clinton's secretary of state Madeleine Albright, and his friendship with rock singer and political activist Bono. Yet not very many African Americans or gay rights advocates would admit to any mellowing in the man whom they viewed as their enemy.

The "White Hands" spot was controversial but effective. Courtesy, Julian P. Kanter Archive/University of Oklahoma.

Helms left the political stage in 2003, when he decided not to seek reelection for a sixth term in the U.S. Senate. His seat was filled by Elizabeth Dole, whom most view as a political moderate.

So how did such a controversial politician, someone who advocated policies considered by many to be vitriolic and hate filled, survive in elected office during four different decades? Some observers, such as Howard Troxler, believe the answer is that Helms was an unswerving ideologue but a charming politician. "He got reelected because a lot of people were mad," Troxler says. "You can argue all day that they were wrong to be mad, that they were backward or unsophisticated to be mad. But they were mad anyway, and anybody who ever thought it could be wished away with a big-city smirk and a roll of the eyes was wrong. This is what Jesse Helms knew."[10]

Homo Sapiens, Thespians, and Extroverts

George Smathers v. Claude Pepper, Democratic Primary, U.S. Senate, Florida, 1950

This campaign has become the stuff of political legend. "Are you aware that Claude Pepper is known all over Washington as a shameless *extrovert?* Not only that, but this man is reliably reported to practice *nepotism* with his sister-in-law, he has a brother who is a known *homo sapiens*, and he has a sister who was once a *thespian* in wicked New York. Worst of all, it is an established fact that Mr. Pepper, before his marriage he habitually practiced *celibacy*."[1]

These, according to the legend, are the words of one George Smathers, a Democratic congressman from Florida, who in 1950 defeated that state's incumbent U.S. Senator, Claude Pepper, in the Democratic primary. The thing about legends, though—particularly political legends—is that sometimes they are not entirely true, and sometimes they are not true at all.

As for this legend, there is simply no proof one way or the other that Smathers ever made the above remarks attributed to him by history. Smathers supposedly made these historic comments about Senator Pepper as he campaigned through north and central Florida in the spring of 1950.

According to the legend, he spoke to crowds of voters in the small towns of the region. To the mostly rural voters of the area, his accusations against Pepper, using words like "homo sapiens" and "thespian" (which to rural small town voters probably sounded a lot like "homo sexual" and "lesbian"), were nothing short of shocking. Many of these voters, for reasons that will be discussed, were predisposed to believe bad things about Senator Pepper, and so the shock value of these statements may have contributed to his reelection defeat.

Claude Pepper on the campaign trail. University Libraries, Florida State University, Tallahassee, FL.

For his part, Smathers always vigorously denied that he ever made the comments. If he did, there were no TV cameras or radio microphones to record them for posterity. One can understand why he would deny making the comments. For one thing, no one wants to be labeled a mudslinger. And his U.S. Senate colleagues might take a dim view of someone who said such inflammatory and misleading things about their opponent, particularly an incumbent senator like Claude Pepper.

But even if the legend is true, it probably isn't the main reason for Pepper's defeat. Smathers, and Pepper's other political enemies, had plenty of other ammunition to use in the 1950 campaign. Even without these legendary slanderous remarks, the statements and tactics that actually were used in this campaign, and that are verified by history, qualify it as one of the most negative ever. Indeed, NBC newsman David Brinkley called it "the dirtiest in the history of American politics."[2]

In hindsight, it now seems clear that Pepper was one of the first political victims of Cold War politics and the Red Scare of the 1950s.

RED PEPPER

Claude Pepper was a New Deal Democrat and an ally of Franklin Roosevelt. He was elected in 1936 to finish out the term of Senator Duncan Fletcher, who died in office, then elected to his first full term in 1938. In the 1940s he became known as somewhat of a radical, pushing legislation for a minimum wage, federal support for health insurance, equal rights for blacks and women, and federal labor legislation.

George Smathers and wife, with the Peppers. University Libraries, Florida State University, Tallahassee, FL.

Pepper was also strongly interested in foreign policy and international affairs. He was a strong proponent in the late 1930s and early 1940s of defeating fascism. He advocated closer ties to Russia, and met with Soviet leader Joseph Stalin to discuss Russia's relationship with the United States. His ties to Soviet politics and causes led him to oppose the Truman doctrine of aggressively confronting communist expansion throughout the world. He voted against President Truman's request to send American forces and economic aid to Greece and Turkey in order to strengthen them from communist takeover.

Pepper was a thorn in the side of Harry Truman, and he wasn't shy about letting people know it. In a speech to the National Citizens Political Action Committee, Pepper replied to those who urged a hard line against the Soviet Union. "There are still selfish and unscrupulous men who place their desires for personal power and profit above the welfare of the nation and the world," he said. People wondered, Was he talking about Truman? "Chief among the weapons of these sinister forces today is the weapon of anti Sovietism. Not a morning passes but that I read in the newspaper some new and conscienceless attack upon our great ally that, be it remembered, which for nearly two years singlehandedly held the line against the engulfing hordes of the Nazi juggernaut."[3]

The Truman administration was trying to act with broad consensus in facing down Soviet expansionism in Europe and elsewhere, and Claude Pepper, a senior member of the Senate Foreign Relations Committee, was getting in the way. By the mid-1940s, he had gained a fair amount of notoriety for his foreign policy views.

To counter Western criticisms of the Soviet Union, Pepper in turn criticized the U.S.–British alliance, with scathing attacks on British imperialism along with what he said were American designs on the rest of the world. His inflammatory statements began to attract national attention, most of it negative.

In August 1946, for example, he was negatively portrayed in the *Saturday Evening Post* in an article called "Pink Pepper." The article focused on his liberal politics and pro-Soviet statements. It attacked him as self-centered and egotistical, and said he was not acting in the national interest. It referred to

The "Red Record" of Claude Pepper. University Libraries, Florida State University, Tallahassee, FL.

him as the "most dangerous man in the Senate since Huey Long,"[4] which was quite an insult.

By the late 1940s, Pepper was increasingly seen as out of the mainstream of foreign policy. But he didn't seem to care. He voted against parts of the Marshall Plan, which was crucial for rebuilding postwar Europe. He said U.S. foreign policy was undermining the authority of the United Nations. He believed that peace would be better achieved through the United Nations, not through the actions of individual countries like the United States and Great Britain.

He even opposed Harry Truman's nomination for

president in 1948. He campaigned for Truman and the Democratic ticket that fall, but Truman kept him at a distance, as did an increasing number of American politicians and Florida business and civic leaders.

Political observers in Florida noted that Pepper's controversial views on foreign policy and his pro-labor positions had damaged him politically. He was no longer seen as a New Deal Democrat, but as an extremist.

ENEMIES IN FLORIDA

One of Pepper's most ardent foes was a Florida businessman named Ed Ball. In the 1940s Ball had become a force in state business and politics as the head of the DuPont family trust and its business interests. Chief among these was a controlling interest in the Florida East Coast railway (FEC). Senator Pepper was a leader in the fight among labor unions to force a labor settlement on Ball and the railway. Ball never forgave Pepper, and he became an active force in the 1950 campaign to unseat him.

Ball joined a growing line of Florida businessmen and state economic interests that wanted to see Pepper gone. Pepper's controversial foreign policy views made it easier for the anti-Pepper forces, as it gave them a popular rationale to oppose him. For example, the Associated Industries of Florida, the principal political arm of the state's business community, distributed anti-Pepper newsletters across the state. One of these famously trumpeted a pro-Pepper article from an American communist newspaper, the *Daily Worker*.

The Florida business community, led by Ed Ball, began actively looking for a candidate to oppose Pepper in the 1950 election. Almost immediately, speculation centered on George Smathers.

THE PERFECT CANDIDATE

Smathers had upset a four-term congressman in 1946. He was a young, tall, athletic lawyer, and a marine combat veteran. He also vehemently disagreed with Pepper on foreign policy, preferring the policies of Truman. In other words, he was the perfect candidate to oppose Pepper.

Smathers came from a political family with good connections. In fact, while at the University of Florida, Smathers had run the campus organization for Pepper's 1938 senate campaign. Smathers maintained a friendly relationship with Pepper all the way up to 1950, even though the two disagreed on many issues, especially foreign policy. Pepper had helped the young

Smathers obtain an appointment as assistant U.S. attorney in Miami in 1941. Then Smathers volunteered for the Marine Corps and served several tours of duty in World War II.

In 1945, with the war winding down, he sought Pepper's assistance in gaining an early discharge from the service. He wrote to Pepper and shared his admiration for the senator's work on behalf of the poor and disadvantaged. Pepper later used these letters against Smathers in the 1950 campaign as examples of his betrayal and disloyalty.[5]

For more information on Claude Pepper, visit the Claude Pepper Museum at Florida State University in Tallahassee, FL. Or visit online at http://www.claude pepper.org.

Smathers was encouraged to run against Pepper by many in Florida, including Ed Ball and others in the business community. But it was President Truman who got Smathers in the race. Smathers had met the president on several occasions but was not well known to him, so Smathers was understandably surprised when he was summoned to the White House to meet with him. After some brief small talk and pleasantries, Truman shook Smathers to the core when he said, "I want you to beat that son-of-a-bitch Claude Pepper!"[6]

INTENSE PERSONAL ATTACKS

As soon as Smathers got into the race in January 1950, the fireworks started. It isn't clear whether the Smathers campaign worked with the business groups represented by the Associated Industries of Florida, but anti-Pepper literature sprang up all over the state. Observers have long suspected that Ed Ball was heavily involved in the production of those leaflets, many of which were virulent attacks on Pepper's character and morals, but there is no proof.

Some of the anti-Pepper literature focused on Pepper's views on civil rights for blacks and other minorities. A Pepper speech to a black church in Los Angeles in 1949 was used to attack him for advocating "social equality between the races." During the campaign, Pepper had to walk a fine line that would not upset the white southern constituency, which would decide the election, but that would not betray his core beliefs in social fairness.

Photos were distributed of Pepper meeting with well-known blacks, such as the actor Paul Robeson. Indications were that some of the photos may have been doctored, but in any case, they were met with outrage by Pepper, who accused his opponents of "hateful" and crass politics.

But the core of Smathers's campaign against Pepper, as well as the attacks by others against him, was Pepper's controversial foreign policy views. Given the growing Cold War politics of the time, and the extent to which President Truman and the U.S. Congress were trying to forge an anti-Soviet consensus, it was inevitable that Pepper's pro-Soviet sympathies would cause trouble for him.

Smathers went after Pepper as a closet socialist and communist sympathizer. Of Pepper's economic views, he said, "When they socialize the doctors, then they socialize the lawyers. . . . Then next they will socialize insurance men, the farmer will be next. . . . They plan to socialize everybody." He told a large gathering of supporters in Miami, "I brand such false prophets [as Claude Pepper] as dangerous and un-American."[7]

The campaign quickly took on intensely personal overtones as Pepper fought back against the charges. He took full advantage of the fact that Smathers had once supported him and appealed to him for help. Pepper released the letters Smathers had written to him asking for help in obtaining early release from the Marine Corps. He played the part of the older, senior mentor and benefactor who had been betrayed by the young, opportunistic politician.

Pepper also went after some of his other detractors. Specifically, he attacked Ed Ball as a tool of the wealthy and powerful. He tore into Ball as a front for the DuPont family, and he cast Smathers as a "DuPont lawyer." Pepper wanted to use the image of DuPont as a wealthy and politically powerful force for the rich against the poor, even though it was stretching the truth because there were virtually no members of the famous DuPont family involved with the Florida DuPont business interests that Ed Ball was administering at that time.[8]

But that didn't bother Pepper. He attacked the DuPont lawyers and Dupont elitists at every opportunity. He used it so often, it became absurd to many people, and Pepper was criticized for trying to use class warfare to pit the rich against the poor.

THE FINAL BLOW

In the final days of the campaign, a very critical anti-Pepper booklet was printed and distributed throughout Florida cities. Called "The Red Record of Claude Pepper," it was a textbook example of how to smear an opponent. It contained a number of excerpts from Pepper's speeches, highlighting his support for the Soviet Union, his opposition to President Truman's policies of containment, and his support for organized labor. It also featured photos of Pepper with well-known socialists and other left-wing political activists.

The material in the booklet was used to make the claim that Pepper was a dangerous extremist with more loyalties to the Kremlin than to his own country. It strung together enough of Pepper's quotes and votes in Congress to make him look like a communist sympathizer. It definitely stretched the truth and manipulated the circumstances, but as a tool of political attack, it was devastatingly effective.

Pepper and his supporters were beyond the point of anger. He pointed the finger at Ed Ball and the DuPont lawyers, but there was no evidence to tie them to the "Red Record." Pepper's counterattacks and denials were lost in an avalanche of unfavorable media coverage and finger pointing.

On election day, Smathers defeated Pepper by more than 60,000 votes—virtually a landslide in Florida in 1950. The anti-Pepper forces had carried the day and ended the career of a longtime nemesis. Or had they?

George Smathers went on to serve three terms in the U.S. Senate, serving with distinction on a number of Senate committees. He left the Senate in 1969 and resumed a lucrative law practice in Washington, D.C. and Miami.

But Claude Pepper wasn't through. He worked in the private sector for twelve years, then came back to politics in 1962. He ran for a newly created congressional seat in south Florida and won. He was elected to thirteen consecutive terms in the U.S. House of Representatives, where he became a champion of senior citizens and the poor, leading the charge on health care, Medicare, Social Security, and social welfare issues.

He died in May 1989, while still serving in the U.S. Congress.

VOTE FOR THE
CROOK—IT'S IMPORTANT

Edwin Edwards v. David Duke, Governor, Louisiana, 1991

Question: *When should you vote for a candidate that has been investigated four separate times by federal grand juries for racketeering, bribery, and extortion?*
Answer: *When his opponent is the grand imperial wizard of the Ku Klux Klan.*

This could probably only happen in Louisiana—a state that is to colorful and memorable politics what Milwaukee is to beer. Edwin Edwards was as colorful and bold a politician (some would say shameless) as Louisiana had seen in a while. And that state has seen its share of colorful and bold (OK, shameless) political figures. Remember Huey Long, the Kingfish? And his brother Earl, who was twice elected governor, then hospitalized for mental illness, then elected to the U.S. Congress?

For much of its recent history, the politics of Louisiana have had clear fault lines—the first being religion. Thirty percent of the voters come from heavily ethnic Cajun Catholic areas, which are often the regions that provide the swing votes in close elections; approximately 25 percent of the state's voters are from mixed-religion New Orleans; and the remaining 45 percent are from the heavily Protestant area north of Baton Rouge, the state capital.

Another fault line in Louisiana's politics is race. Around 30 percent of the voters are African American. These voters are normally a reliable source of

David Duke in England, 1978. His controversial past brought Louisiana unwanted attention. AP/Wide World Photos.

support for Democratic candidates. Louisiana's white voters often split their vote along economic lines. Middle- to upper-income white voters normally vote Republican, while lower-income and blue collar white voters lean toward Democrats. One result of this mixture is a historical tendency to back either very conservative candidates or reformist mavericks.[1]

Another Louisiana tradition is populism. Populist candidates craft their appeals to the common people, and often wage war against the "powers that be," such as when Huey Long railed against corporate interests such as big oil companies. The 1991 campaign for governor featured in some ways a contest between the more traditional Huey Long–type of liberal populism, embraced by Edwin Edwards, and a more radical, right-wing type of populism, pushed by David Duke.

But of course Duke's style of right-wing populism catered toward extremist teachings about race, ethnicity, and religion. Though he tried to disguise his radical views in the 1991 campaign, he was well known for saying that blacks are lazy, are predisposed to crime, and have lower IQ scores because they are genetically inferior to whites; that whites suffer from reverse discrimination; and that the lynching of blacks was justified because it was punishment for "serious criminal behavior such as rape and murder."[2]

Duke didn't leave the Jews out either. Along with anti-black literature and speeches, he peddled anti-Semitic teachings. He insisted that "conniving" Jews run the economy and the media; that they use blacks as pawns against white Christians; that the Holocaust was "greatly exaggerated;" and that Jews declared war on Adolf Hitler first, so his actions were in self-defense.

THE CAST OF CHARACTERS

Edwin Edwards was elected governor in 1972, 1976, 1984, and, of course, 1991. His motto during his four terms as governor was *laissez les bon temps roulez* (let the good times roll). And they did. He was an old-school politician, sort of a throwback to machine politics and the corruption that goes with it. But he did it in style. For one thing, he was a quote machine. He left political historians with some very memorable quotations. Among them, "The only way I can lose this election is if I'm caught in bed with either a dead girl, or a live boy." And this one during one of his corruption trials, "I never speak ill of dead people or live judges."[3]

It was in his third term that he was indicted by federal prosecutors on multiple counts of bribery and obstruction of justice. His first federal trial ended in a hung jury; his second trial ended with an acquittal, leaving him free to run for political office again.

His opponent, Duke, was not as colorful or as clever, but in many ways more dangerous. Duke bore all the markings of a classic sociopath or narcissist—dispensing hate, using financial shenanigans to finance his schemes, and manipulating those around him to further his social and political aims. "On the surface, he is charming, friendly, and boyishly handsome," writes Tyler Bridges, who wrote a biography of Duke. "But beneath the mask lurks a twisted fanatic."[4]

Edwin Edwards contributed greatly to Louisiana's "colorful" political heritage. Louisiana State Archives.

A MISSPENT YOUTH?

Duke was exposed to racist and neo-Nazi literature when he was in high school. As a student at LSU in the early 1970s, he organized a group called the White Youth Alliance. This group was affiliated with the National Socialist White People's Party (NSWPP), a neo-Nazi party in Virginia. Duke was known for distributing racist and Nazi propaganda on campus and organizing campus events in which he and his followers would parade around with swastika armbands.

After college, he started a Louisiana chapter of the Knights of the Ku Klux Klan (KKK), and was appointed its grand wizard. Duke was a new kind of Klan leader. Far from the old, redneck type of leader associated with the KKK, he was a college-educated, well-dressed, rather charismatic leader. He was politically savvy, and very adept at fund-raising and working a room.

Duke first sought elective office in 1975 when he ran for the Louisiana state senate. As a candidate for public office, he de-emphasized his affiliation with the Ku Klux Klan, but ran on a platform of "white rights." He would follow this pattern in future political campaigns—camouflaging as best he could his racist, extremist views, while still holding true to his political goals. He lost the 1975 race, but set the tone for future runs for office.

> This is the only gubernatorial campaign of the 20th century in which *both* major party nominees were later convicted of felonies and served time in federal prison.

He ran for the state senate as a Democrat in 1979 and lost again. Then in 1980, he broke from his association with the Klan, ostensibly for public relations reasons, and formed the National Association for the Advancement of White People (NAAWP). He said it was an attempt to further the cause of white rights without the baggage and stereotypes of the old Klan image. He spent the 1980s raising money and building the National Association for the Advancement of White People into a regional political organization.

In 1989 he ran again for the Louisiana state house as a Republican, and this time he won. Now a government official, he tried to rehabilitate his public image by projecting a more statesmanlike, shrewd, policy-oriented message. The charade was hard to maintain, though, as he was exposed by his critics for selling neo-Nazi literature from his legislative office, an issue that would haunt him in his future political efforts.

The next year, he ran against incumbent U.S. Senator Bennett Johnston. In what many in Louisiana dubbed "Dukespeak," he carefully couched his radical public agenda in code words that sounded to most like racial appeals. Duke's radicalism was publicly rejected by a number of Republicans, leading eight Republican members of the U.S. Senate to endorse the Democrat Johnston. Duke lost to Johnston, but pulled in over 45 percent of the vote.[5]

THE WIZARD AND THE LIZARD

Then in 1991 came the race for governor. So how did Louisianans find themselves in this situation, with a race for governor between a former Ku Klux Klan leader and a discredited former governor? Many blame the state's electoral system for statewide elections.

Louisiana is the only state in the country to use a "non-partisan primary" to elect its statewide officeholders. All candidates for an office, regardless of party affiliation, run on the same primary-election ballot. If a candidate gets over 50 percent of the vote, he or she wins the office outright. In statewide elections, this rarely happens because the number of candidates running makes it practically impossible for any one of them to get over 50 percent of the votes. So the top two vote getters, regardless of party, face each other in a run-off election in December. There could be two Republicans facing each other, or two Democrats.

During Edwards's third term as governor in the mid-1980s, he was dogged by allegations of corruption and investigated by the federal government. He ran for reelection in 1987 but lost to fellow Democrat Buddy Roemer. However, during Roemer's only term as governor, he switched parties and became a Republican. He may have thought that Louisiana was becoming a more Republican state and wanted to ride that wave, or that as the incumbent governor he could survive switching parties. In either case, he turned out to be wrong. Party switchers in general do not have a very good record of holding on to power.

Escaping a federal criminal conviction, Edwards ran again for governor in 1991 against Roemer. Several other candidates were on the ballot, including David Duke, running as a Republican. The campaign was dominated by Edwards, Roemer, and Duke. Many Louisianans thought their choices were bleak.

It is interesting that Roemer, the incumbent governor, came in third on primary day to Duke and Edwards. Edwards led with 34 percent of the vote, followed by Duke with 32 percent and Roemer with 27 percent. Thus, the fall campaign between the Klansman and the crook, or the "wizard and the lizard," as some called it, was set.

One of the advantages that Duke had in the race was that his notoriety, or infamy, for running for statewide office on such extremist, radical views had caught the attention of the national media. In November 1991, Duke appeared on *Good Morning America*, *Today*, *Crossfire*, *The Phil Donahue Show*, *Nightline*, *Larry King Live*, and other national news programs. These programs liked interviewing Duke because it attracted viewership and increased ratings. Duke liked appearing on these programs as it provided him free airtime to broadcast his message to the voters of Louisiana. Edwards, meanwhile, had to scrape by with paid advertising.

Duke made full use of his national exposure. He urged viewers to write his campaign for more information and asked that financial contributions be sent to his campaign headquarters in Louisiana, for which he gave the full address and ZIP code. It worked quite well, at least financially; Duke received campaign contributions from viewers in forty-six states.[6]

He also used the airtime to make his case to Louisiana voters through the use of outlandish claims, such as "the U.S. Postal Service drops the test scores of whites and elevates them for blacks," and "billion dollar-a-year" companies were eager to come to Louisiana if he was elected governor. He was also very savvy in his negotiations for interviews. For example, in several of his TV appearances, he won guarantees from the program's producers that they would not show old photos of him in Klan uniform and would not display racist statements he had made on the TV screen.[7]

A REASONABLE PRICE?

It was a far different case with the media inside Louisiana. After all, they had to live with the aftermath of the campaign—the folks at *Good Morning America* didn't. Louisiana newspapers had long been active participants in the state's raucous politics, and 1991 was no exception. The *New Orleans Times-Picayune* waged an aggressive campaign, not necessarily in support of Edwards but definitely against Duke.

The *Times-Picayune* had not been a supporter of Edwin Edwards, but the paper enthusiastically endorsed him while blasting Duke as a dangerous extremist. It was a well-coordinated media campaign, with columnists, reporters, and photographers doing whatever they could to prevent Duke from becoming governor. It failed traditional standards of journalism, to be sure, but the overall goal of defeating the former Klan leader was seen as "a reasonable price to pay."

Jim Amoss, editor of the *Times-Picayune*, explains: "Newsrooms pride themselves on being at the epicenter of momentous events, monitoring tremors, privy to the excitement, yet always at a dispassionate distance. For Louisiana journalists, our recent governor's race broke that mold. Our state was shaken to its core. And the newsroom of the *Times-Picayune* quaked with it, knowing that our future was at stake. It was a battle for the soul of the electorate, and we found ourselves in the thick of it."[8]

ANYBODY BUT DUKE

Another part of the campaign against David Duke was waged by Louisiana's business community. Mainstream business leaders decided Duke's name would hurt the state's business prospects, particularly its convention and trade-show business, and the tourism industry. In what some might call image politics, Louisiana trade and business groups blanketed the state with anti-Duke TV advertising and newspaper ads, threatening dire economic consequences if Duke actually became governor.

And although Duke ran as a Republican, the Republican Party establishment loudly rejected Duke and his political beliefs. President George H. W. Bush had campaigned for the party-switching Buddy Roemer in the primary, and although he did not endorse the Democrat Edwin Edwards in the general election, the president was openly disdainful of Duke throughout the fall campaign. The national Republican Party did what it could to distance itself and its officials from any kind of relationship with Duke, even running radio ads in Louisiana criticizing his racist statements from past campaigns.

Edwards and Duke attacked each other as unfit for office. Of the three-time former governor, Duke said he was an example of the corrupt, immoral system of domination that "big-government elites" had used to enrich themselves at the expense of the state's good, hardworking people. Edwards dismissed Duke as a Nazi nutcase. Asked by a reporter what he had to do to defeat Duke in the election, Edwards replied, "Stay alive."

In one of the campaign's more high-profile incidents, Duke attacked Edwards for encouraging black voter registration. This represented one of the few instances in the campaign in which Duke let his true colors show, accusing Edwards and other state officials of enticing blacks to register to vote with offers of fried chicken, an old racist stereotype. He then accused Edwards of being a member of the National Association for the Advancement of Colored People (NAACP). Duke had repeatedly renounced his past association with the Klan and emphasized his rebirth as a Christian, but attacks like these, as well as the use of other code words for race and ethnicity, made it a hard sell to many Louisiana voters.[9]

END OF THE LINE

In the end, the voters were pretty clear. Edwards crushed Duke in the election, winning 61 percent of the votes to Duke's 39 percent. Duke won over 60 percent of the white vote, but his strident image and controversial campaign had pushed black voter registration and participation to all-time highs. That, combined with the revulsion that many middle-class, moderate whites held for Duke, made the outcome inevitable.

The rest, as they say, is history. Edwards went on to serve his fourth term as Louisiana's governor, after which he was indicted yet again by federal prosecutors on charges of extortion and bribery. This time he was convicted. His appeals ran out in 2000, and he now sits in the federal penitentiary in Fort Worth, Texas, serving a ten-year prison sentence.

As for David Duke, he continued to try to use the world of politics and public policy to keep himself afloat, both professionally and personally. In the mid- to late 1990s, he entered several political campaigns, only to drop out after dismal showings in the polls. All the while, he continued to appeal for financial contributions from his supporters. He briefly had a radio talk show in New Orleans, in which he railed against the worldwide Jewish conspiracy and the danger blacks posed to America.

After his failure to win public office, Duke dropped all pretense of moderation or reform of his old extremist views. He renewed his association with anti-black and anti-Semitic neo-Nazi organizations. In 1998 he wrote a 700-page autobiography called *My Awakening*, modeled on Adolf Hitler's *Mein Kampf*. In it, Duke calls for an Aryan revolution to cleanse America of "undesirables" and defend the white race. So much for moderation.

Duke also ran afoul of federal authorities, just as his old nemesis Edwin Edwards did. The campaign contributions he had solicited in the 1990s were used by Duke for personal investments and gambling trips to Las Vegas and the Bahamas. This was an often-used tactic by Duke: beg supporters for money to support political activities, then use the money for personal use. Duke also filed a false tax return in 1998, claiming income of only $18,000 when it was actually $65,000—another federal offense.[10]

In 2002 Duke pleaded guilty to federal authorities and negotiated a prison term. He entered federal prison in 2003. The unkindest cut of all? His felony conviction makes him ineligible to run for political office.

Who's the Boss? Richard Daley and the Chicago Political Machine

Richard Daley v. Robert Merriam, Mayor, Chicago, 1955

In the movie *The Untouchables,* which is about fighting crime during prohibition-era Chicago, the Sean Connery character turns to Kevin Costner (Eliot Ness) and explains, "They put one of yours in the hospital, you put one of theirs in the morgue! That's the Chicago way!" Although the Daley era in Chicago didn't involve sanctioning murder and gangland violence, it involved pretty much everything else.

Chicago is a tough city, and through most of the 20th century, it was run by a political machine the likes of which this country has rarely seen. There have been lots of big-time political bosses in America's large cities—George Washington Plunkitt of Tammany Hall in New York in the 1800s and, more recently, Marion Barry of Washington, D.C. But for pure political muscle and unashamed strong-arming of every official in the way, none match Mayor Richard J. Daley, who ran Chicago from 1955 until his death in 1976.

His election in 1955 set the stage for a brutal twenty-year reign. But first he had to dispense with his opponents in the election. His victory over his Democratic primary opponents and then Republican nominee Robert Merriam is remembered as a vicious struggle for the heart and soul of Chicago.

Daley was born and bred in the city's politically powerful Eleventh Ward, which produced not only Daley but the three mayors preceding him. The machine system that Chicago's power brokers used to run city services, elect their preferred candidates, and intimidate potential adversaries was brutal. Either you produced, or you were replaced.

Richard J. Daley was among the most powerful political bosses in American history. Photograph, ICHi-25546; photographer—Pete Peters, *Chicago Sun-Times*. Courtesy, Chicago Historical Society.

Loyalty to the city's Democratic Party and to the leadership was crucial for survival. The center of the political universe was the Cook County Democratic Party. The chair of the county party ran the show, and from there, power trickled down to other city and county officials, such as aldermen and precinct captains.

The power of any political machine stems from its ability to provide jobs for its supporters and government contracts and other financial incentives for its financial contributors. And the Chicago machine was one of the most brutally effective in history. In other words, it was crooked, from top to bottom. The Cook County Democratic chair and the city and county officials working for the machine could get literally anything for anybody it wanted.

POLITICS, CHICAGO STYLE

Daley's rise to power started in 1947, when he became precinct captain of the Eleventh Ward. By 1952 he was vice-chair of the Cook County Democratic Party and on his way up in the machine system. He had cultivated enough favors and political support by 1954 to become chair. Later that year, his supporters had him "drafted" as a Democratic candidate for mayor in the 1955 election.

Getting the Democratic nomination was usually the key to getting elected in big city politics. Opposing Daley for the nomination were incumbent mayor Martin Kennelly and former Daley ally Ben Adamowski. Kennelly, mayor from 1947 to 1955, had run into serious political problems, mostly through efforts to reform parts of city government. Adamowski had been a loyal machine member of the state legislature, but had a falling out with Daley and his allies in the capital.[1]

Kennelly's efforts to resist the machine by reforming the civil service sec-

tor and cracking down on gambling and vice had hurt him politically. The machine decided to back Daley over the incumbent mayor. Daley campaigned using the resources of the machine, promising jobs and favors to those who supported him. But what won him the nomination was his support from the

black communities. Daley had worked black neighborhoods hard, visiting local shops and restaurants, and walking through neighborhoods. Mayor Kennelly had alienated some black leaders by not consulting with them on key decisions. Daley exploited that opening.

Kennelly tried to run a reform campaign, and appealed to independents and Republicans to cross over and vote in the Democratic primary for mayor. But that didn't happen—at least not in large enough numbers to offset the power of the machine and its candidates.

Through the power of the machine, and support among key ethnic groups in Chicago's south side and the

Robert Merriam ran as a "reformer." Photographic print, ICHi-38532; Courtesy, Chicago Historical Society.

black community, Daley prevailed over his two primary opponents, winning 49 percent of the vote. Now he turned his attention to the general election and the Republican opposition.

THE OPPONENT

The Republican nominee, Robert Merriam, was actually a Democrat. He had been an alderman from the city's north side, known for an interest in reform. The dashing and charismatic thirty-six-year-old Merriam, whose district included the University of Chicago and Hyde Park, was known as "the

WASP prince of Chicago."[2] He was the son of a renowned university professor, he himself held a master's degree, and he had been a World War II hero at the Battle of the Bulge.

Merriam and Daley were a study in contrasts. Merriam had good looks, style, and sophistication, while Daley—a short, balding, working-class sort—had spent decades of his life plodding his way up machine politics. Merriam was a smooth speaker. Daley spoke in a heavy Chicago accent, sprinkling his sentences with "dis" and "dat."

But the fact is, Daley fit much more the lifestyle and expectations of most of Chicago's citizens. His working-class background and regular-person demeanor appealed to more Chicagoans than Merriam's upper-crust pedigree and high-minded talk of reform. From a standpoint of style, Daley was south side; Merriam, north side.

On the city council, Merriam was the leader of a group of reformers known as the economy block, for their interest in reducing the wasteful spending of city dollars. Many reform-minded city officials, as well as the Republican Party, encouraged Merriam to challenge Daley and the political machine. Although not all Republicans wanted to turn the party over to a Democrat, no better potential candidates stepped forward, and the Republican governor of Illinois, William Stratton, urged them to accept Merriam and use his crossover appeal to help expand the base of the Republican Party.[3]

Daley made the most of his affiliation as a Democrat. He routinely reminded Chicago voters that Merriam was a Republican. Of course, he did not bother to explain that Merriam had jumped ship from the Democratic Party machine because of concerns about corruption. Daley taunted Merriam for not being a loyal member of either party. He claimed that Merriam was trying to convince Democrats that he was not a Republican and trying to convince Republicans that he was not really a Democrat. In one debate, he declared, "I can't think of anything harder than mating an elephant with a donkey."

> Richard Daley's son, Richard M. Daley, is the current mayor of Chicago. Since 1989, he has served five terms as mayor of the City of the Big Shoulders.

But Merriam's only real chance of winning was to do just that. The idea was to make it a "fusion" campaign, he would explain later. A coalition of disaffected Democrats, Republicans, and independents could stop the Democratic machine if they could be convinced that it was in their interests. He was moderately successful in attracting some independents, but not very many Democrats. Not even Daley's primary foes, Kennelly and Adamowski, would come out and endorse Merriam.

A BLOOD MATCH

Basically, Merriam said that Daley was corrupt and would run a corrupt city. Like Kennelly and Adamowski did in the Democratic primary, Merriam warned Chicago voters that they would be in for dark times with Daley as their mayor. He argued that the mayoral election of 1955 would decide whether the city would fall victim to "the arrogant bosses" of the Chicago political machine. "Their transparent and nefarious manipulations," he said, "proved that the Democratic Party under Richard Daley cannot be trusted to govern the city in the interests of all the people."[4]

He also tied Daley to the mob and organized crime. He said the machine was backing Daley so that Chicago could become a "wide open city" for mob gambling, prostitution, and the drug trade. "Every syndicate operation is going to open up in Chicago: open for high stakes, high pressure gambling, crooked dice games, and all the rest," he declared.

Daley reacted with calm anger. "It's a lie," he reported. "I will follow the training my good Irish mother gave me. . . . If I'm elected, I'll embrace mercy, love, charity, and walk humbly with God."[5] *Kum ba yah*, Mayor Daley!

As he did in the primary, Daley ran his campaign as the candidate of the machine—and everything that goes along with it. As in the primary, he courted the black vote, but also remained close to ethnic leaders who were hostile to civil rights for blacks. He presented himself to the black community as someone who would fight for equal rights. He even got an endorsement from a black Chicago newspaper—"Elect Daley," the headline blared.

Many blacks were told Daley would take a firm stand on issues of importance to the black community. But how firm the stand was would change, depending on who was in the room. When speaking before white audiences, Daley was indifferent, in some cases even hostile, to equal rights for blacks. He maneuvered as best he could to attract black support without alienating his white, ethnic base.

He had voiced support for integrated public housing to black leaders, but when asked by reporters where it would be located, he replied, "Let's not be arguing about where it's located." His precinct captains quietly reassured white neighborhoods that they could count on a Mayor Daley to "hold the line" on integration. The South Deering Improvement Association, very much opposed to racial integration, announced it had struck a deal with Daley. The association endorsed him and campaigned for him throughout north Chicago.

Dirty Tricks

The machine also used more blatant racial appeals, but did so very quietly and behind the scenes. In neighborhoods such as the Bungalow Belt—working-class white neighborhoods on the south side—it circulated fake letters from a made-up group called the American Negro Civic Association praising Merriam for his strong support for integrated housing in Chicago. Daley's forces also spread rumors in some of these neighborhoods that Merriam's wife was black.

Not to leave the Catholics out, they stirred them up by circulating copies of Merriam's divorce papers from his first marriage. Daley's campaign sought to emphasize his strong family, in comparison to Merriam's two marriages, by speaking emotionally of his "sainted mother, and his seven children kneeling at the side of their beds in prayer."[6]

Probably the low point of Daley's campaign, because it gave credence to Merriam's corruption charges, was a scandal involving one of Daley's machine-sponsored aldermen, David Becker. The Chicago Bar Association had brought formal charges against Becker for receiving kickbacks. Daley at first stuck by Becker—he was, after all, one of his. But when evidence surfaced and questions started being asked, Daley dropped Becker from the machine ticket for alderman and replaced him with a ward captain.

At least Merriam had most of Chicago's newspapers on his side. At the time, the Chicago papers leaned Republican, and although they looked at Merriam with suspicion for just having joined the Republican Party, they looked at Daley and his machine with absolute revulsion. The *Tribune*, the *Sun-Times*, and the *Daily News* all endorsed Merriam. Daley's machine did get one endorsement, from the *Herald-American*, but even that came about as a result of a financial deal. In return for its endorsement, Daley's precinct captains would sell subscriptions.

Election-Stealing 101

Merriam and the Republicans were concerned that the Daley machine would try to steal the election. They had reason to be concerned; there was considerable evidence to bolster charges of corruption and vote buying. Merriam charged that the machine consisted of a bunch of "dictators who would spend millions of dollars to try to buy the votes they cannot honestly win."

The Merriam campaign obtained photos of a machine precinct captain named Sidney "Short-Pencil" Lewis reportedly stealing votes. (The "short-pencil" came from stuffing ballots and writing in votes for voters that did not exist.) To prove his vote-stealing claims, Merriam's campaign sent out 30,000 letters to registered voters in machine precincts. Almost 3,000 of them came back either unclaimed or indicating that the voter had moved and left no forwarding address.

Merriam used this as proof that the machine had as many as 100,000 "ghost voters" hidden away on the Chicago voting rolls. He filed a formal complaint with the Cook County Board of Elections, but it didn't get very far. The head of the elections board, Sidney Holzman, was a high-profile member of the Daley machine.

When Merriam complained that no justice could be found in Chicago, and that Holzman was part of the "Daley machine Politburo," Holzman compared Merriam to Adolf Hitler. Merriam, he said, was "following Hitler's tactics which consisted of this—if you tell a lie often enough, people will begin to believe you."[7]

MONEY TALKS

Daley had a sizable financial edge over Merriam. His machine had raised about a million dollars; Merriam and his reformers had raised about a third of that sum. One of the things the Daley campaign bought with their campaign funds was walking around money—a Chicago tradition. "Walking around money" is a term well known to many big cities and some not-so-big cities. It is purportedly used for election-day operations and get-out-the-vote efforts. But most of it finds its way into the pockets of voters. Or some of it is used to buy whiskey that finds its way into the pockets of voters. The money was usually distributed by precinct captains, who knew how to use it to best effect in their neighborhoods.[8]

In the final week of the campaign, the Daley machine had more dirty tricks up its sleeve. Republican voters got letters urging a vote for Daley on letterhead of the fictional Taft-Eisenhower league. (Robert Taft was the Republican leader of the U.S. Senate, and we all know who Eisenhower was.) Rumors were also circulated that anyone who had voted in the Democratic primary could not vote for Merriam now.

Merriam needed a large turnout to overcome the power of the Daley machine. He didn't get it. Most veteran Chicago politicos thought the machine
could turn out anywhere from 600,000 to 700,000 voters. So, Merriam
would need a total turnout of about 1.5 million to have a chance of winning.

When all the votes were in, only about 1.3 million people voted. Daley
got 708,000 votes, or 55 percent, to Merriam's 600,000. It was close—in
fact, one of the closest mayoral elections in Chicago history—but the machine prevailed.

So began the Daley era in Chicago.

Polluting the Garden State

Frank Lautenberg v. Pete Dawkins, U.S. Senate, New Jersey, 1988

I'm running against a Swamp Dog.

—Pete Dawkins

New Jersey has seen its share of tough political races. This 1988 U.S. Senate race set a state record for spending in a political campaign and is remembered as one of the dirtiest on record. According to *Newsweek*, there was so much mud flying between the two candidates that New Jersey voters "practically had to wear hip boots to get to the polls."[1]

Challenger Pete Dawkins called the incumbent, Senator Frank Lautenberg, a "swamp dog." Lautenberg called Dawkins a "carpetbagger," accusing him of polling in several other states before running in New Jersey. Dawkins was not a New Jersey native, but he denied the charges. Television ads by Lautenberg, such as the one urging Dawkins to "be real," drove Dawkins's negatives up to 35 percent by the end of the campaign.

It was not supposed to be that way. Pete Dawkins was a "dream" candidate for the Republicans in 1988. He was running against a vulnerable incumbent in Lautenberg, who was finishing his first term with public approval ratings in the forties. Lautenberg had been elected in 1982 by the smallest of margins over Republican Millicent Fenwick, even though he had outspent her $6 million to $2 million.

Dawkins looked like a "hot" political property, as the Republican Senatorial Campaign Committee made the New Jersey Senate race their number-

Frank Lautenberg. New Jersey State Archives, Department of State.

one priority in 1988. And what a résumé he had: a successful battle against childhood polio; first captain of the Corps of Cadets at West Point; football co-captain and winner of the Heisman Trophy; president of the class of 1959; Rhodes Scholar at Oxford; military service in Korea and Vietnam; winner of the Distinguished Service Medal, Legion of Merit, and two Bronze Stars; the youngest brigadier general in the Army; and so on.

After his military service, he went to work for the Shearson Lehman investment banking firm on Wall Street, where he made a bundle. His political prospects were boosted when New Jersey's popular incumbent governor, Thomas Kean, signed on as the chair of his senate campaign committee. And George H. W. Bush was expected to carry New Jersey easily over Michael Dukakis in November, enhancing the Republican senate nominee's odds.

Yet despite all of this wonderfulness, he was received coolly by the local New Jersey media. One reporter scrutinized Dawkins—still trim and athletic at age fifty, with only a dusting of gray in his sandy hair—scanned his biographical summary, and sniffed, "He looks like the kind of guy who wouldn't have a grease spot under the car in his garage."[2]

And Dawkins did have one major chink in his otherwise impressive armor. He had just barely moved into the state when he announced his intentions to seek federal office representing New Jersey. Dawkins and his all-

American family—including his pert and peppy wife Judi and their two children straight out of central casting—moved to Rumson, New Jersey, in February 1987, and he announced his candidacy for the U.S. Senate in June.

He was born and raised in Michigan and, as a military professional, had moved around quite a lot, having family residences in fifteen or twenty states

Pete Dawkins: the perfect candidate? Getty Images.

over the course of his career. When he left the service in 1983, he lived and worked in Manhattan up to the time he moved his family to the Garden State in 1987.

BATTLE OF THE RÉSUMÉS

Frank Lautenberg had also made a bundle as the CEO of Automatic Data Processing (ADP), one of the nation's most successful corporations, so he was welcome in America's boardrooms. But he was also welcome in some of America's most liberal living rooms. He was an early supporter of George McGovern's 1972 presidential campaign, gun control was one of his top priorities, and he steadfastly opposed most of Ronald Reagan's legislative agenda in the 1980s.

But because he grew up in poverty and made his money the old-fashioned way, by earning it on his own, he was held in high regard by most of his colleagues, regardless of party or ideology. According to a profile of the senator in the *New York Times*, "he wears carefully tailored suits but takes off his coat and appears in shirtsleeves when he shows up at town meetings and suburban shopping malls."[3]

But many of the political observers and analysts who followed New Jersey politics thought that "good old Frank" was going to be extremely vulnerable to a good challenger in 1988. For all his positives, he had not quite lived up to the high expectations that accompanied his victory in 1982.

Ross Baker, a political scientist at Rutgers University in New Jersey, said that Lautenberg had earned "a gentleman's C" in his first term, not becoming a high-profile senator or making himself influential in Washington.[4] Part of the problem, some analysts thought, was that he was overshadowed by the senior senator from New Jersey, Bill Bradley. Senator Bradley was a national figure, and one of the party leaders who was thought to have a shot at the presidency some day.

VOTE NEGATIVE

Dawkins was the first to go on TV, but his ads were positive at first. He spent roughly $2 million on biographical-type ads introducing him to New Jersey voters. His adman was none other than Roger Ailes, the TV advertising pioneer behind much of Richard Nixon's and Ronald Reagan's success. Ailes is now the chair of FOX News.

One of the spots produced by Ailes anticipated the "carpetbagger" charges. In the ad, Dawkins is walking in his front yard, with the sun shining through the trees. "I wasn't born in New Jersey," says Dawkins, "but I live here now. . . . Judi and I came back here to live because New Jersey people made us feel the most at home."[5]

Lautenberg held his fire until after Labor Day, feeling less of a need to introduce himself to New Jersey voters, and hoarding precious campaign dollars until they would do the most good. But when he started, he let loose a torrent of slashing attacks against Dawkins.

His ads were produced by Bob Squier and Carter Eskew, two old hands at political communication. One of his better-known ads goes after Dawkins's "transient" image. Squier and Eskew used Dawkins's 1987 announcement speech against him: "I've lived in a lot of places," he is heard saying, "but I never found a single place that had as good people or as much promise as I've found right here in our Garden State."

As he finished his statement, the words "Be Real Pete!" flash on the screen and an announcer says, "Come on, Pete; be real." The implication is that Dawkins is a shallow manipulator and is merely using New Jersey as a stepping stone into national politics.

There were indications that Lautenberg had a point. In a less-than-flattering article about Dawkins, *Manhattan Inc.* dramatized the carpetbagger issue: "One of the numbers on Dawkins's speed dialer belonged to a well-known political consultant with the Republican polling firm of Robert Teeter." (Teeter was President Bush's pollster.) "From there it required only a bit of digging to discover that the Teeter organization was polling for Dawkins in four states—Michigan, Connecticut, New York, and Colorado. . . . New Jersey was notable for its absence from the list."[6]

The Teeter firm issued a blanket denial, but the author of the article, Robert Anson, stood by the story. "Teeter does not explain how the name of an official in his organization wound up on Dawkins's office speed dialer when the non–New Jersey polling was being conducted," he said. "Equally difficult to explain is why that official was talking openly of the polling, where it was being conducted and why the exact quote was 'We're looking for a place for him to run.'"

The carpetbagger issue undeniably hurt Dawkins. In a response ad that aired a few days later, an "offended" Dawkins sits at a desk with a large American flag in the background and looks earnestly at the camera: "I'm the guy Frank Lautenberg has been attacking personally in his TV ads. . . . This election shouldn't be about where you were born or mudslinging. I'll leave that to Frank Lautenberg."

In fact, he really didn't leave it to Lautenberg. The Dawkins team went negative, too. A new Dawkins ad accused Lautenberg of taking campaign contributions from some of New Jersey's "worst toxic polluters." In the same ad, an announcer accused Lautenberg of using his Senate seat to line his own pockets with money. "Senator Lautenberg personally pocketed tens of thousands of dollars trading stocks of companies that do business with the government. . . . He'll deny anything to get elected—as long as he can make some money on the side."

Pollution is a sensitive issue in New Jersey; therefore, Lautenberg and Dawkins spent considerable time and effort portraying each other as environmental disasters. For example, New Jersey's beaches are a national tourist attraction. At one Dawkins news conference, he presided over a pile of hypodermic needles and other toxic trash that he said routinely wash up on New Jersey shores. Senator Lautenberg, he said, was partly to blame.

Dawkins said he would fight to restore $72 million in funds that were cut from the Coast Guard budget "with the support of Senator Frank Lautenberg." He also said he would end "sewage-sludge dumping" and develop a tracking system for hospital waste.

In response, Lautenberg got "really" nasty. One of his ads called Dawkins a liar and a hypocrite. He said Dawkins "misled us" when he moved to New Jersey. An announcer then says that the Dawkins campaign "lied" about his wounds in Vietnam. (Does that sound familiar?) As photos of Dawkins and newspaper headlines pop up on the screen, the announcer finishes: "Dawkins is a hypocrite because he himself is financed by polluters. . . . He'll move anywhere and say anything to get elected."

THIS MIGHT BE FUNNY IF IT WEREN'T SO SERIOUS

From that point on, the campaign got so negative and biting, it was almost funny. One Lautenberg ad pilloried Dawkins for "personally polluting an entire beach" when he was with the army in California. "You know what he did to California's environment," says an announcer. "Think what he could do to New Jersey's."[7]

Another part of Dawkins's strategy was to portray Lautenberg as too liberal for New Jersey. He called the senator a "taxer and a tariffer." He said Lautenberg was bad for New Jersey because he supported protectionism, while representing a state to which foreign trade was extremely important, producing $5 billion and 200,000 jobs.

He claimed to be a moderate pragmatist on economic issues, while Lautenberg was an "ultra-liberal." Compared to Frank Lautenberg, he said, Ted Kennedy looks like a centrist. Finally, he dismissed Lautenberg as "ineffective." He recalled that in his 1982 race against Millicent Fenwick, Lautenberg made a major issue out of New Jersey's 46th-place ranking in its return of federal tax dollars. "That was a proper issue," said Dawkins. "But after six years with Lautenberg in the Senate, know where we are? We're 50th. Dead last. In the cellar."

As the campaign spat and hissed its way toward the finish, Dawkins challenged Lautenberg to join him in signing a pledge to end negative campaigning. Lautenberg refused. In addition, news coverage of the campaign had featured the mudslinging so prominently that the Lautenberg campaign refused to preview its upcoming ads for reporters.

Of course, as the *National Journal* commented, if "the reporters happened to live within a 100-mile radius of the Garden State, they could just tune in along with millions of TV viewers in Connecticut, New Jersey, New York and Pennsylvania and watch the carnage in their living rooms."

DREAM TURNS TO NIGHTMARE

In the end, Dawkins didn't turn out to be the dream candidate the Republicans had hoped for. Lautenberg rang up the largest margin of victory in his Senate career, taking 54 percent of the vote. In fairness to Dawkins, Lautenberg probably wasn't as vulnerable as many state observers had thought.

His narrow win over Fenwick in 1982 can be attributed more to the competitive nature of party politics in the Garden State in the 1980s than to his "weakness" as a candidate. And his lack of national "stature" in his first term is really no different than the first-term experiences of the vast majority of U.S. senators in their first terms.

But some of the credit should go to Lautenberg's use of the carpetbagger issue. He had the facts, or at least what seemed to be the facts, on his side. And it helped to blunt the impact of Dawkins's charges against him. Dawkins had a golden résumé but could not convert it into a defeat of a senate incumbent. But there are few who can. Defeating an incumbent U.S. senator is just about the hardest thing to do in politics.

It was an extremely negative campaign—a harbinger, really, of things to come for New Jersey and other states in the 1990s. But this incumbent was able to capitalize on an inherent weakness in his challenger and rode to an easier-than-expected victory.

LAUTENBERG, ACT II

Frank Lautenberg retired from the Senate in 2000, declining to run for a fourth term. He would have been seventy-seven when his next six-year term was scheduled to begin, and he wanted to spend more time with his wife and relax a little. Life has a funny way of working out.

In 2002 the reelection campaign of embattled incumbent U.S. senator Robert Torricelli was in trouble. He had been plagued by ethics scandals related to financial improprieties and was formally rebuked by his Senate colleagues. Polling by both parties showed that he was vulnerable to his little-known Republican challenger, Douglas Forrester.

In September, the Democratic Party convinced Senator Torricelli that for the good of the party, he had to leave the race. But who could be found to replace him on the ballot, and would a ballot change be upheld by the courts?

As New Jersey Democrats looked around the state for a suitable replacement, several incumbent congressmen politely declined. There were no state-level Democratic officials with the interest, or the stature, to join a Senate race so late in the year.

Former senator Lautenberg became a consensus choice. But he had to be convinced, as he was not eager to jump back into politics. The national Democratic Party prevailed on Lautenberg to join the race in order to prevent the seat from going to the Republicans. At the time, the Democrats had a one-seat edge in the Senate, and the loss of Torricelli's seat would turn control back over to the Republicans.

So Lautenberg, ever the good soldier, signed on. The two parties fought out the ballot issue in the New Jersey courts. The Republicans argued that New Jersey law did not allow a ballot change so close to an election. But the court ruled that a political party should have an opportunity to decide who will represent them in an election, and that the voters should have an opportunity to make that choice for themselves.

The court allowed Lautenberg on the ballot, and after a thirty-four-day campaign, he won the election, returning to the Senate at age seventy-eight.

GOD SAVE THE REPUBLIC, PLEASE

Rutherford Hayes v. Samuel Tilden, President, 1876

And you thought the disputed 2000 election between Bush and Gore was bad. At least that one was resolved by the time the electoral college met in December. The 1876 mess between Rutherford B. Hayes and Samuel Tilden wasn't resolved until early March of the following year—only days before the scheduled presidential inauguration.

Ironically, the year 1876 was America's centennial. The country's 100-year anniversary was celebrated with small-town barbecues and big-city parades. The National Centennial Exposition in Philadelphia was the center of the nation's love affair with democracy. It was only fitting, then, that a presidential election should feature America's democratic system in action. But this election was not America's finest hour.

The campaigns of the 1870s and 1880s were intensely personal and nasty. The Hayes-Tilden campaign set a new standard for nastiness, maybe because the campaign lasted so long and involved so much drama and intrigue.

In 1876 the Republicans were at a crossroads of sorts. The Civil War had been over for more than a decade, but its aftermath created administrative and political headaches that were very difficult to manage. The divisive period of Reconstruction was coming to an end, and there were calls for its repeal, particularly from the Southern states under its thumb.

The country had survived two scandal-plagued terms of President Ulysses S. Grant, but the Republican Party's image was badly tarnished. To make matters worse, the country had gone through a severe economic downturn since the Panic of 1873. Falling crop prices, rising unemployment in the cities, and widespread corruption at all levels of government—Republicans were blamed for it all.

"Inoffensive"

Hayes's best quality as a potential candidate for president was that he wasn't as "offensive" as some of the other Republicans running for the presidency. For example, James G. Blaine, the U.S. senator from Maine, was an early front-runner but had been severely damaged by allegations of corruption.

Another potential candidate, Benjamin Bristow, was a favorite of many re-

formers in the party, but he had been so critical of the party and its policies that he was unacceptable to many. And Roscoe Conkling, one of the big-city political bosses, was seen as too corrupt and therefore unacceptable to the reformers.[1]

Rutherford Hayes had been elected governor of Ohio in 1875 in a tough election against a strong opponent. And Hayes was not "unacceptable" to a significant block of Republicans, as were Blaine, Bristow, and Conkling.

Hayes was a war hero, well liked by the regular Republicans as well as the reformers. He had a reputation for integrity (very important in the post-Grant period); he

Samuel Tilden of New York. Library of Congress.

had supported the Reconstruction legislation of the 1860s as a member of Congress; he was a champion of "Negro suffrage;" and he came from a large swing state with significant electoral votes. Also, the convention was in Cincinnati that year, guaranteeing a mass of supporters for the Ohio governor.

The Corruption Breaker

The Democrats were more unified in their choice of New York governor Samuel Tilden. He was the ideal candidate to take on the Republicans and

"Grantism"—the corrupt stranglehold the Republicans had on the federal government.

Tilden's credentials as a reformer were second to none. As a member of the New York State Democratic Committee from 1866 to 1874, he played a leading role in the breaking up of the notoriously corrupt Tammany Hall and its leader, William "Boss" Tweed. As leader of the infamous corruption ring that controlled government in New York, Boss Tweed controlled every political appointment along with the funding of government programs.[2]

Under Tilden's direction, reform leaders in New York exposed and destroyed Tweed and his associates. Many went to jail, including Tweed himself,

Rutherford Birchford Hayes. Library of Congress.

sentenced to twelve years in state prison. Elected governor in 1874, Tilden went on to bring yet another corrupt organization to justice—the Canal Ring, which had arranged financial payments and bribes to government officials.

Given his prominence as a crusader against public corruption, and his position as governor of a large, electoral-vote-rich state, Tilden was easily nominated for president at the Democratic convention, beating his closest competitor 535 to 60.

THE MUD FLIES

Both Hayes and Tilden were considered reformers. Both men advocated reform of the civil service system, which had crept into corruption and inefficiency since the days of Andrew Jackson and patronage. Both also believed in removing federal troops from the South and in bringing the period of Reconstruction to a desirable close.

But though they were both considered honorable men and indeed had much in common, the campaign among the loyalists for each side devolved into name calling, innuendo, and mudslinging.

The Democrats in particular had a wide range of ammunition to choose from. There were the scandals of the Grant administration, the economic problems following the Panic of 1873, the James G. Blaine financial shenanigans, widespread corruption in the Southern Reconstruction governments, accusations of payoffs from big business to Republican officials, and more.

But the Republicans could still count on a certain measure of support for their handling of the Civil War and Reconstruction. In fact, some Republicans used the Civil War as a battering ram against all Democrats. Presidential historian Paul Boller characterizes the Republican position as, "not every Democrat was a rebel, but every rebel was a Democrat."[3]

In a well-publicized speech that is not exactly a model of self-restraint or political moderation, the writer Robert Ingersoll, a Hayes advocate, put it this way: "Every man that endeavored to tear the old flag from the heavens that it enriches was a Democrat. Every man that tried to destroy this nation was a Democrat. . . . The man that assassinated Abraham Lincoln was a Democrat. . . . Soldiers, every scar you have on your heroic bodies was given to you by a Democrat."[4]

And Republican officials unleashed a tirade of insults toward Samuel Tilden. He was accused of evading taxes; promoting slavery; making millions of dollars as an attorney for some of the leading robber barons of the day; coddling some of the corrupt figures in the Tammany Hall organization; and, maybe worst of all, scheming to relieve the Confederates' debt if he was elected president.

In response, the Democrats cranked up their own mud machine. Hayes was accused of stealing the pay of dead soldiers in his Civil War regiment, cheating Ohio out of millions of dollars while governor, and even "shooting his mother in a fit of insanity."

Neither Hayes nor Tilden approved of such smear tactics and lie telling, but both were tarred with the filth being spread by campaign loyalists. By the end of the campaign, Tilden had been called a liar, a thief, a drunkard, a syphilis carrier, and a swindler. The nicknames were nasty: Slippery Sammy, Soapy Sam, Ananias Tilden. One campaign book dismissed him as a criminal, a disgrace to New York State, and a "menace to the United States."[5]

MESSY ELECTION

On election day, it looked as if Tilden had won. He received about 250,000 more votes than Hayes nationwide. Of the states that had certified their votes, Tilden led in enough states to give him 184 electoral votes, one short of the number needed to win the electoral college. But twenty electoral votes in four states were in doubt: South Carolina (7), Louisiana (8), Florida

(4), and one of Oregon's three electoral votes. Tilden needed only one more electoral vote to claim the presidency, and Hayes needed all twenty.

Tilden thought he had won, and so did most everyone else, including the newspapers. But there was the matter of that one electoral vote. The chair of the Republican Party, Zachariah Chandler, took matters into his own hands. He claimed all three of Oregon's electoral votes, then instructed the Republican leaders of South Carolina, Louisiana, and Florida to hold the line for Republicans in their state. The next day, Chandler and the leadership of the Republican Party made a stunning announcement: "Hayes has 185 electoral votes and is elected!"[6]

Both sides knew it would be close, and accused their opponents of trying to rig the election. There was widespread voter fraud and intimidation tactics, especially in the Southern states under Reconstruction governments. Hayes had said that if he lost, it would be by "crime and bribery."

After the election, it was learned that in the three Southern states, voting had been sullied by bribery, forgery, violence, and ballot-box stuffing. Democrats intimidated black voters to keep them away from the polls, while Republicans "assisted" blacks in voting, sometimes assisting them in voting two or three times.

Because of their race and their association with the Republican Party, Southern blacks were often intimidated with threats or acts of violence by groups of Democrats and other organizations to keep black men from voting. For example, in one Louisiana parish, East Feliciana, the majority of registered voters were black and Republican, but in 1876, only one Republican voted in that entire parish.

In South Carolina, the paramilitary Red Shirts aggressively prevented blacks from voting. And in Florida, Democrats distributed Tilden tickets decorated with Republican symbols among the illiterate former slaves. In all three states, ballot boxes were stuffed with multiple Democratic votes. Had elections in 1876 been free and fair, Hayes might well have carried a number of Southern states and avoided the whole post-election mess.

CONSTITUTIONAL CRISIS

But here's where it gets really messy. In the three Southern states, both parties were claiming victory. In all three states, both Republicans and Democrats claimed that the opposition was guilty of widespread voter fraud, and submitted their own separate electoral vote tallies to Congress. The Republicans vote total, certified by the governor, showed that Hayes had won, while the Democratic vote total, certified by the legislature, showed that Tilden had won.

Oregon was different. Only one electoral vote was in dispute there. The statewide vote went for Hayes, but Oregon's Democratic governor claimed that one of the state's three electors, a postmaster, was constitutionally ineligible to serve as an elector because he was already a federal official. So the governor substituted an elector in his place. Naturally, the substitute was a Democrat.

There had been disputed elections before, in 1800 and 1824, but none quite like this. There was no precedent for it. The Constitution simply didn't provide for a situation in which multiple Electoral College returns were sent to Congress.

Under the Twelfth Amendment, the vice president opens and counts the electoral votes from the states before a joint session of Congress. But there is no authority given to determine contested returns. The Democrats did not want the Republican-dominated Senate to determine which votes were valid, and Republicans feared that the whole election could be thrown into the Democratic-controlled House of Representatives, as in 1800.

But Congress had to act—the country needed a president. In January 1877, it passed a law forming a fifteen-member Electoral Commission to settle the dispute. Five members of the commission were from the House of Representatives, five were from the Senate, and five were U.S. Supreme Court justices.

Congress did make an effort to fairly balance the members of the commission. The House was controlled by Democrats, so its five-member delegation included three Democrats and two Republicans; the Senate was controlled by Republicans, so it had three Republicans and two Democrats. The Supreme Court justices consisted of two Republicans and two Democrats, plus a fifth chosen by them.

Initially, the four supreme court justices chose David Davis, an independent. But soon after, Davis was elected to fill a vacant Senate seat from Illinois. This may have been part of a political ploy that backfired. Illinois Democrats threw their support behind Davis for the Senate seat, perhaps thinking that this would sew up the election for Tilden. But as soon as he became a senator, Davis disqualified himself.[7]

Davis was replaced on the commission by Justice Joseph Bradley, a Republican. Bradley had a reputation as an independent free thinker, so he was thought to be impartial. Republicans now had an eight to seven advantage on the commission, and despite his independent streak, Bradley voted with the other Republicans on the commission on every crucial decision.

After the commission voted to award Louisiana's electoral votes to Hayes, the Democrats knew it was over. Tilden had carried Louisiana by 6,300 votes in the election, but the Republican-dominated state government threw out 15,000 votes that were "tainted." Thirteen thousand of those were Democratic votes.

Out of frustration and some measure of political calculation, the Democrats on the commission delayed the counting of the remaining electoral votes, threatening to plunge the nation into chaos by leaving it with no president on inauguration day, March 4. Some Democrats had hoped to extract some concessions from Hayes and his congressional allies.

Among their objectives was the removal of the handful of troops that protected state governments in New Orleans, Los Angeles, and Columbia, South Carolina. Also, they desired a federal subsidy for the Texas & Pacific Railroad, and cabinet appointments for certain Southerners who had been members of the Whig Party before the Civil War.

During the controversy, both sides hurled accusations, and debate sometimes reached a fever pitch. General William Sherman even ordered four artillery companies to Washington to help maintain order. The crisis sent newspaper sales soaring, as some commentators wondered if the controversy could set off a new civil war. Fortunately, cooler heads prevailed.

In secret meetings in late February, Hayes supporters agreed to withdraw federal troops from the Southern cities in question and appoint at least one Southerner to the new cabinet. This tacit agreement defused the crisis and led many Democrats to drop their objections.

As the presidential inauguration drew closer, some somber-minded Democrats, such as House Speaker Samuel Randall, feared the dispute would weaken the Democrats more than the Republicans. With some concessions from Hayes now in the bank, Randall convinced Democrats on the commission to allow the electoral vote count to be completed. With just two days to spare, the commission completed its business and declared Hayes the winner.

"His Fraudulency"

But not all Democrats were satisfied. In many Democratic circles, in party publications, and in newspapers throughout the South, Hayes was dubbed "His Fraudulency." Other names for him included "Rutherfraud Hayes," "The Usurper," and "Boss Thief."[8]

Samuel Tilden went to his grave thinking he had been rightfully elected president of the United States. As for Hayes, he never quite lived down the image of "His Fraudulency." Though many Americans thought his election was tainted, at least by the fraudulent acts of some of his supporters, the Hayes administration is credited with formally ending Reconstruction. During his presidency, he also advanced the cause of civil service reform, as he had promised to do, and helped the country achieve a measure of financial stability by returning to the gold standard.

By the end of his term in 1880, economic prosperity had returned. But ill feelings over his election, and his dedication to a "single-term presidency," led him not to seek reelection.

RUDY AND THE JETS

Rudolph Giuliani v. David Dinkins, Mayor, New York City, 1993

Willie Horton, David Duke, Jesse Jackson, Adolf Hitler . . . all of these political figures were prominently mentioned in the 1993 race for mayor of New York City, but not one of them was on the ballot. The most notable feature of this ugly campaign between Democrat David Dinkins and Republican Rudolph Giuliani was the constant accusations by each of them that the other was playing racial politics.

The two men faced each other only four years earlier to decide who would succeed three-term incumbent mayor Ed Koch. That 1989 campaign also descended into racial and religious pandering, with both sides competing to see who could be the most "outraged" and "horrified" at the behavior of their opponent.

It's no secret that New York City politics is tough, just as it is in most major cities, such as Chicago, Los Angeles, Philadelphia, and Boston. NYC is an interesting case, however, because although it is a heavily Democratic city (Democrats outnumber Republicans about 5:1), black voters make up less than a third of registered voters. And although white voters are less than half the population of the city, they make up more than half of its registered voters.[1] Dinkins's victory over Giuliani in 1989 was very close—one of the closest in the city's history—making the rematch between the two an automatically competitive and compelling race.

The swing vote in NYC, at least in the 1990s, was often a coalition of white liberals—overwhelmingly Democrat—and Hispanic voters. Dinkins won these voters in high enough numbers in 1989 to give him the edge over

Rudolph Giuliani. Courtesy NYC Municipal Archives.

Giuliani. But by 1993, these voters were ambivalent to Dinkins's record and his leadership, making them prime targets for Giuliani's campaign.

BLACK V. WHITE?

The tone for their rematch was set more than a year before the election, when Giuliani accused then mayor Dinkins of using the racial card and trying to turn black New Yorkers against him. Giuliani was responding to comments made by Dinkins's Deputy Mayor Bill Lynch on a radio show, in which Lynch compared Giuliani to former Louisiana KKK leader David Duke.[2]

The week before, Giuliani had appeared at a demonstration by off-duty police officers at city hall. At the demonstration, some officers held racist signs and shouted racial slurs in their protest of Dinkins's personnel policies. Of Lynch's comments, Giuliani said, "to compare me to David Duke is sick and indicates that what you're interested in is not racial peace but racial polarization."

Dinkins defended Lynch and accused Giuliani of inciting the off-duty police officers at the rally. "If you put that issue before editorial boards or the general public," said Dinkins, "it would be Mr. Giuliani that would be found guilty of using race."[3]

David Dinkins was NYC's first black mayor, and New York was actually one of the last of the major cities to elect a minority or woman as mayor. He took office pledging to move beyond racial politics, with the stated intention of being mayor for "all New Yorkers." But as he entered his reelection campaign in 1993, he was a wounded incumbent, struggling to not become the first black mayor of a major city to lose a first-reelection bid.

Part of his problem was the recession of 1991–1992, which had wounded all big city mayors, as well as governors, who were trying to keep their budgets afloat while providing government services. But another part of his problem was that in a racially and ethnically diverse city, many felt that he had not kept his promise to rise above racial politics.[4]

Mayor Dinkins was loudly accused of siding with blacks in several high-profile incidents involving racial and religious conflicts. There were clashes between blacks and Hasidic Jews in the Crown Heights neighborhood that drew national attention. Some Jewish groups accused the mayor of casting blame on the Jewish community for the troubles. Then there were conflicts in some neighborhoods between blacks and Korean-owned grocery stores, leading to boycotts of the stores.

Mayor Dinkins was caught in the middle. "I don't think most people feel he's really delivered on his promise," said Thomas H. Kessner, a historian at the City University Graduate Center. "But then again, how does one transcend race when race played such an important role in defining who you are, and in defining the country and the city?"[5]

David Dinkins. Courtesy NYC Municipal Archives.

Giuliani was able to exploit some of the mayor's vulnerabilities. One of the challenges facing Giuliani as a candidate was to soften his image among moderate voters and women. Both as a federal prosecutor and in his 1989 campaign for mayor, he had developed an image as tough and uncompromising. But the 1989 campaign left some bitter feelings. He and his advisers knew that he would have to go on the attack against Dinkins, but first they wanted to show a warmer, more human side of Giuliani.

A media campaign in July and August portrayed him as a warm family man, playing with his kids and going to Yankee games. Polls indicated some softening in his image among voters, thanks to the positive advertising, which helped clear the way for the inevitable negative campaigning and attack advertising that were to come.

Feeling the pressure, the normally low-key and affable Dinkins prepared for a knock-down-drag-out fight with the hard-charging Giuliani. The mayor created a stir when his campaign hired former Watergate prosecutor Terry Lenzner to provide opposition research on Giuliani.[6] Hiring opposition-research specialists was becoming more common in congressional and U.S.

Senate races, but was rare in a mayoral race, even in a high-profile place like NYC.

Lenzner had served on the Senate Watergate committee that investigated the "dirty tricks" attributed to the Nixon White House and the Nixon re-election committee. The speculation was that Mr. Lenzner was hired by Dinkins for the same purpose—to find and expose "dirty tricks" and other irregularities by Rudolph Giuliani.

> After the September 11 attack in New York City, Rudolph Giuliani campaigned hard for the reelection of President George W. Bush in 2004. He is rumored to be a major contender for the Republican presidential nomination in 2008.

Giuliani blasted the hiring of a "private investigator" to check up on him. He said it marked a new low point in Mayor Dinkins's campaign to smear him and accused the mayor of digging for dirt in his personal life. "It's unethical," he said, and should not be tolerated. The Dinkins campaign defended the hiring, saying Mr. Lenzner was not hired to look into Giuliani's personal life but his record as a public official.[7]

Then the TV ad wars started. A Dinkins ad against Giuliani focused on his lack of support for civil rights and his failure to hire minorities as a federal prosecutor. The ad shows a series of unflattering black-and-white photos of Giuliani, accompanied by ominous music and a narrator's voice:

> He was the third-highest official in Washington of the Reagan Justice Department that led an attack on the environment, tried to overturn a woman's right to choose, and turn back the clock on civil rights. . . . As U.S. Attorney in New York, of the 146 people he hired, only 15 were Latino or black. He was accused of abuse of power, and federal courts rebuked his conduct. Rudolph Giuliani: Can we elect a man who's fought against everything we stand for?

Naturally, Giuliani reacted with outrage. At a fund-raising dinner a few days after the ad began running, Giuliani accused Dinkins and his people of trying to divide the city by race in order to win. "Shame on them," he railed. He also ran TV ads responding to the Dinkins TV spot. In one, his wife Donna reacts with disgust to Dinkins's charges. In another, Herman Badillo, a candidate for NYC comptroller, chides Dinkins for injecting racial politics into the campaign. "We don't need these anti-Semitic and racial attacks. The city needs us all to get along. David, you know better," Badillo says in the ad.[8]

It didn't help that only a week earlier, a major Dinkins supporter, Rev. William Jones, pastor of Bethany Baptist Church in Bedford-Stuyvesant, had remarked to a reporter that there were "fascist" elements surrounding Giuliani's campaign. He may have been referring to earlier comparisons to David Duke, but the remark was seized on by the Giuliani campaign. In a campaign statement and in public appearances, Giuliani said the remark was "an anti-Italian slur." Apparently by that, Giuliani, who is Italian, was accusing the Dinkins side of comparing him to Italian fascist leader Benito Mussolini.

In the same week, the head of a black police officers' union attacked Herman Badillo, who is Hispanic, and noted that Badillo was not married to a Hispanic woman but a Jewish woman. Mayor Dinkins distanced himself from both of his supporters' remarks and said he would tolerate no ethnic, racial, or religious discrimination of any kind.

THE CLINTON EFFECT

Some observers have focused on President Bill Clinton's role in injecting race into the NYC mayoral campaign on behalf of the mayor. At a September 26 dinner for Dinkins, the president himself brought up the issue of a racial divide in New York City: "too many of us are still too unwilling to vote for people who are different than we are," he said. His remarks were widely interpreted as scolding white voters for being too "unwilling" to vote for black candidates. But many, including some of Giuliani's supporters, accused the president of stirring up racial animosities with his remarks, particularly because in the 1989 mayoral election more than one-third of white voters did vote for the black candidate (Mayor Dinkins), while over 90 percent of black voters supported Dinkins.

Unfortunately, the race issue did not go away; it only got hotter. New York congressman Charles Rangel, an African American Democrat, and Badillo, the Giuliani ally who was running for comptroller, waged their own separate "race" campaign. In commenting on the mayoral campaign, Congressman Rangel said that one of Giuliani's main assets is that he is "white." Badillo then reminded Rangel that he himself had won in an overwhelmingly white congressional district, and then added, "By the way, he (Rangel) is half Puerto Rican." During a TV interview, Congressman Rangel responded angrily, saying that "Mr. Badillo is an orphan who doesn't even know who his own parents are."[9]

The Dinkins campaign charged the Giuliani camp with using the race issue for its own purposes. Dinkins's campaign consultant wondered why, if the race issue was hurting Giuliani so much, he was keeping it alive through his TV ads and campaign speeches. Political observers believed that Giuliani's ads complaining about the "race issue" were aimed at NYC Hispanic, Jewish, and liberal white voters, many of whom were undecided and could provide the margin of victory for the winning candidate. It also helped to mobilize some of Giuliani's core constituents, especially Italian Americans.

The *New York Times* agreed. It editorialized about what it called the "inflated grievances" and "artful cynicism" of Giuliani's TV advertising campaign. "Not since the heyday of Lee Atwater [President George Bush's political consultant in 1988] have we seen such devious artistry when it comes to stirring feelings of racial paranoia among whites. That is the rationale behind the attempt to wrap Mr. Giuliani in the victim's mantle, and thus make a campaign that stands to benefit from racial fears appear to be the victim of those fears."[10]

The same editorial did, however, criticize David Dinkins for not acting quickly enough or forcefully enough to disassociate himself from the racial comments of his supporters. According to the *Times*, "The Mayor's tepid disavowals opened him to the accusation that these statements were coordinated with his campaign. It is not enough for the mayor to say mildly that 'I do not agree with every statement made by every supporter.' What was needed was prompt, outright repudiation" of the racial remarks of his supporters.

On election day, Giuliani won 51 percent of the vote to 49 percent for Dinkins, almost exactly the reverse of the outcome of their 1989 race. Race was a factor in the outcome, as a number of whites and Hispanics that had voted for Dinkins in 1989 switched to Giuliani in 1993.

But it was not the only issue—nor, some would argue, was it the main issue. There was the anti-incumbent mood of the general public in the early 1990s, for one thing. President Bush lost in 1992, then Dinkins in 1993, followed by a host of U.S. congressmen and senators in 1994. The recession, crime, and failing schools were all part of the equation. Dinkins had presided over a city characterized by high taxes, welfare dependency, and escalating violent crime.

According to *New York Newsday*, Dinkins also failed to capitalize on his strengths, such as the newspaper endorsements that came his way, the power of the Clinton White House, and his own moderate image among the voters.[11] He also may have underestimated the appeal of Giuliani's media campaign with key swing voters.

For his part, Rudolph Giuliani went on to become "America's Mayor." In his two terms as New York City mayor (1994–2002), he was largely credited for reducing violent crime, increasing tourism (which are related), ridding the streets of vagrants and pushy squeegee car-window washers, lowering taxes, and working to end mafia control of service industries in NYC. Then, of course, came his starring role in the September 11 saga, for which he is given credit for calming the citizenry and leading the government through those very tough days.

A Jersey Street Fight

Robert Torricelli v. Richard Zimmer, U.S. Senate, New Jersey, 1996

Well-known radio shock jock Howard Stern just could not make up his mind. He had been hosting an on-air interview/debate/shouting match between Representatives Richard Zimmer and Robert Torricelli for the better part of an hour, yet still could not decide who he should support. He did like the trash talk Zimmer displayed toward his opponent, but he was irresistibly drawn to the low blows Torricelli gave Zimmer. Finally, Stern announced to his listening audience that he had fallen in love with both candidates and was endorsing both of them.

This 1996 campaign to fill the U.S. Senate seat of the retiring Bill Bradley has now become somewhat of a legend in New Jersey politics and in U.S. Senate election history. Due to a series of very hostile negative ads from both candidates, this campaign quickly became known as "the nastiest campaign in the country."[1] Everything from "mafia ties" to radio jingles of "liar, liar, pants on fire" were featured in this very ugly campaign. Voter participation in this race was shockingly low, even among voters. Of those who turned out to vote, 10 percent refused to vote for either candidate.[2]

Zimmer was a conservative Republican and Torricelli a liberal Democrat, both of whom represented New Jersey congressional districts in the U.S. House. They also represented some very stark differences in public policy as well as their campaign styles. Torricelli was brash, abrasive, and aggressive (his nickname was the Torch). Zimmer was more restrained and cerebral. Yet both candidates went for the jugular in this matchup.

Zimmer accused Torricelli of nurturing ties to organized crime in the

Robert Torricelli was known for "smashmouth" politics. U.S. Senate Archives.

Northeast, accepting money from terrorist groups, intimidating critics, and laundering money for a Korean embezzler. Not to be outdone, Torricelli accused Zimmer of also taking money from mob interests, supporting toxic dumping, "favoring" breast cancer, and encouraging teenage drunken driving. While indulging in this orgy of mudslinging, both candidates had the nerve to sign pledges not to engage in negative campaigning and then claimed, with straight faces, to have abided by them.[3]

Zimmer, an ardent advocate of welfare reform, campaigned on a total rewriting of the tax code, and was named the most fiscally conservative member of the U.S. Congress by the National Taxpayer's Union. He led the fight to enact Megan's Law, signed into law by President Clinton in 1996, which informs neighbors when a convicted sexual offender moves into a neighborhood. He was also a strong supporter of the death penalty, and introduced into Congress the No Frills Act, which would eliminate prisoner perks, such as cable television, gym equipment, and other forms of entertainment.

Torricelli, a former aide to Walter Mondale, opposed welfare reform in Congress, voted against the term-limits amendment, and opposed many of the crime-reform proposals championed by Zimmer. In contrast to Zimmer, Torricelli was also a strong supporter of Goals 2000, the education reform package sponsored by President Clinton.

Zimmer's campaign was advised by Arthur Finkelstein, a renowned Republican operative famous for hard-hitting negative attacks on opponents. A large component of the Zimmer campaign's strategy was to paint Torricelli as a big-government, big-spending liberal.

CASH AND CARRY

Torricelli, who was ranked the biggest tax-and-spend liberal in the New Jersey congressional delegation by Citizens Against Government Waste, had significant union support. Organized labor, including the AFL-CIO, con-

Happy Republicans. Zimmer, left, shares a laugh with state senator Walter Foran. New Jersey State Archives, Department of State.

tributed heavily to Torricelli's campaign, produced independent television commercials critical of Zimmer, and implemented its own get-out-the-vote drive on election day. This led Zimmer to accuse Torricelli of selling out to special-interest money.

In fact, Torricelli was so successful at raising money from advocacy groups that he was asked by the Democratic Senatorial Campaign Committee to provide lectures on fund-raising for would-be candidates. He had contacts in the defense industry, with insurance companies, with oil companies, and with the office of the governor of the Virgin Islands, among others. He would tell them, "All I ask is that you open your home, have some friends or associates in, and I'll do the rest."[4]

He raised $399,000 in south Florida, mostly from Cuban Americans attracted to his anti-Castro positions. He also raised money from Portuguese Americans, Greek Americans, Chinese Americans, Pakistani Americans, and Iranian Americans, all based on various foreign policy positions he espoused. In total, he raised over $9 million, and another $3 million was spent on his behalf by independent groups.

Torricelli's fund-raising success came in a year that became notorious for campaign finance abuse and excess. In 1996, multiple inquiries were triggered into both national parties' use of soft money, the Clinton reelection campaign's fund-raising appeals to foreign nationals, and the role played by offshore banks and financiers. The financial scandals increased the appearance of corruption and led to stepped-up activity in Congress to reform campaign finance, including the McCain-Feingold bill.

Political observers regarded the Zimmer-Torricelli race as a prime example of a crumbling system. Interest groups and political party organizations poured cash into a race denounced from the beginning for its lack of substance; its focus on money; its reliance on misleading, negative television ads; and its vicious personal attacks.

Zimmer also criticized Torricelli for voting against the death penalty, voting to continue prisoner perks, spending more money than any other New Jersey congressman on taxpayer-funded franking privileges (free use of the U.S. mail), and voting to raise income taxes.

The Torricelli campaign, whose media consultant was Robert Schrumm, a consultant noted for his work for Bill Clinton in 1996, Al Gore in 2000, and John Kerry in 2004, attempted to portray Zimmer as a "Newt Gingrich crony," and criticized him as too extreme to represent New Jersey voters. Torricelli mirrored President Clinton's attacks on Republicans nationally by accusing Zimmer of trying to abolish Medicare, and criticized him for votes to reduce funds for the Superfund cleanup program, abolish the Department of Education, weaken safe-drinking-water standards, and allow ocean dumping.

An R-Rated Campaign

Although both candidates attacked each others' legislative record and policy statements, the contest garnered national attention as a hostile, negative campaign because of the personal invective featured in the race.

Throughout the campaign, Zimmer repeatedly attacked Torricelli's character and ethics.[5] For example, Zimmer's TV ads accused Torricelli of cozying up to criminals because his office had assisted the fifteen-year-old daughter of a federal fugitive. Zimmer also questioned Torricelli's patriotism and his commitment to America's allies, citing a 1993 speech to the radical Islamic group Hamas. Zimmer also accused him of accepting campaign contributions from the group.

One of Zimmer's TV ads showed a man combing the Internet for the word "liberal." Sure enough, up pops a photo of Torricelli on a Web page, www.lib.torricelli.com. It is supposed to be a Web page dedicated to the liberal voting record of Robert Torricelli. One problem, though: the Web page doesn't actually exist anywhere on the Internet and never did.

Another Zimmer ad attacked Torricelli's ethics for revealing confidential information he obtained as a member of the House Intelligence Committee. In 1995 Torricelli had revealed to the media that a Guatemalan military officer on the CIA's payroll was responsible for killing an American and a Guatemalan guerrilla leader, leading House Speaker Newt Gingrich to accuse him of violating his oath not to disclose classified material. Gingrich said Torricelli should be removed from the committee.

Zimmer also accused Torricelli of having one of the worst voting records in the House of Representatives, alleging that Torricelli missed more than 650 votes. Zimmer said that Torricelli had voted to cut $750 million in aid to Israel, had voted to raise taxes and increase spending on frivolous government programs, and did not completely support a balanced budget amendment.

For his part, Torricelli did not let the attacks go unanswered, calling Zimmer a liar in one TV ad and portraying him as an extremist who cannot be trusted.[6] Torricelli defended his own ads as more issue-based than Zimmer's. "You cannot have a campaign where I don't criticize my opponent's voting record," said Torricelli. "That would be absurd. That would make the Lincoln-Douglas debates out of bounds in fair politics. . . . the Federalist Papers would no longer be fair game. That is different from my turning on an advertisement which I consider to be a disgrace."[7]

GLOVES COME OFF

Probably the most controversial TV advertisement in the campaign—and the one that Torricelli was referring to—was a Zimmer spot that many accused of blatantly trying to deceive the public. The ad was designed to mimic a television news update. An actor portraying an anchorman on a TV news set reads a list of Zimmer's charges against Torricelli as the caption "Breaking News" runs across the screen. Several TV stations refused to run the ad without their own disclaimer, due to their opinion that the caption "paid for by . . . ," which is required by law, was too small and too brief to provide an adequate warning to viewers.

Of course, Torricelli also skirted campaign laws with some of his tactics. In October, 144,000 gun supporters in New Jersey received a mailing purportedly from the Coalition of New Jersey Sportsmen. The words "Election

Alert" were in bold letters at the top. The one-page bulletin said that Zimmer would be "as bad for gun owners as his Democratic opponent, Robert Torricelli."

The letter went on to say that Zimmer would like gun owners to think he is stronger on gun rights than Torricelli, but that is "Not So!" It went on to recommend that gun supporters vote for a little-known Conservative Party candidate or not vote at all. No one will ever know how many votes this mailing siphoned away from Zimmer in the election.

But federal prosecutors investigating allegations of financial misconduct indicated that Torricelli's campaign staff arranged the $50,000 mailing. Two witnesses to a federal grand jury told the *New York Times* that the Torricelli campaign was involved. A Justice Department inquiry later looked into the case and added it to a series of charges against Torricelli.

When the two candidates met in formal debate, the tone of the exchanges were equally as harsh. The citizens of New Jersey, in particular the media, came to be frustrated, and even angered, when the campaign became a national symbol of mudslinging. The *Asbury Park Press* editorialized that

> the truest demonstration of the depths to which the two candidates have plunged was their most recent, and final, debate. Pity the poor voter who tuned into that debacle believing it to be the path to making an informed vote. Rather than educate, Torricelli and Zimmer used the forum to once again obfuscate. Questions that demanded straight answers about ideologies and voting records were twisted into vituperative broadsides about each other's failings. (October 16, 1996)

With three weeks to go before the election, while Zimmer continued to pound away at Torricelli's ethics, Torricelli announced that he would take the high road. He vowed to talk exclusively about issues and challenged Zimmer to do the same. He said he had made this decision because he wanted to win the campaign with some "self-respect" and an ability to govern.

JUDGMENT DAY

Leading up to the election, the polls indicated that it would be a very close race, too close to call. Zimmer even led in some surveys. But on election night, Torricelli defeated Zimmer 55 percent to 44 percent. There was an unusually large number of undecided voters, with as many as 15 percent of those surveyed right before the election who had not yet decided how to vote.

Apparently, a significant majority of those deciding who to vote for in the final days went with Torricelli. Why?

There could be a lot of reasons. For one thing, President Clinton enjoyed a 49 percent to 41 percent margin over Bob Dole, which undoubtedly helped Torricelli. Zimmer also suffered for his association with Newt Gingrich, who was very unpopular in pre-election surveys.

One could also make the argument that the Zimmer campaign violated the rules and standards for safe and effective negative campaigning. In fact, Zimmer's attacks on Torricelli's character are examples of the kinds of attacks that produce the dreaded "boomerang effect," hurting the attacking candidate more than the target.

Torricelli certainly believes this to be the case. Torricelli asserted that Zimmer's advertising strategy was "central to his defeat." Speaking of the mock newscast aired by the Zimmer campaign, he said that "almost from the moment that these fake news ads aired, the election began to slip away from Mr. Zimmer."

Although Torricelli's statements are not exactly objective, it does seem to be the case that Zimmer's ads and statements created significantly more backlash than did Torricelli's. Although Torricelli did criticize Zimmer, it was more often on issues and voting record, whereas Zimmer relentlessly made the campaign a debate on character and ethics. Therefore, Zimmer's charges were perceived as personal attacks to many New Jersey voters, especially the undecided ones.

HAUNTED BY THE PAST

Torricelli remained a controversial figure after winning this election, and eventually his aggressive fund-raising caught up to him. For practically his entire term in the Senate, he was dogged by rumors of financial wrongdoing and various types of corruption. Finally, while running for reelection in 2002, his unpopularity forced him to drop out of the campaign so that the Democrats could field a candidate that might actually win. The Democrats turned to former senator Frank Lautenberg, who went on to defeat the Republican challenger Douglas Forrester.

Beginning in 2000, questions surfaced about Torricelli's relationship with campaign donor David Chang. A series of damaging disclosures detailed gifts that Chang gave to Torricelli and the favors he did for Chang in exchange. Chang began cooperating with a Justice Department investigation and, in 2000, pleaded guilty to illegally donating more than $53,000 to Torricelli's campaign. He told prosecutors he had showered Torricelli with cash, a Rolex watch, suits, and other gifts in exchange for official favors.

When the revelations became public, Torricelli was "severely admonished" by the Senate Ethics Committee. His poll numbers began plunging in his 2002 reelection campaign against the Republican Forrester, prompting his quick exit from the race.

In This Corner, Little Lord Fauntleroy

John Tower v. Robert Krueger, U.S. Senate, Texas, 1978

My kind of Texan doesn't shake hands with that kind of man.
— John Tower

I know it is Texas, but this one got really nasty. I do not think these two men liked each other very much. John Tower was a three-term U.S. senator seeking reelection in a state that had become accustomed to tough, bare-handed political fights. His opponent was Bob Krueger, a two-term U.S. congressman representing west Texas.

The thing that Tower and Krueger had in common was that they were both college professors before they were elected to office. But that's where the similarity ends. Tower was short, feisty, folksy, and plainspoken; Krueger was tall, reserved, and rather urbane for a Texas politician. Tower was married with several children; Krueger was single. Tower had been a political science professor; Kruger was a scholar of Shakespearean literature.

Tower, in particular, enjoyed highlighting the differences between the two of them. During the course of the campaign, some Tower supporters even raised "questions" about the fact that Krueger had never served in the military (important in a state like Texas) and, at age forty-three, had never been married.[1]

As the only Republican elected statewide, Tower presented a big and tempting target for Texas Democrats. This was especially true because in the Senate, Tower became a pillar of the Republican's conservative wing, and

John Tower was a consummate politician. Photograph from the 1972 campaign brochure, "Number One Senator For Texas," Box M211 Folder 10; John G. Tower Collection, Southwestern University, Georgetown, TX.

Democrats nationwide looked to knock him off at reelection time. At the time, Texas was still largely a Democratic state, so it seemed very doable.

The patrician and sophisticated Krueger had spent more time back east than he had in Texas. After getting a degree from Oxford University in Elizabethan literature, he served as dean of the College of Arts and Sciences at Duke University. In 1974 he moved back to his native west Texas and was elected to represent the sparsely populated Twenty-first Congressional District, which had more tumbleweeds than people.[2]

The campaign between the two was, for the most part, devoid of substantive issues and became instead a contest of personalities and personal will. They were actually not that far apart on the issues. Both supported the state's powerful oil and gas industry, and both men aggressively raised money from those interests. Perhaps Krueger was not as liberal as some of the state's Democrats would have preferred, but he had the financial base to compete, along with the strong desire to defeat Tower that motivated most Democrats.

In his campaign for the Democratic nomination, Krueger seemed to be dismissive of Tower, as if the Democratic nominee, whomever it was, would easily go on to beat Tower. Krueger carried this attitude into the fall campaign. He castigated Tower for wasting his—and the peoples'—time in the Senate. He made effectiveness an issue in the campaign. According to Krueger, for example, Texas had lost eleven military bases in the 1970s because Tower wasn't "tending to your business."[3]

For his part, Tower took to calling Krueger "Little Lord Fauntleroy," which was a reference to his high-brow education and penchant for "the finer things."[4] Tower knew that Texans did not take kindly to folks who thought they were above the crowd, and that's the picture Tower tried to paint of Krueger.

WINE AND WOMEN?

Krueger's response touched off a nasty personal battle that had Texans riveted to their TV sets and newspapers for weeks. Krueger's campaign decided to make public some of the rumors that had been circulating about Tower in Washington, D.C. The word in the halls of Congress among staffers and journalists was that Senator Tower liked to chase women and whiskey, not necessarily in that order.

A Krueger campaign official wrote an op-ed piece and sent it to newspapers across Texas, describing in detail what was being said about Tower's personal life in Washington. The editorial asked Texans if it was in their best interests to have their U.S. senator the object of so much speculation and rumor. After the op-ed piece ran, the talk in Washington had become the talk in Texas.

Bob Krueger. Texas State Library & Archives Commission.

So the Krueger campaign achieved its goal, which was to make Tower the issue in the campaign. Tower reacted with predictable indignation. He was so angry that he canceled four joint TV appearances he was to have with Krueger. He could not stomach seeing Krueger, the senator explained, because he was "uninhibited by the truth." But then came a turning point in the story.

Both men attended a highly publicized Texas barbecue and candidate forum. When they encountered each other in the crowd, Krueger extended his hand in greeting, and Tower refused to shake his hand. A newspaper photographer captured the moment on film, and the next day, the front page of the local paper ran the photo showing Tower refusing to shake the hand of his opponent.[5]

Now, civility and manners are a big deal in Texas, and refusing to shake hands with someone, even an opponent, is considered the height of bad manners. The Krueger campaign made the most of the moment, cutting a TV ad showing the photo and raising questions about Tower's temperament.

Public opinion soured on Tower. Now there were the rumors about his personal life, plus front-page evidence of rude and inappropriate behavior. His job-approval ratings fell, and new polls showed Krueger overtaking Tower in the race for Senate.

THE AD

The mood in Tower's campaign headquarters was glum. Things looked bad. Tower's campaign consultant asked him what he was thinking when he refused to shake Krueger's hand. Tower explained that Krueger's actions against him personally were an affront to him and his family, and that he didn't feel a need to show phony warmth toward someone who had defamed him. His consultant then said to him, "Oh, I see. Well, at least that explains it." Then he added, "Why don't you explain it that way to the voters?"

Thinking it was worth a try, Tower and his advisers went in to the TV studio to cut an ad explaining his side of the story. The result, according to journalists, historians, and political scientists, was TV advertising magic. The ad showed Tower sitting on the edge of a desk and addressing the camera.

Holding up the newspaper with the photo of him refusing to shake Krueger's hand, Tower said, "Perhaps you've seen this picture of my refusal to shake the hand of my opponent. I was brought up to believe that a handshake is a symbol of friendship and respect, not a meaningless hypocritical gesture. My opponent has slurred my wife, my daughters, and falsified my record. My kind of Texan doesn't shake hands with that kind of man. Integrity is one Texas tradition you can count on me to uphold."[6]

Tower's campaign threw all of its TV advertising budget into running this one spot all across Texas. It worked like a charm. When enough Texans had seen the ad of Tower explaining his action and the reasons behind it, his poll numbers recovered. Within two weeks, polls showed Tower once again leading the race.

This ad has gone down in history as a classic example of TV advertising that works. That's a hard commodity to produce in the world of political advertising. One of the controversies in that field lies in disagreements over what moves votes. Political consultants, journalists, and other observers all have their theories on advertising and political campaigns, but proof of something actually working can be hard to come by. This ad was so direct in its effects on the race that its effectiveness was never in dispute—not even by the Krueger campaign.

Political scientist Kathleen Hall-Jamieson describes it as a textbook example of "reframing."[7] Tower's image and poll numbers were hurt because voters didn't know or understand the context behind his actions, she explains. But when that explanation was given and the context was supplied, the effects were transforming.

The vitriol that defined this race and rancor were fueled by more than just personal smears. Both candidates reached inside their grab bag of political stereotypes and pulled out weaponry that suited their needs. Tower depicted Bob Krueger as a lackey of big labor and trade unions. One of his TV ads shows him heroically resisting a bulldozer driven by George Meany, president of the AFL-CIO—the nation's largest union. In Meany's pocket is a slip of paper that reads: "Krueger's Vote."

But the advertisement conveniently overlooks one crucial fact: Krueger has a mixed record on labor issues, and would hardly be in the pocket of the AFL-CIO. For example, in the U.S. House, Krueger voted against giving different unions the right to picket at common sites. On a separate bill, he voted against repealing right-to-work laws, which would have strengthened the role of unions in employment practices. In his last year in Congress, the AFL-CIO gave him a rating of 39 out of 100.

In fact, some Democrats in Texas expressed a certain lack of enthusiasm when it came to Krueger's voting record. In 1977 he earned only a rating of 20 out of 100 from Americans for Democratic Action, a liberal Democratic advocacy group. In Congress, he voted for food-stamp cutbacks, relaxation of urban air-pollution standards, construction of the controversial B-1 bomber, subsidies for agribusiness, and other items objectionable to many

You Want a Senator Who Lays It on the Line, Right? But Not on Both Sides of It.

KRUEGER

— vs —

KRUEGER

ENERGY:

President Carter's energy proposals are "courageous and thoughtful."
—*San Antonio Light, 4/29/77*

CONSERVATION:

"No issue more strongly concerns me than that of protecting the environment for future generations. I will do nothing to betray you, me, or the environment."
—*Texas Observer, 4/28/78*

LABOR REFORM:

Krueger said his vote for the Labor Reform bill was the "single most important vote in 1977" for organized labor.
—*El Paso Times, 3/27/78*

BUREAUCRACIES

"Government bureaucracies in general, and OSHA in particular, have already intruded too much in our public and private lives. . . ."
—*Copperas Cove Press, 6/11/78*

BALANCED BUDGET:

"If the frustration of our citizens is to be ended, a balanced budget must become a reality."
—*Houston Post, 7/5/77*

"His (Carter's) plan was bad to begin with."
—*Longview Journal, 4/23/78*

Arguing that his change of position (now favoring extension of the Rio Grande Park System) was not a "switch." Krueger said he was merely "changing my vote, not my position."
—*Houston Post, 6/28/78*

Krueger told a group of Dallas lawyers at a private meeting that his vote for the Labor Reform bill may have been a "bad judgment." — by news account —
—*El Paso Times, 3/27/78*

On June 16, 1977, Robert Krueger voted against reducing the OSHA budget by 6.3 million dollars.
—*Congressional Record, 6/16/77*

In San Antonio, Krueger referred to balanced budget votes as one of those "demogogic votes."
—*San Antonio Light, 11/1/77*

Here's what other people say about Bob Krueger:
" . . . a politician in the worst sense of the word, a politician who is willing to bend the rules, shave the facts and skate close to the edge."
— *Joe Christie*

You may not agree with John Tower on every issue. But you can trust him. He's consistent. He won't waffle. He doesn't distort the issues. Let's keep integrity and honesty in the U.S. Senate. Let's keep Senator John Tower.

Senator Tower needs more than your vote — he needs your help. Three hours of your time, over the entire semester, at the Baylor (Waco) phone bank, will result in 50 people being contacted to support Senator Tower who otherwise would not be contacted. To help, call ROSEMARY TOWNSEND at 776-0951 or MIKE TUCKER, Young Texans for Tower Chairman at Baylor, 756-3905.

John Tower

HE STANDS FOR TEXAS.

The Tower campaign attacked Krueger's integrity. Photograph from "Krueger vs. Krueger" flyer, Box M212 Folder 13; John G. Tower Collection, Southwestern University, Georgetown, TX.

Democrats. Some of these votes can be explained by his support for Texas oil and gas interests, but not all.

In his campaign literature and TV spots, Senator Tower was portrayed as the fearless defender of "our fellow Texans against the forces moving to destroy America's economic, social, and moral values." He railed against "Eastern labor bosses," the supporters of the Panama Canal treaties, school busing, and the opponents of a constitutional amendment to allow prayer in public schools. It was largely in this vein that Tower staked his reputation as a conservative stalwart against the forces of big government and big labor.

JIMMY CARTER AS BOGEYMAN

The policies of President Jimmy Carter became a central element in the race between Tower and Krueger. For one thing, Tower made a big deal out of his opposition to the Panama Canal Treaty, which was pushed heavily by the president. Tower characterized it as "giving away our national sovereignty." Polling by the Republican National Committee found the Panama Canal issue to be a potent one, and Republican candidates in 1978 got as much mileage out of it as they could.

As the Democratic nominee, Krueger really had little choice but to be an ally of President Carter. But when Carter abandoned his pledge to deregulate the oil and gas industry, it cut Krueger's legs out from under him. Deregulation was a buzzword in the 1970s and 1980s, and it was seen as very important to Texas business interests. Krueger had recognized this early on, and had made deregulation an important part of his efforts in the U.S. House. He had introduced a deregulation bill and fought for its passage—something not even Tower could claim.

But the president's lack of support for the deregulation issue hurt Krueger's cause in Texas and forced him into the uncomfortable position of disagreeing with the president, at least on that one issue. It also played into Tower's hands. He, too, had been a proponent of deregulation, and the issue played to his strengths in 1978.

¿CÓMO ESTÁ?

With Krueger's background and education, it's not surprising that he spoke fluent Spanish. And with the growing Hispanic population in Texas, that was a definite plus. Tower didn't know much Spanish, but he did understand the power of advertising. To offset Krueger's potential advantage with the Spanish-speaking population, Tower hired an ad agency in Austin that specialized in Spanish-language advertising.

The Ed Yardang Agency created a series of TV and radio spots targeted to the Hispanic community that helped John Tower create positive name identification with Hispanic voters. One of the TV ads showed Senator Tower, dressed in a traditional Mexican shirt, meeting with Mexican Americans, eating traditional Mexican dishes, and attending a street festival, all the while laughing and smiling with his new friends. The voiceover in Spanish urged Hispanic Americans to support the senator.

The agency also created several radio ads touting the senator's support for the Hispanic community. The senator did have somewhat of a record in this regard, as he had cast a vote for bilingual education in a Senate debate in 1972. In Spanish-speaking parts of Texas, billboards could be seen that said "Tower, Con Nosotros" (Tower, he's with us).

The advertising campaign resulted in an astonishing 37 percent of the Hispanic vote for Senator Tower on election day. Prior to this election, no Republican politician had ever received more than 5 percent of the Hispanic vote in Texas. Viva Tower!

EPILOGUE

John Tower went on to defeat Representative Krueger and became chairman of the Senate Armed Services Committee in 1981. He decided not to seek reelection in 1984 and became a consultant to the defense industry. In the wake of the Iran-Contra scandal that plagued President Ronald Reagan's second term, Tower was named to head a bipartisan study committee to investigate the incident and issue a report of its findings. Known as the Tower Commission, this group met for approximately six months interviewing key witnesses. The commission issued a final report, largely clearing President Reagan of wrongdoing but holding his national security staff and intelligence agencies responsible for the screwups.

Then in 1989, upon President George H. W. Bush's election win, Tower was the incoming president's first choice to be secretary of defense. But in confirmation hearings on Capitol Hill, the old stories about Tower's personal life and times came back to haunt him, and he withdrew from consideration. The charges and countercharges from his confirmation hearings, as well as from his Senate career, are chronicled in his 1991 book, *Consequences: A Personal and Political Memoir.*

Tragically, Tower died in a plane crash in 1991, along with his daughter and former astronaut Sonny Lanier.

Bob Krueger did make it to the Senate eventually. In 1992 President Bill Clinton appointed him to the Senate to fill the unexpired term of Lloyd Bentsen, who had become Clinton's secretary of the treasury. Though Krueger lost the election to hold on to that seat, he was later appointed by President Clinton ambassador to Burundi.

Currently, he consults for various firms on international trade issues, and he writes and speaks on various public policy issues.

SEX, LIES, AND VIDEOTAPE

Charles Robb v. Oliver North, U.S. Senate, Virginia, 1994

The 1994 election year was very memorable. It was the year of the "Contract with America," the Clinton health-care debacle, and a Republican majority in Congress for the first time in a generation. It also featured a good many tough, competitive congressional races, none more so than the campaign for U.S. Senate in Virginia between incumbent Democrat Charles Robb, Republican nominee Oliver North, and independent candidate Marshall Coleman.

The race attracted national attention for obvious reasons. It was expected to be a slugfest, but it also had star appeal. Oliver North was the star witness in the Iran-Contra hearings of 1986, during which he became something of a celebrity. He was later convicted on federal charges relating to the Iran-Contra scandal, but that conviction was overturned on appeal because North had been granted immunity during the congressional hearings. Though to many this was a technicality, having no criminal conviction, he was cleared to run for federal office.

Both North and Robb were damaged goods, politically speaking. When Robb was first elected to the U.S. Senate, there were whispers of a future presidential run. He seemed to have it all. He was a former marine, had been a popular governor of Virginia, and even had a political pedigree—he was married to one of former president Lyndon Johnson's daughters. But then the rumors and allegations began to surface about drug use, adultery—the stuff of which negative campaigns are made.

HELLO, MISS VIRGINIA!

When he was governor, Robb was apparently very active on the party circuit in Virginia Beach. These parties became controversial when stories of drug use emerged in the media. There was never any evidence that Robb himself had used drugs, but he was known to have attended a number of parties in the early 1980s at which cocaine and other drugs were openly being used, according to those in attendance.[1] Whether Robb had used drugs himself or not, the story was hugely embarrassing.

Charles Robb. U.S. Senate Archives.

Then there was the sex scandal. Several years earlier, Robb had apparently had a fling with the former Miss Virginia, Tai Collins. When media reports surfaced of the affair, Robb admitted that he had had a brief encounter with Collins—"just a massage and wine," he insisted.[2] In 1991 Collins was on the cover of *Playboy*, and in an article called "The Woman Senator Charles Robb Couldn't Resist," she openly discussed the encounter with Robb.

The political damage to Robb from these events was significant. Speculation about a future presidential run vanished. His stock in the U.S. Senate plummeted, so much so that he was listed as one of the most vulnerable U.S. senators by the Republican Senatorial Campaign Committee leading up to the 1994 elections.

Another problem for Robb was the antagonistic relationship he had with another former Virginia governor, Douglas Wilder. The feud between the two dated back to Wilder's tenure as a state senator from Richmond and Robb's term as governor from 1982 to 1986. Never allies, they were openly critical of each other and grew to be bitter enemies. Wilder served as Virginia governor from 1990 to 1994.

The feud became very public and very hostile in 1991, when Senator Robb and his staff were accused of illegally wiretapping Governor Wilder's telephone. Private conversations by Wilder were recorded and then leaked to the press in an effort to embarrass him.[3] Following an investigation by the U.S. Justice Department, Robb was not indicted, but three former aides were convicted on

minor charges. Wilder ac-
cused Robb of trying to undermine his governorship and
his short-lived presidential
campaign. Wilder referred to
Robb as an "unindicted co-
conspirator" in the wiretapping case.[4]

The feud seemed to come
back to haunt Robb in late
1993, when Wilder, whose
term as governor was winding down, said he intended
to challenge Robb for the
Democratic Party nomina-
tion for the U.S. Senate.
After consulting with Virginia Democratic Party officials, however, he had second
thoughts about a primary

Oliver North accepts the nomination. AP/Wide
World Photos.

challenge and dropped out of the race. Robb, weakened by the scandals, had
two other challengers in the Democratic primary, though neither had statewide
name recognition or the ability to raise the money necessary to challenge Robb.

WILDER CHANGES HIS MIND; COLEMAN CHIMES IN

When it became apparent that Robb was going to win the party nomination for Senate, Wilder reversed course again, and began organizing an independent campaign. The campaign became a three-way race between Robb,
North, and Wilder. Republicans were jubilant and Democrats were worried
because it now became likely that Robb and Wilder would split the Democratic vote and hand the Senate seat to Oliver North.

But the dynamics of the campaign changed again. It became a four-way
race with the entrance of former Virginia attorney general Marshall Coleman, a Republican, as an independent candidate. Oliver North had been opposed for the Republican nomination by Jim Miller, former Office of
Management and Budget director under Ronald Reagan. North's candidacy
had brought considerable anxiety to Virginia Republicans all along. Many
feared that he was a loose cannon, and that his Iran-Contra history had

tainted him as a public official. Miller picked up the support of many of those Republicans.

North, however, had the support of the Christian Coalition and other conservative groups very active in Republican Party politics. Another advantage North had over Miller was that in Virginia, the Republican Party chooses its candidates for statewide office at a party convention, not in a primary. At a convention, the candidate with the most support from the "activist" groups, such as the Christian Coalition, has the advantage because it can mobilize support and control a small vote much easier than in a statewide election.

Even though Miller had significant support from a number of nationally known Republicans, including Ronald Reagan and Virginia's senior U.S. senator, John Warner—a Republican—North prevailed at the convention. North's nomination propelled Coleman into the race, ostensibly to give Virginia voters who disliked both Robb and North another choice. Coleman's candidacy was widely expected to balance out the race once again, and wipe out any advantage North gained from Wilder's entrance into the campaign.

Heading into the general election, the fact that there were four candidates in the race added to the circuslike atmosphere surrounding the campaign, as the national press anticipated a free-for-all. North had become a cause célèbre among the Christian right, which represented a significant fund-raising and volunteer force. North's campaign, more so than Robb's, reached out to a national audience, as North's advisers implemented an intensive direct-mail effort around the country, which brought in significant money from outside Virginia.

WILDER CHANGES HIS MIND AGAIN

The dynamics of the campaign shifted yet again in September, when Wilder, languishing in the polls and unable to raise much money, abruptly dropped out. That left it a three-way race again, but this time with two Republicans (North and Coleman) and one Democrat. Advantage Senator Robb!

Republicans were distressed that their opportunity to defeat a vulnerable Democratic U.S. senator was being threatened by Marshall Coleman, a Republican, running as an independent. To defeat an incumbent in a statewide race, they surmised, North would need every possible vote, and Coleman's candidacy gave those voters who were disenchanted with Robb another choice. Indeed, that was Coleman's strategy: "You don't trust North, but you're bothered by Robb's character problems, then vote for me."

The North campaign lambasted Coleman as a turncoat, and insisted that all he was doing was helping Robb get reelected. Initially, the Robb campaign ignored Coleman, assuming that he would take away more Republican votes than Democratic ones.

Since clinching the Republican nomination, North had spent most of his time raising money, and was receiving the lion's share of media coverage. That changed in late August when Robb, sensing a need to gain some momentum, went on the offensive. Senior Democrats had relayed concerns to the Robb campaign that North had seized strategic control of the race and was setting the tone.

At a news conference called by his campaign in Arlington, Robb characterized the contest with North as a battle of "the mainstream and the extreme."[5] Citing differences with North on gun control, abortion, and education funding, Robb asserted that North's brand of conservatism was out of touch with reality. Robb also went on the attack with regard to North's role in the Iran-Contra scandal. Emphasizing his own preference for outlawing assault weapons, Robb noted that North opposed outlawing them: "I can understand why. If you have sold arms to the ayatollah, you might not be quite as sensitive to firearm laws."[6]

Robb's campaign manager was Susan Platt, a well-known Democratic Party operative in Virginia. His media consultant was the wily veteran David Doak, of Doak/Carrier & Associates. Their game plan was to portray North as an extremist—someone with whom mainstream Virginia voters should be uncomfortable. At the same time, they needed to defend Robb's record in the Senate and downplay the character issue.

The Robb campaign repeatedly called North a liar. Courtesy, Julian P. Kanter Archive/University of Oklahoma.

The North campaign responded to Robb's broadside by saying that it was Robb who was the extremist. A North spokesman called Robb a "rubber stamp for the Clinton agenda of socialized medicine, record tax increases, and massive defense cuts."[7]

In marketing North to Virginia voters, his campaign workers had their work cut out for them. North's media consultant was Mike Murphy, who had emerged in the 1990s as one of the top Republican strategists in the country. He also had a reputation for going for an opponent's jugular. When asked about going negative, Murphy responded as most consultants do: "People say they don't like negative ads, but negative information is an important part of their decision-making. It works. Campaigns are a 'whatever works' kind of world."[8]

Conventional wisdom regarding the North-Robb confrontation would have had the North campaign bashing Robb for the better part of a year. But Murphy took a different strategy. Instead of going after Robb early, the campaign worked to polish and soften North's public image. From June to Labor Day, the North campaign spent over $800,000 in TV advertising aimed primarily at reintroducing North to a public that knew him only as a shadowy Iran-Contra figure. "There was a hell of a story to tell there and the media wasn't going to tell it," said Murphy. "Father, Silver Star winner, patriot—our campaign shorthand was 'helluva guy.' "[9]

THE MUD STARTS FLYING

In September, as part of public appearances and stump speeches, the candidates turned up the rhetoric. Robb and campaign surrogates tagged North as a lying crook, calling him "the colonel of untruth." In turn, North called Robb a liar and castigated him for a "liberal lifestyle" of infidelity.[10] But neither candidate went negative in TV ads until the second week in October—later than many analysts expected. According to *Washington Post* reporter Peter Baker:

> some political analysts attributed the delay to the fact that both Robb and North are regarded so poorly that they needed to spend more time burnishing their own images with positive ads before turning negative. They also suggested that neither major party nominee wanted to make the contest ugly early enough to provide an opening for Coleman to capitalize by appearing above the fray. (October 7, 1997)

Actually, it was Coleman who launched the first TV attack, airing an ad in early October attacking both Robb and North as extremists. A few days later, Robb aired his first negative ad, in which he attacked North's credibility. Robb's ad had the added benefit of having Republicans question North's honesty, citing statements by Ronald Reagan, Senator John Warner, and former national security adviser Robert McFarlane.

The conventional wisdom of the past—that challengers attack early and often while incumbents are less likely to go negative—has been turned on its head in the last decade, and the North-Robb campaign is a good example. Robb's campaign felt little hesitation in beating North to the punch on television. The feeling was that North had made up a lot of ground in the summer and early fall with his soft, positive spots, and so Robb had to remind voters of how North came by his reputation.

North and Murphy were ready to return fire. Two days later, the North campaign aired its first attack ad on television, and it was a doozy. The ad shows a close-up of Robb as newspaper headlines reporting his attendance at drug parties roll across the screen, followed by the names of Robb's associates convicted of drug charges, and finally the *Playboy* cover featuring Tai Collins. As the images are seen, the following audio is heard:

Why can't Chuck Robb tell the truth? About the cocaine parties where Robb said he never saw drugs—then four of his party friends were sent to prison for dealing cocaine. Or about the beauty queen in the hotel room in New York. Robb says it was only a massage. Chuck Robb lived a lie and violated his oath of good faith to the people, writes the *Richmond Times/Dispatch*. Character counts, and North has it all over Robb.

The very next day, Robb responded with a second ad that called North a liar:

After lying about President Reagan and even lying to schoolchildren, now Oliver North is lying about Chuck Robb. Chuck Robb has never had anything to do with illegal drugs—period. But what North doesn't understand is the real issue in this campaign is the candidate's record of public service. Chuck Robb has a proven record of public service, while North's public record includes putting himself above the law by selling arms to terrorists and backdating documents to conceal that some of the money went to his personal use. Oliver North—people are starting to wonder if he knows what the truth is.[11]

In the third week of October, the polls showed North with a slim lead over Robb, with Coleman trailing a distant third. The Robb campaign's own polling revealed something they had not expected: Marshall Coleman's independent campaign was actually hurting Robb more than North. This was especially true in the northern suburbs of Virginia, where Robb was counting on substantial support to offset North's strength in the rural areas of the state. Something had to change if Robb was going to hold on to his seat. Something did.

WILDER MAKES A DECISION

On October 21, former governor Douglas Wilder, the man who had called Robb "unfit for office," formally endorsed him. Thus ended weeks of speculation about whether Wilder would eventually endorse Robb over their common enemy, Oliver North.

A number of Democrats, including President Clinton, had asked Wilder to consider endorsing Robb for the good of the party and to help preserve the Democrats' majority in the Senate. Democrats were also hopeful that Wilder, the nation's first elected black governor, would shore up Robb's standing in the black community. A low voter turnout among blacks, they feared, would hurt Robb and help North.[12]

North dismissed Wilder's endorsement, saying Bill Clinton was simply trying to salvage his "liberal monopoly" on political power. Experts disagree on how much Wilder's endorsement aided Robb with black voters, but the endorsement undoubtedly provided Robb with needed momentum heading into the last two weeks of the campaign, when many undecided voters begin to make up their minds.

The Robb campaign also benefited by opening a new front in the air war. Based on internal polls showing Coleman hurting Robb in northern Virginia, Robb aired a TV ad critical of Coleman for altering his position on abortion. Robb, an advocate of abortion rights, said Coleman had shifted ground "on issues where you shouldn't shift ground." Coleman had softened his previously tough stand against abortion by saying that government cannot settle the issue and that he would not seek to promote or ban abortion as a U.S. senator. Robb accused him of flip-flopping on the issue.[13]

One of Robb's perceived strengths in northern Virginia was the abortion issue. Northern Virginia, a suburb of Washington, D.C., where significant numbers of government employees live, tends to be more moderate than the rest of the state, especially on the abortion issue. According to the Robb campaign, it needed to seize this issue to reinforce Robb's position in the northern part of the state. The attacks on Coleman helped solidify Robb's support.

In the last week of the campaign, sensing the public's attitude that the campaign couldn't go any lower and hoping to avoid backlash from all of the mudslinging, North and Robb's TV ads, though still critical of each other, began to be more issue based. For example, North's ads focused on his opposition to taxes and congressional pay raises, while linking Robb to President Clinton.

In the final days of the campaign, the momentum seemed to be with Robb. Douglas Wilder, his once bitter enemy, campaigned beside him. Former first lady Nancy Reagan was quoted as saying North "has a great deal of trouble separating fact from fantasy." Opinion polls showed that North's negatives were up, and that more people distrusted him as compared with earlier in the campaign.

On election night, Robb won 46 percent of the vote, compared to 43 percent for North and a disappointing 11 percent for Coleman. Wounded by character questions, Robb had been pushed to the brink of defeat, but in the end, the power of incumbency, Wilder's support, and the lingering doubts Virginians had about North were just too much for the former NSC colonel to overcome.

North's electoral strategy of linking Robb to the unpopular President Clinton and counting on significant support from Virginia's rural areas didn't work. Neither did his attacks on Robb. If the election had been held in September, North very likely would have won. Through the summer and early fall, North's campaign was humming. He was raising tons of money and spending tons of money on positive TV ads polishing his image.

After the negative campaigning blitz, though, from mid-October through the election, voters were reminded of North's negatives. In the final analysis, it may well be that the voters, though no longer enamored of Senator Robb, considered his shortcomings to be of a personal nature, while those of North were more linked to professional and public accountability.

CLAYTIE VERSUS THE LADY

Clayton Williams v. Ann Richards, Governor, Texas, 1990

If there was ever a candidate who should have won an election and did not, it is Clayton Williams. As the Republican nominee for governor of Texas in 1990, he had everything going for him. He had the swaggering, John Wayne cowboy image, which Texans admire. He was a self-made millionaire, and had the fund-raising edge to go along with it. He was a conservative in a conservative state that was trending Republican, as most other southern states were in the 1990s. And he faced an opponent in Democratic nominee Ann Richards who had a controversial public image and a history of personal problems.

Newsweek described the contest as between "a millionaire political novice who sits on a white horse, tips his Stetson hat when he greets a woman and has settled at least a couple of disagreements with fisticuffs . . . and a feminist and recovering alcoholic who put her white bouffant on the national map by telling the country (at the 1988 Democratic National Convention) that President George Bush was 'born with a silver foot in his mouth.' "[1] A cowboy versus a feminist? In Texas?

But something happened that cost Clayton Williams the election. He opened his mouth.

His campaign advisers probably wish he had developed laryngitis—a bad enough case that would have lasted through election day. From the moment he secured the Republican nomination, he said one dumb, insulting thing after another. The end result, according to most analysts and observers, was that he snatched defeat from the jaws of victory.

Clayton Williams giving his concession speech. Texas State Library & Archives Commission.

BAD WEATHER?

The most famous, or infamous, example of his bad judgment and bad timing was when he compared bad weather to rape. Speaking of the cold, foggy weather at his west Texas ranch, he compared it to rape, saying, "If it's inevitable, just lie back and enjoy it."[2] The remark was widely reported and created a firestorm. Naturally, everyone who heard it cringed, especially women and women's advocacy groups. The head of the Texas Women's Political Caucus, Marilyn Rickman, said the remark was inexcusable. "Rape is never a joke under any circumstances," she said.

Predictably, the Richards campaign pounced on the remark as an example of Williams's insensitivity toward women and his general unfitness for high political office. Richards said that Williams "seemed not to realize that rape is a crime of violence." Of course, politically, it was a crime of stupidity that did violence to his own campaign.

And certainly, many Texans raised their eyebrows when Williams said in late spring that he thought he would do very well with Mexican American voters in Texas because "I like Mexican food and Mexican music."[3]

But the verbal sparring between the two candidates has become famous. Williams and his side did all they could to present Richards as an elitist liberal and a gay and lesbian sympathizer who hangs out with Jane Fonda and Ted Kennedy, and who would rather serve the interests of Hollywood than Texas. The Richards team dismissed Williams as a junk-bond peddler and

Ann Richards was not your typical politician. Texas State Library & Archives Commission.

polluter, and a guy who is as ignorant "as a box of rocks" when it comes to state government.[4] In a speech, Richards jeered him as a "media cowboy who rides off into the sunset and kisses the horse instead of the girl."

DIVERGENT PATHS

The two candidates had very different primary contests to win their nominations. Williams sailed to a surprisingly easy victory over his Republican opponents. Richards, on the other hand, slugged it out with Attorney General Jim Mattox and former governor Mark White in what is remembered as one of the nastiest, roughest Democratic primaries in Texas history.

Much of the fighting revolved around Richards's past alcohol use and allegations from Mattox that she had also used illegal drugs. In a televised debate, Mattox and White made a big deal of never using drugs, while Richards refused to say one way or the other, which fueled the story. In one of Mattox's TV ads, the announcer asks, "Did she use marijuana, or something worse, like cocaine?" The Richards campaign responded with attacks on Mattox's ethics, accusing him of financial wrongdoings. One of her ads focused on Mattox's indictment on bribery charges, but made no mention of his acquittal in a jury trial.

Perhaps what saved Richards in the primary campaign was the female vote. Many Democrats, especially women, came to see the race as a "feminist crusade," according to the *New York Times*.[5] Richards won the primary runoff over Mattox surprisingly easy, winning by a wide margin. The battle-scarred Democrat then faced off with the swaggering Williams.

In the meantime, Williams continued his act of political self-destruction. His comments and demeanor began to contribute to the "gender gap," the tendency for men to support Republicans and women to support Democrats—the plague of many Republican candidates. For example, not long after his blunder about rape and bad weather, he admitted that as a youth in Texas he had been "serviced" by prostitutes. When asked by a reporter whether he had ever patronized a prostitute, he replied, "of course," insisting that it was just part of growing up in west Texas.[6]

But some of his sexual adventures may not have been limited to his youth. Rumors swirled among the Texas political and media world about "honey hunts" at Williams's ranch. According to several firsthand accounts, Mr. Williams served as host at these social occasions, in which prostitutes were hidden on the grounds of his ranch and party guests were set out to find them. Although his campaign handlers denied these accounts, they nonetheless contributed to his mounting image problems.

As summer turned to fall, however, Williams still maintained a lead in the polls, especially among men. Although he had clearly stumbled, Richards still had the same vulnerabilities: a liberal woman in a conservative state that was trending Republican.

The late summer and early fall featured a knock-down-drag-out brawl between the two. Ironically, only a few weeks earlier, both candidates had vowed to avoid mudslinging and concentrate on the issues. So much for good intentions.

ROPE HER AND TIE HER?

The verbal war of words began to heat up with the weather. Speaking to reporters, Williams said he looked forward to the fall campaign against Richards because he was going to "rope her like a calf and drag her through the dirt." Nice imagery!

In August, the war of TV ads began. Richards lambasted Williams as a corrupt oil tycoon, mired in business debts and fighting off lawsuits. Williams accused Richards of financial mismanagement as state treasurer. He called on Richards to explain her investment of state funds in savings and loan thrifts when the savings and loan financial crisis was brewing in the late 1980s. He also claimed that some of these same thrifts had contributed to Richards's campaign. The Richards campaign released documents showing that the state had not lost money in the thrifts, and that none of them holding state money had contributed to her campaign.

The response from the Williams campaign was to call for a truce on negative ads. Richards refused. Her campaign's position was that Williams had called for a truce only because he couldn't defend what he was saying in his ads. A Richards spokesman said they would continue running the anti-Williams spot because it was accurate. "It's a 30-second documentary," he said.

More damaging to Richards, though, was a set of radio ads by Williams tying her to Michael Dukakis (the 1988 Democratic presidential nominee, an avowed liberal), as well as to Jane Fonda, flag burning, gun control, and gays. Richards dismissed the ads as "trash."[7]

SORRY POLITICS

The *Houston Post* lamented that "never have we had sorrier politics than we've had lately. . . . In fact, Texas may just soil the record books by waging even crummier campaigns for high office than those that smeared around George Bush and Michael Dukakis two years ago." A popular joke making the rounds in Texas at the time was: "Clayton Williams and Ann Richards are on a life raft that's sinking. Who will be saved? The people of Texas."

Some Texas Democrats worried that for all the fighting between the two, Richards wasn't making enough headway in the polls. The furious attacking from both campaigns led a few Democratic insiders to worry that Richards was drowning out her issue positions and policy stands. These concerns were backed by surveys showing that the negative evaluations of both candidates were increasing, potentially reducing voter turnout that would be crucial to a Richards victory.

Weeks later, the Richards camp released a poll showing that she was only 6 points behind Williams, not the 10 to 15 points shown in other polls of Texas voters. Williams's response was that he hoped Richards "didn't go back to drinking again." He added that there was no way the race was that close. His remark about her alcohol problems were seen as tasteless, and served as further evidence to many female voters that he was an insensitive, "Cro-Magnon" cowboy.

Is Chivalry Dead?

The turning point in the campaign may have come in late September, at a joint appearance before a luncheon meeting of the Dallas crime commission. Whether Williams simply lost his cool or was trying to stage some sort of morality play is unclear, but he confronted Richards in a way that reinforced the doubts many Texas voters had about him. Reacting to her recent attacks on his banking and insurance dealings in his oil business, Williams approached Richards at the luncheon, pointed his finger at her, and said, "Ann, I'm calling you a liar today." She answered, with a note of sarcasm, "I'm sorry Claytie," and extended her hand to his. He pulled his hand away, refusing to shake.[8]

Then, at the end of Williams's prepared remarks to the group, he stunned the audience of Dallas business and law enforcement leaders by launching a vicious attack on Richards, seated a mere few feet away. "I know politics is a tough business, but even politics has its boundaries," he said, his face red with anger. "Ann, you crossed over the line." Comparing her tactics to those of Senator Joseph McCarthy during the communist witch hunts of the 1950s, he said, "Ma'am, have you no sense of decency? Ma'am, have you at long last lost all your decency?"

Not a smooth move. Talking to reporters afterwards, Richards dismissed Williams's behavior as that of a desperate candidate in a free fall. "I think this is a very tough thing for him. It's tough to go through this kind of pressure. I feel very sad. I can't believe he would refuse to shake my hand. I think he's lost control," she said. Many in attendance agreed.

It did not help matters that Williams had rebuffed calls for a debate with Richards. Williams had refused to debate her unless she signed a pledge promising not to attack him. The Richards campaign rejected his offer as nothing more than a cheap ploy to avoid a direct debate. "I think he's in serious trouble," Richards said. "And he doesn't want to debate me because of that."

DIRTY TRICKS?

In October, the issue of whether Richards had ever used illegal drugs surfaced again, but in a way that seemed to hurt Williams more than Richards. The *Albuquerque Journal* had reported that a New Mexico tour operator had seen Richards using cocaine at a Dallas bar in 1977. The tour operator, J. D. Arnold—who had once worked for Jim Mattox, Richards's opponent in the Democratic primary—said he received a call from someone advising him to tell his story to the Williams campaign. Arnold then received a call from the sheriff's office in San Antonio. It was well known that the San Antonio sheriff was a well-connected supporter of Clayton Williams.[9]

Williams and his campaign staff insisted they had no knowledge of the story or the investigation, but Richards called a press conference to accuse Williams of orchestrating the whole thing. She also produced two eyewitnesses who were with her the night of the alleged cocaine use in Dallas, who said there was no drug use. "The whole thing stinks to high heaven," said Richards. "Williams's campaign has not only lost its momentum, but its moral compass as well."

Through most of October, the Williams campaign changed tactics—pub-

> Ann Richards lost her reelection campaign to future president George W. Bush in 1994. That same year, New York governor Mario Cuomo was also defeated for reelection. This was the year of the "Contract with America" and Newt Gingrich, when a number of incumbent officeholders at both the federal level and the state level went down to defeat.

licly, anyway. The campaign became more conservative and close to the vest. It seemed Williams had been told by his campaign handlers not to wander from the script in public. His talks with the press became very short, lasting only a few minutes before or after an appearance, only to be rescued by his staff and hustled away. It was a stark contrast to the Republican primary back in the spring, when he would wax on and on about his upbringing, his politics, and his views on Texas life and government. But then again, those free-talking ways seemed to be what got him into trouble.

And he was in trouble. His lead was shrinking. According to tracking polls, he had squandered his lead among some critical demographic groups, such as suburban voters and middle- to high-income voters, who were turned off by his fiery rhetoric and slips of the tongue. In the Republican primaries, his campaign prided itself on his unusual and frank demeanor. "Let Claytie be Claytie," they said. But it went too far.

As the *Washington Post* said, "Sometimes he taps into the Texas myth a little too far. When he uses rodeo lingo to describe his campaign, or when he acknowledges he visited prostitutes across the border as a youth . . . people start remembering that there was a time in Texas when women were treated like cattle, blacks were slaves, Mexicans were second-class citizens and many cowpokes were greedy, uneducated, and crude."[10]

Shortly before election day, most tracking polls showed the race a dead heat. Williams had lost his 15-point cushion from when the campaign began. The Richards campaign and other Democratic consultants said that Williams had overexposed himself. "He spent about $16 million educating Texans about who he is," said one Democratic official. "Well, now they know who he is, and they don't like him." Even one Republican media consultant said that this was a case where "familiarity (with the voters) bred contempt."

ONE MORE BLOW

The truth is, Richards had not so much caught up with Williams as he had simply slid down even with her, and maybe even a notch or two lower.

But there was one more blow to the Williams campaign, and it came two days before the election. Williams had long refused Richards's repeated calls for him to release his income tax returns, saying they were irrelevant. But under tremendous pressure from the media in the final days of the campaign, the Williams camp responded to the income tax issue. In response to a reporter's question, Williams said, "Yes, I've paid lots of income taxes—lots, lots. . . . I'll tell you, when I didn't pay any income taxes was 1986, when our whole economy collapsed." It was a startling admission, especially with the election only forty-eight hours away.

Richards blasted him. "He said it was a bad year," she said at a campaign rally. "It was a bad year for a lot of Texans in 1986. I paid my taxes in 1986; how about you?"

THE FAT LADY SINGS

On election day, Richards beat Williams 51 percent to 49 percent. She did it by carrying a good bit of territory that should have belonged to Williams, such as upscale Republican suburbs in Dallas and rural sections of east Texas. And, of course, she cleaned up with the state's female voters, winning over 60 percent of women's votes.

One of the dirtiest campaigns in Texas history was over. Gone, but not forgotten.

RICHARD NIXON VERSUS THE UNITED STATES OF AMERICA

Richard Nixon v. George McGovern, President, 1972

No look at dirty politics would be complete without some words about Nixon's near-total destruction of the Democratic Party in 1972. Ostensibly, the campaign was about the Republican nominee Nixon and the Democratic nominee George McGovern, but it was much bigger than that. Nixon's campaign was waged against the entire Democratic Party and, ultimately, against the rule of law.

President Nixon's campaign committee, the Committee to Reelect the President (CRP, or CREEP as it was known), actively coordinated with White House staff to weaken Democratic candidates for president throughout 1971 and 1972. This was accomplished through espionage, wiretapping, blackmail, forged documents, financial payoffs, burglary, cover-ups, and purgery, all sanctioned by the highest authorities in the land—the president, his senior staff, and the attorney general's office.

As a campaign strategy, it was incredibly effective—that is, until everyone involved went to jail or resigned from office. What Watergate came to symbolize was an organized conspiracy from the highest office in the world to subvert the democratic process and evade any form of accountability. The general election campaign between Nixon and McGovern was just one act in this ongoing tragedy. Shakespeare would probably blush.

The feeling among Nixon and his confidants was that they had already had one election stolen from them (1960) and that his amazing political comeback in the late 1960s was endangered by Vietnam, civil rights, and economic uncertainties. They would have to take matters into their own hands and determine the direction of the next campaign. To accomplish this, the White House–directed group of "plumbers" and dirty tricksters formed to go after the Nixon administration's enemies would widen its scope and go after the president's potential Democratic opponents.

As they sized up the field of potential Democratic candidates for president, they realized that Senator Ted Kennedy, whom Nixon had feared as a potential rival, was damaged goods after the incident at Chappaquiddick, and would likely never be president.[1] Former vice president and 1968 presidential nominee Hubert Humphrey was likely to run, but as Lyndon Johnson's vice president, he was still tainted by Vietnam in a party that had moved closer to the political left since 1968. That left U.S. Senators George McGovern and Edmund Muskie.

Of the two, the Nixon team strongly preferred to run against George McGovern rather than Muskie. McGovern, from South Dakota, was an antiwar candidate from the party's left wing and seen by most as "hopelessly liberal." He had been a relatively minor figure in the Democratic Party before 1972. Muskie, from Maine, was also critical of the war and favored liberal or progressive social and economic policies, but had more credibility and substance than McGovern as well as stronger leadership qualities. Muskie had been governor of Maine, he was seen as an effective leader in the U.S. Senate, and he had gained national exposure as Humphrey's running mate in 1968. Some even compared the lanky, angular Muskie and his commonsense wisdom to Abraham Lincoln.

There was also an added irritant in the mix. Governor George Wallace of Alabama, who had run an insurgent campaign in 1968 as the nominee of the American Independent Party and had actually won the electoral votes of five southern states, would be running as a Democrat this time, and was expected to do very well in the South.

However, few thought a segregationist like Wallace could actually win the Democratic nomination, and even fewer thought he could win the general election. Of course, unbeknownst to Nixon or anyone else, Wallace had a date with destiny in the form of assassin Arthur Bremer, who wounded Wallace as he was campaigning for the nomination in 1972, confining him to a wheelchair for the rest of his life and dooming his campaign for the presidency.

DIRTY TRICKS FOR TRICKY DICK

CREEP hired a team of political operatives to "disrupt" the campaigns of Democratic candidates for president. This team was directed by Donald Segretti, a lawyer and campaign operative from California. Segretti and his group were basically the "dirty tricks" squad for the White House and for CREEP.[2]

The main goals of this group, as Segretti and his accomplices later told reporters and investigators, were to torpedo the campaigns of Democrats they thought to be a serious threat to Nixon's reelection, and to wreak havoc among the Democratic campaigns, creating ill will and sore feelings. "The main purpose was that the Democrats not have the ability to get back together after a knock-down drag-out campaign," according to Segretti.[3]

Their style of disrupting and harassing rival political campaigns was known to them as "ratf###ing." Their main target early in 1972 was Ed Muskie. According to the political pundits and pollsters, Muskie was the man to beat for the Democratic nomination. As the front-runner for the nomination, expectations for him were high heading into the New Hampshire primary—some estimates had him winning 65 percent of the vote.

But then came the "Canuck letter." Segretti and Ken Clawson, a White House communications deputy, had cooked up a letter and sent it to William Loeb, the publisher of the *Manchester Union Leader*—an influential conservative newspaper in Manchester, New Hampshire. The letter claimed that at a campaign meeting in Ft. Lauderdale, a Muskie campaign aid had cracked a joke about French Canadians living in New England. "We don't have blacks, but we have Canucks," the aid supposedly said. To this, Senator Muskie was reported to have agreed and laughingly said, "Come to New England and see."[4] ("Canuck" is a derogatory term for French Canadians.)

Two weeks before the New Hampshire primary and one day before Muskie was to campaign there, the *Union Leader* published an anti-Muskie editorial on its front page, entitled "Senator Muskie Insults Franco-Americans."[5] The paper accused Muskie of hypocrisy for supporting blacks while condoning the term "Canucks." A copy of the Canuck letter accompanied the editorial.

The very next day, Loeb reprinted a two-month-old *Newsweek* article about Senator Muskie's wife, entitled "Big Daddy's Jane." This piece reported that

Richard Nixon was on top of the world in 1972. Library of Congress.

Mrs. Muskie was a chain-smoker, drank too much, and used off-color language on the campaign plane.

The next morning, the Muskie campaign started to unravel. The senator appeared in front of the headquarters of the *Union Leader* in a driving snowstorm. Standing on a flatbed truck, he addressed a gathering of supporters, along with the media covering his campaign, and attacked Loeb as a "gutless coward." As he spoke about the charges against his wife, his voice halted as he choked back tears. It was a dramatic moment. For a moment, it appeared as if he could not go on, but he struggled to finish his condemnation of the *Union Leader*. TV cameras recorded the incident, and it led most evening news broadcasts.

Senator Edmund Muskie. U.S. Senate Archives.

There is widespread agreement among observers, journalists, and even Muskie's campaign staff that this incident had a disastrous effect on his campaign. It shattered the calm, cool, reasoned image that Muskie had cultivated in the months leading up to the primaries. The image TV viewers got of Muskie was of someone unable to control his emotions and unpresidential.

There were other dirty tricks just before the New Hampshire primary. In late February, voters began receiving late-night phone calls from people who said that they had just arrived from Harlem and were calling to solicit votes for Muskie. Presumably, New Hampshire voters would not welcome late-night calls from campaign workers from Harlem, one of New York's largest African American communities.

On March 7, Muskie did win the New Hampshire primary, but by the disappointing margin of 47 percent rather than the expected 60 to 65 percent. Even though he came in first, it was seen as a loss, and the image of Muskie crying in the snows of New Hampshire defined him for many Democratic-primary voters.

But Nixon's dirty tricks squad wasn't through with Muskie, or with the other Democratic candidates. Ahead of the Florida primary, Muskie was again the victim of political sabotage. Three days before the vote, letters written on "Citizens for Muskie" stationery were sent to Democratic Party workers charging that Hubert Humphrey had been arrested for drunk driving in 1967. Also, according to the letter, at the time of his arrest, in the car with Humphrey was a prostitute.

Another letter on Muskie stationery charged that Democratic U.S. senator Henry Jackson had fathered an illegitimate child in 1929 and had been arrested for committing homosexual acts in 1955 and 1957. Yet another phony letter, this time on the letterhead of former U.S. senator Eugene McCarthy, urged his supporters to vote for Hubert Humphrey.

Segretti and his unit put up posters along Florida highways that read, "Help Muskie in Busing More Children Now." An ad planted by Segretti in a Miami newspaper asked, "Senator Muskie, would you accept a Jewish running mate?" And at a Muskie press conference in Florida, Segretti and an accomplice released handfuls of white mice with ribbons tied to their tails. The ribbons read, "Muskie is a rat fink."[6]

Due to the combined effects of his fall from grace in New Hampshire and Segretti's political sabotage, Muskie finished a disappointing fourth in the Florida primary. His star had fallen, and he was no longer considered the front-runner. The dirty tricks had worked.

In April, after he was unable to come back and win primaries in Wisconsin, Pennsylvania, or Massachusetts, Muskie suspended his campaigning and effectively left the race. So the Democratic field was down to Humphrey, McGovern, and Wallace. As Muskie had faded, McGovern had picked up steam, coming in first in Wisconsin and Massachusetts, and second in Pennsylvania. The Nixon team was starting to feel better about its prospects for reelection.

After the assassination attempt on Wallace, he was forced to leave the race, and the nomination came down to either Humphrey or McGovern. The two

Senator George McGovern of South Dakota. U.S. Senate Archives.

Democrats savaged each other leading up to the crucial California primary. Humphrey criticized McGovern's positions as "dangerous" and irresponsible, particularly his goal of slashing the size of the military to "pre–Pearl Harbor" days. Humphrey TV ads raised fears that McGovern's plans would make America a "second-class world power."

To many Democrats in 1972, Humphrey was too closely associated with Lyndon Johnson's Vietnam policies. McGovern's strong antiwar stance and his preferences for reduced military spending seemed to fit better with what most Democratic voters wanted. McGovern won the California primary, but by a smaller margin than had been expected. Humphrey's attacks had taken a toll.

McGovern had proven to be a survivor and a tougher candidate than most observers had believed. He had developed a strong following among many young college activists who had built a grassroots network in some of the key primary states. With his win in California, McGovern had now come from behind and won enough delegates in enough primaries to be the front-runner for the nomination, but the Democratic Party had splintered.

Not everyone in the party could get behind the McGovern agenda, which not only called for the immediate withdrawal of U.S. troops from Vietnam but also called for amnesty for those avoiding military service. He also favored busing to achieve school integration, abolishing capital punishment, and banning handguns. There were also hints at support for gay rights, which added to the controversial image of his campaign.

After the Democrats' disastrous convention in Miami, in which, due to floor demonstrations and out-of-control delegates, McGovern gave his acceptance speech at 3:00 A.M., the party seemed to be in turmoil and out of the political mainstream. The Republicans—and the Nixon White House—were ecstatic. Their plans were working to perfection.

DEMOCRATS FOR NIXON

The antiwar, antimilitary posture carved out by McGovern and the Democrats presented a problem to many moderate American voters, which the Nixon campaign was able to exploit. It created a group called Democrats for Nixon, which drove home the message that McGovern was so liberal and so out of touch with the mainstream that many Democrats could not support him.

The group took out ads in major newspapers and ran TV spots urging Democrats who were concerned about America's role in the world and with McGovern's "Far Left" agenda to support President Nixon. The effort was boosted by the support of high-profile entertainers, such as Sammy Davis Jr., and a number of other leading Democrats. The group was chaired by former Texas governor John Connally.

Democrats for Nixon became a very effective way to attack McGovern be-

The Nixon campaign ridiculed McGovern's defense policies. Courtesy, Julian P. Kanter Archive/University of Oklahoma.

cause as a group "independent" of Nixon's reelection campaign, it carried more credibility with the voters. The group made three very memorable TV ads attacking McGovern and his record.

The group took advantage of the split between regular Democrats, many of whom had supported Hubert Humphrey or Ed Muskie, and the more liberal supporters of McGovern. In fact, it used Humphrey's own words against McGovern in a TV spot that featured McGovern's proposals to slash military spending along with a quote from Humphrey that McGovern's plans for military reductions "are cutting into the very fiber and the muscle of the defense establishment."[7]

Another effective ad by this group focused on jobs and welfare. A construction worker with a lunch pail is shown, while an announcer details McGovern's support for expanding unemployment compensation and welfare benefits. As the list of McGovern's positions grows, the look on the worker's face grows more worried and shocked.

Probably the most effective of the anti-McGovern spots was the "weathervane" ad. A photo of McGovern flips one way and then another as an announcer reads McGovern's changing positions on some key issues:

In 1967, Senator George McGovern said he was not an advocate of early withdrawal of our troops from Vietnam. Now of course he is. Last year the senator suggested regulating marijuana along the same lines as alcohol. Now he's against legalizing it and says he always has been. Last January Senator McGovern suggested a welfare plan that would give a thousand dollar bill to every man, woman, and child in the country. Now he says maybe the thousand dollar figure isn't right. Throughout the year he has proposed unconditional amnesty for all draft dodgers; now his running mate claims he proposed no such thing. In Florida he was pro-busing; in Oregon he said he would support the anti-busing bill then in Congress. Last year, this year. The question is, what about next year?

The Nixon campaign team liked the Democrats for Nixon ads so much that they shelved other ads that had been produced with the campaign's tag line, the Committee to Reelect the President. President Nixon confided to senior staffers and campaign personnel that he believed these ads to be "the best political TV ads" he had ever seen.

THE EAGLETON AFFAIR

McGovern's campaign was also hurt by revelations that his running mate, Senator Thomas Eagleton from Missouri, had undergone electroshock treatment while hospitalized for depression. Eagleton had neglected to tell McGovern about it, and the campaign had apparently not looked into Eagleton's background thoroughly enough.[8]

In addition, the whole situation was handled poorly, which harmed McGovern's image as a decision maker. At first he said he backed Eagleton's candidacy 1,000 percent. But after a barrage of criticism from editorial writers, Democratic Party contributors, and his own campaign staff, McGovern did an about-face and dropped him from the ticket.

It was hard for McGovern to find a suitable replacement for Eagleton. Several high-profile Democrats were approached by the McGovern campaign, but they all refused. Finally, it settled on former Peace Corps director and ambassador to France, Sargent Shriver. Shriver was the husband of Eunice Kennedy. He was hardly a national figure, but it was the best they could do on short notice, and Shriver was not expected to provide any further embarrassment to the McGovern campaign. Somewhere, Donald Segretti was smiling; he didn't even have to lift a finger.

NIXON, THE WORLD LEADER

The general-election campaign that fall was a mismatch. The Nixon campaign knew it was going to win, but now it wanted a blowout. Nixon ran as a world leader, above the realm of petty partisan politics. His TV ads featured him visiting China, walking on the Great Wall, and meeting with Soviet leader Leonid Brezhnev. They cast McGovern as a minor figure on the Far Left of the Democratic Party, with a radical agenda.

They had succeeded in destroying the candidacy of a Democrat they did not want to run against (Muskie) and marginalizing the eventual nominee of the Democratic Party. What could have been a major weakness for Nixon—Vietnam—turned out to be his ace in the hole. The country trusted Nixon much more than McGovern to handle the war and manage America's role in the world.

The McGovern campaign tried, in vain, to get the country to focus on political corruption. After the Watergate break-in, with no evidence to tie Nixon or his campaign to it, the McGovern campaign continuously brought up the issues of ethics and corruption, but no one was listening. In the closing weeks, McGovern ran a series of radio ads critical of Nixon's handling of the presidency. And he hired Tony Schwartz (who had created the "Daisy Girl" spot for Lyndon Johnson in 1964) to produce some anti-Nixon TV spots.[9]

But by this time, McGovern's candidacy was adrift. After months of acrimony within the Democratic Party and among its candidates, and after the barrage of Nixon ads painting him as some kind of Far Left wacko, McGovern and his campaign simply had no credibility with voters.

> Nixon resigned the presidency after the House Judiciary Committee voted to enact articles of impeachment. Had Nixon not resigned, the next step would have been for the full House of Representatives to vote on impeachment. Then the Senate would have held a trial to consider whether the president should be removed from office. President Bill Clinton was impeached by the full House in 1998, but a trial by the Senate resulted in an acquittal.

On election day, George McGovern suffered one of the most severe beatings in presidential history. In a landslide of epic proportions, Nixon won forty-nine states in the electoral college to McGovern's one. He didn't even carry his home state of South Dakota, carrying instead Massachusetts.

Twenty-one months later, Richard Nixon would resign from the office of the presidency in disgrace, the first American president to do so. Most of his top White House advisers were convicted of various felonies resulting from the Watergate cover-up, such as obstruction of justice and perjury. Haldeman, Erlichman, Colson, Dean, Magruder, and others all did time in federal prison. Donald Segretti served a six-month prison term, then went home to California to practice law.

"Bye-Bye Blackbird"

Harold Washington v. Bernard Epton, Mayor, Chicago, 1983

A number of American political campaigns, and several in this book, have featured overt appeals to racism. But none have been more coarse and openly hostile to racial tensions and sensitivities than the 1983 race for mayor of Chicago between Harold Washington, a Democrat, and his Republican challenger, Bernard Epton. This was a shockingly brutal campaign, even for the rough-and-tumble world of Chicago politics.

Although he was a longtime fixture in Illinois politics, Harold Washington was not the mayoral nominee that many Democrats wanted in 1983. He had won a bruising primary against Democrats Jane Byrne, the incumbent mayor, and Richard M. Daley, son of the late mayor Richard Daley and scion of the famous Daley political machine. In the Democratic primary, neither Byrne nor Daley wanted to attack Washington because they were trying to win votes in the black community. In the general election, however, Epton and his campaign forces felt no such hesitation.

As a candidate, Washington did have some significant vulnerabilities. In the 1970s he had not filed income taxes for four straight years. His debt to the IRS lead to a short prison term. He had had his law license suspended for taking clients' money without performing services. It also came to light that he had not paid a series of electricity and water bills, also leading to legal action against him. Thus, his political opponents had considerable ammunition to throw at him, completely apart from race, creating an image problem that Washington would have to overcome.

Primary Colors

But perhaps a larger hurdle for Washington's candidacy was the fragmented nature of his core constituency, Chicago's black community. A gulf of mistrust, resentment, and political turf battles existed between black voters in the western precincts of Chicago, which tended to be middle class, and the less affluent black communities on Chicago's south side, where Washington was from. This split, most observers believed, would make it difficult for Washington to form a winning coalition in the Democratic primary for mayor and overcome the strength of incumbent mayor Jane Byrne or the historical legacy of Richard Daley.

Harold Washington. Photographic print, ICHi-18094; Courtesy, Chicago Historical Society.

But Washington's appeal across the divide in the black community was stronger than either Byrne's or Daley's, strategists thought. Washington gained in the polls, especially after a debate in which Washington held his own against his two opponents.[1]

But the biggest blow against Mayor Jane Byrne's candidacy may have been self-inflicted. It was reported in the newspapers that a prominent Byrne supporter and a top Democratic Party official named Ed Vrdolyak had told his precinct captains that Washington's candidacy represented a dire threat. Reportedly he said "It would be the worst day in the history of Chicago" if Washington won. "It's a racial thing, don't kid yourself. . . . We're fighting to keep things the way it is," he said. The reaction from the black community was immediate and predictable. Washington became a hero and a cause to rally around.[2]

In the three-way primary, Washington outpolled Byrne and Daley by almost 100,000 votes, winning over 80 percent of the black vote in the process. But this fight was only the beginning.

Washington and his campaign advisers, along with a number of Chicago political observers, thought that since Washington was the Democratic Party nominee, the predominantly white Democratic political machine would support him as it had supported past Democratic candidates. They were wrong.

BLACK AND WHITE

Racial politics and sensitivities in Chicago were simmering underneath the surface, as they were in most big cities in the 1970s and early 1980s. Yet no one was prepared for the racial warfare that ensued in the general-election campaign. The intensity and the harsh nature of the racial overtones in the campaign were surprising to many, but then again, there had never before been a black nominee for mayor of Chicago.

What was left of the Democratic Party political machine that had dominated Chicago for decades was split over Washington's candidacy. For the first time in a long time, party labels meant little because race became the main issue. Some Chicago Democrats were uncomfortable with Washington, not just because of race but because he had promised to dismantle the system of political patronage (giving jobs and favors to political supporters) on which many had come to rely.[3]

The thing is, Bernard Epton was no racist—or at least he had not been one up to that point. Epton was Jewish, a native of Chicago, and a successful insurance lawyer, and had been active in politics since he was a teenager. He had served in the Illinois House of Representatives for fourteen years, at the same time Harold Washington was in the state legislature. Though a Republican, he voted with the Democrats on most social issues, thereby gaining a reputation as a moderate. In fact, he was lauded by one Chicago minority newspaper for "supporting causes affecting the black and the poor."[4]

Chicago had always been a Democratic city; Republicans had not done well in elections there since the 1920s. Epton had no opposition in the Republican mayoral primary and had very low name recognition in the Chicago area. So he was not considered a factor in the campaign for mayor—that is, until Washington became the Democratic Party nominee. It seemed that virtually overnight, Bernie Epton became a household name.

Republicans suddenly saw an opportunity to actually win the election, which had not happened since 1927. Money started flowing to Epton's cam-

Bernard Epton. Abraham Lincoln Presidential Library.

paign, from Republicans and disaffected Democrats. The campaign manager for the state's Republican governor went to work for Epton. And Epton signed John Deardourff, a big-time Washington, D.C., consultant, to direct his media efforts and serve as chief strategist.

Washington had another problem. His campaign wasn't, shall we say, a model of organizational effectiveness and efficiency. Going into the general-election campaign, Washington and his advisers were overconfident and complacent. Much of his staff was inexperienced and untrained in the art of campaign communication. For Washington's candidacy, this ineptness reinforced the doubts many voters held about his ability to be mayor and pull Chicago together.

To most observers, it didn't really matter what Epton or Washington said during the campaign, or what issues or policies they emphasized. The fact was, Epton was white and Washington was black, and in Chicago politics in 1983, that was all most people needed to know. Some of Epton's precinct workers reported hearing comments like "people feel threatened, and they're going to vote." "People in my area just don't want a black mayor; it's as simple as that."

Washington's standing in the black community and Epton's Republican label meant that Epton had very little chance of gaining a significant measure of black support—something that had been crucial to Byrne's and Daley's primary strategy. Many felt that this left Epton free to not worry about alienating black voters. Strategically, he could then concentrate on increasing turnout in white and other ethnic precincts. As soon as the campaign got underway, the flood of white volunteers, many of them Democrats, and the energy and enthusiasm at Epton's campaign events signaled to Epton that white voters, regardless of party, were streaming to his candidacy.[5] From that point on, his campaign was targeted mostly to undecided white voters. The goal was to convince undecided whites that Washington was not competent to serve as mayor of a large city like Chicago.

EPTON COMES ALIVE

Soon after, Epton's campaign went on the attack. Epton accused Washington of ignoring his responsibilities as a member of the U.S. Congress and proposing job schemes that would bankrupt the city. He told a cheering crowd of supporters that he was "perfectly willing to get rough. . . . I used to think Harold was an amiable and an intelligent fellow. I guess I was wrong on both counts."[6]

Attacking one's opponent usually comes later in a campaign, after a candidate has had a chance to establish his image with the voters first. But Epton's campaign felt a need to go after Washington early and drive up his negatives with undecided voters. He made Washington the issue in the campaign. Of course, the downside to this strategy was that it outraged and energized Chicago's black communities, who were solidly behind Washington.

The only televised debate between the two became very nasty very quickly. Epton criticized Washington's integrity, bringing up his past legal problems as well as his brief stay in jail. "Will he tell the truth? Will he obey the law?" Epton asked. Washington fought back against what he called this "scurrilous" attack. The next day, Epton launched a television ad campaign depicting Washington as a tax fraud, a shady lawyer, and an ex-convict. Pretty rough stuff.

Epton and his advisers denied they were trying to take advantage of the racial climate in Chicago with their withering attacks on Washington. For its part, Washington's campaign insisted that Epton's attacks were all about race, portraying Epton's attacks on his integrity as a smoke screen to give whites a reason to vote against him without admitting it was about race.

New accusations against Washington hit the airwaves almost daily. He was portrayed as a slumlord and a deadbeat who refused to pay his bills. These ads created an image in the minds of many voters, particularly white voters, of someone irresponsible and incompetent. The attacks and accusations also reinforced and encouraged negative stereotypes about blacks.

These troubling developments were also exacerbated by Epton's biting and caustic wit. Upon learning of Washington's return from an East Coast fundraising trip, Epton remarked, "I hope he brought back some brains." He also constantly referred to Washington, an incumbent U.S. congressman, as "Harold," which struck many as demeaning and condescending. Of course, it could have been worse, as Chicago newspaper columnist Mike Royko said, "he hasn't called him 'boy' yet."[7]

It was clear this would not be a normal mayoral election from just observing the traditional Irish celebrations in March. At the annual St. Patrick's Day parade, normally an occasion to showcase the Democratic Party's candidates for office, Washington was relegated to a spot near the back of the parade. When he walked by onlookers, there was only a smattering of polite applause. But at a similar parade on Chicago's east side, Epton was greeted as a conquering hero by the crowds, mostly made up of working-class Catholic Democrats. One incident at this parade seemed a foreshadowing of what was to come: a woman cheering for Epton jumped out in the street and opened her jacket to reveal a T-shirt that said "Vote Right, Vote White."

The racial fears and resentments among white and ethnic communities fanned the flames of Epton's support in those neighborhoods. Their enthusiasm for Epton and their dislike for Washington brought energy and money to Epton's campaign, but it also helped set the tone for the ugliness to come.

One of the goals of Epton's TV advertising campaign was to allay the guilt many Democrats had about supporting a Republican. One such ad quoted John F. Kennedy appealing for bipartisanship: "Sometimes party loyalty asks too much. Surely, this is such a time." Most who saw the ad believed it to be a carefully veiled appeal to racial fears.

Another tactic that garnered a great deal of attention, as well as criticism and disgust, was the use of popular songs put to campaign lyrics in support of Epton. The most well-known example was "Bye-Bye Blackbird," a popular children's nursery rhyme. At some of his rallies, the chant could be heard: "It's not a case of black or white / We need someone to win the fight / Your record, Bernie, shows you're tough / And as for us we have been pushed enough / Bye-Bye Blackbird."[8]

Epton also complained about "reverse racism" in media coverage of he and Washington. He insisted that Washington received greater amounts of coverage by Chicago media and that they "went out of their way" to ignore Washington's past legal problems.

SUNDAY, BLOODY SUNDAY

The low point of the campaign came on March 27, Palm Sunday. Washington was accompanied by former vice president Walter Mondale as they attended services at St. Pascal's Roman Catholic Church in northwest Chicago. It was a disaster—a well-photographed disaster. They were met by an angry mob. Approximately a hundred or so sign-waving, shouting protesters met Washington and Mondale in a confrontation that symbolized the racial division and hatred that characterized this campaign. Shouts of "go home," "carpetbagger," and "tax cheater" could be heard.[9] The animosity of the crowd can clearly be seen in videotapes of the event that were broadcast on the news and later used in some of Washington's TV spots. When Washington and Mondale got to the front of the church, they saw that the words "Nigger Die" had been spray-painted on the front door.[10] The Washington campaign turned video footage and photos of the incident into a very effective anti-Epton TV ad of their own. The animosity on both sides continued to grow.

For his part, Epton did apologize. There is no indication that his campaign organized the protest or even knew anything about it, yet the demonstrators were carrying his campaign signs and shouting his name at Washington and Mondale.

The Epton side did not do all of the attacking. Washington's campaign raised questions about Epton's emotional stability. Medical records were stolen from a doctor's office that detailed Epton's visits for psychiatric evaluation. Epton claimed that the visits were due to severe abdominal pain. Washington also accused Epton of conflict-of-interest dealings while a state legislator because he had voted for insurance bills that would benefit his insurance business. Washington also called Epton's media consultant, John Deardourff, one of the "slimiest, funkiest, lowlife, scurrilous individuals who ever crawled out from under a rock."[11]

The Washington campaign also drew attention to the tag line used in most of Epton's TV ads and in other campaign materials. The slogan was "Epton for Mayor—before it's too late!" This became a source of controversy, as Washington and a number of media observers thought it to have racial implications. The *Chicago Tribune* denounced the slogan as "disgraceful evidence of either insensitivity or outright exploitation; it is a blatant appeal to the worst of Chicago."[12] Epton's campaign insisted it was meant as a message about Chicago's financial problems and Epton's ability to solve them. But in the racially charged climate of the campaign, it was interpreted by most as racial in nature.

"STOP THE N*****"

If the ad campaign and war of words between the candidates was getting hot, the battle at the neighborhood and precinct levels was pure fire and brimstone. In the final weeks of the campaign, racist literature was distributed by some of Epton's workers, apparently without the candidate's knowledge. Leaflets were circulated showing a police badge with the words "ChiCongo Po-lease" around the edges. In the middle of the words was a pair of lips, a watermelon, a can of beer, and the words "say what?" Another leaflet had an unflattering photo of Washington with the words "The White People's Choice? No Way!"[13]

Yet another leaflet fictitiously listed "Brother Mayor's Campaign Promises." Number one was "Raise Whitey's Taxes." The last straw for Washington, and for many people in Chicago, was the circulation of rumors and leaflets accusing Washington of having sexual relations with a ten-year-old girl. One of the leaflets read:

Before you vote you have the right to some answers. Much has been said about the background of the two men who are candidates for mayor.

A rumor has been circulated that Harold Washington was arrested for sodomy with a 10 year old. Is this truth or fiction? We should know the facts before we vote. The Chicago Tribune has completed an investigation of this story and so far failed to release the results—Why haven't we been told? Is this rumor, truth, or fiction? We have a right to know the truth before we vote— Call the Tribune and ask about this. Call 222-3232 and demand that they release the results of their investigation. The citizens of Chicago must know!!

Waving the leaflet over his head, Washington exploded in anger at a campaign event at Mundelein College: "I say to you, Mr. Epton, if you want this job so badly that you will destroy character . . . if the taste of power is so much in your veins . . . and these are the kinds of dogs of racism and scurrilism you are going to unleash, I will fight you day and night." The crowd was stunned but supportive. They began to chant, "We want Harold. We want Harold."[14]

Although Epton had not directed the racist leaflets and whisper campaigns about Washington, many of his campaign volunteers and precinct captains had been directly involved. Epton's daugher Dale, active in her father's campaign, said the campaign had spun out of control. "It was mass hysteria," she said. "At the beginning we said we didn't want anyone to vote for us because we were white, but then we gave up saying it because it just didn't matter, nobody listened to us. . . . Epton offices all over the city were printing their own literature, spending their own money."[15]

The openly racist appeals were likely the decisive element in the campaign, though not the way its sponsors intended. Analysts believe it did not win the Epton campaign many converts because the whites leaning toward him didn't need any convincing, while those undecided voters may have been so shocked by the hostility of it that they ended up voting against Epton. In any case, it undeniably solidified Washington's support in Chicago's black communities and boosted their turnout rate on election day.

A NAIL-BITER

It was close. In fact, the closest mayoral election in over a half century. But when all the votes were counted, Washington had eked out a victory. The difference had been made by the overwhelming turnout of black voters citywide. Washington won 95 percent of the black vote, and black voter turnout was 73 percent, a historic high. In the end, the overtly racist campaign—waged not by Epton personally but by forces working on his behalf—had defeated itself. The race baiting had energized the black community and disgusted a number of undecided whites. (Turnout among white voters was only 58 percent.) Ironically, the forces of racism had succeeded in doing something that no black leader up to that time could accomplish—unifying the black communities of Chicago.

AMERICA, MEET WILLIE HORTON

George H. W. Bush v. Michael Dukakis, President, 1988

The presidential election of 1988 is considered by a number of journalists, political scientists, and other observers of the political process to be one of the major turning points in the more recent history of negative campaigning. Maybe that's because, at least from a political strategist's point of view, it was so brutally effective.

It was a textbook example of how to take your opponent apart, limb from limb. I'm not saying that's a good thing, I'm just saying that the Bush campaign in 1988 achieved precisely what it set out to do. And what had it set out to do? When asked that very question, Bush's campaign czar, Lee Atwater, answered with what has now become a famous quote in the annals of presidential politics: "I'm going to scrape the bark off of Michael Dukakis."[1]

THE WIMP FACTOR

The two candidates faced very different challenges in gaining their party's nomination. For George Bush, the challenge was emerging from the shadow of President Ronald Reagan, the first two-term American president since Dwight Eisenhower and a cultural icon to many American voters.

Even though Bush had a military background and had served in numerous high-level government posts in his government career, his public image was one of timidity and relative weakness in comparison to Ronald Reagan. In fact, Bush had to combat what had come to be known as the "wimp factor" in his quest to follow Reagan into the White House.

George H. W. Bush. Library of Congress.

History was also against Bush. No American vice president had been elected directly to the presidency in 150 years. The last to accomplish that feat had been Martin Van Buren in 1836, who had been Andrew Jackson's vice president.

Bush's nomination as the Republican Party's candidate was never in serious doubt, although he had lost the Iowa Caucus—the first contest on the way to the party nomination. But Reagan had also lost the Iowa Caucus in 1980 and was able to recover. As a matter of fact, the candidate who had beaten Reagan in Iowa was Bush himself.

Bush's competitors for the nomination in 1988—including Bob Dole, the Republican leader in the U.S. Senate, and Jack Kemp, the conservative congressman from New York—told Republican-primary voters that Bush would not be tough enough with Democrats, and that he would not forcefully complete the Republican agenda started under Ronald Reagan. But Bush toughened up for the rest of the primaries, and rode to the nomination, largely on the coattails of his boss, President Reagan.

Of course, at the beginning of the year, Bush gained some assistance in "toughening up" from an unlikely source: Dan Rather of CBS News. Rather was a longtime network news figure, with a reputation for toughness and confrontation.

In January 1988, Rather interviewed Bush on the *CBS Evening News*. The interview turned into an argument on the air. Rather was pressing Bush on the Iran-Contra scandal and asking Bush very pointed questions about what it meant for his candidacy. Then Bush started pushing back. Both men lost their cool. When both men continued talking and refusing to yield, a clearly agitated Rather abruptly ended the interview and went to a commercial.

By this time, everyone who was watching the interview had to pick their jaws up from the floor and put it into some kind of perspective. From the standpoint of many Republicans, the encounter had been an impressive showing by the vice president in the face of an unrelenting enemy. History has judged this encounter to have significantly helped Bush in his battle against the "wimp" label.

THE COMPETENT BUREAUCRAT

The Michael Dukakis experience was totally different. Later in the campaign, he would have his own image problems to overcome, but winning the Democratic nomination was a matter of convincing primary voters that he was the best candidate to take on the Republicans.

The Democratic primaries in 1988 were more a matter of survival than they were about one candidate breaking from the pack. It was a war of attrition; who would be the last man standing? The early front-runner, former senator and 1984 presidential candidate Gary Hart, had dropped out after revelations of extramarital affairs. (Remember the good ship *Monkey Business?*) Congressman Richard Gephardt and Senator Al Gore brought a great deal of political baggage to the campaign, as members of Congress do when they run for president. Reverend Jesse Jackson had run respectably enough in the 1984 Democratic primaries, but still wasn't perceived by most Democrats as a credible candidate to take on Reagan, Bush, and company and win.

Dukakis won it almost by default, but his experience as a governor was a crucial factor in his success. In recent history, governors have had an inside track to the presidency—Carter, Reagan, Clinton, George W. Bush. They are outsiders, not part of the Washington establishment. They also have relevant executive experience, such as dealing with legislatures, putting together a budget, and managing a bureaucracy.

Michael Dukakis. Massachusetts State Archives.

Along the way, the Democrats and Dukakis had their own mini-scandal to deal with. Someone had anonymously sent the media a videotape of Democratic presidential candidate Joseph Biden making a speech that turned out to be almost a total rip-off of a speech given a year earlier by British Labour Party leader Neil Kinnock. Biden, forced to confront the charges of plagiarism, dropped out of the race.[2]

But there were charges of "dirty politics." Who had sent the tape? Who was dragging the Democratic candidates down into the mud? It turned out to be Dukakis's own campaign manager, John Sasso, who had sent the tape. Under pressure, Sasso resigned from the Dukakis campaign, and Dukakis pledged to remain free of dirty political tactics. History's verdict on Dukakis's general-election campaign is that he didn't fight back early or hard enough against the barrage of attacks from Bush. Was this early experience with Sasso and Biden one of the reasons he held back?

The Democratic National Convention, held in Atlanta that summer, is known for two things: Arkansas governor Bill Clinton giving a self-important speech that dragged on for too long; and Dukakis's acceptance speech, in which he exhorted the nation to consider his management experience above all else. "This election isn't about ideology," he said. "It's about competence."

The political battles of the 1980s had been very much about ideology. The decade began with a dramatic shift in the ideological direction of the country under Reagan's "conservative" revolution. The word "liberal" had become a dirty word by the late 1980s, and Democratic politicians did what they could to avoid it.

And George Bush and the Republican Party did whatever they could to hang the "liberal" tag around the neck of Michael Dukakis, which explains Dukakis's effort to make the election about anything but ideology.

THE "L" WORD

If Mike Dukakis didn't want to run on ideology, so, the Republicans reasoned, they would give him an ideological jihad that would force the dreaded "liberal" label on him, like it or not. The truth was, Dukakis had come from a liberal governing and political tradition in Massachusetts, and he would have to defend that record.

Some observers have dubbed the 1988 campaign between Bush and Dukakis as the "issueless" campaign.[3] There were no large, overriding issues as in other election years, so the campaign was fought on smaller, mostly social and cultural issues, such as furloughs for state prisoners, the death penalty, and the Pledge of Allegiance.

Bush's victory hinged on his ability to make Dukakis the issue, not the Reagan or Bush record, jobs, or foreign policy. The Bush campaign leaped on Dukakis's assertion that ideology wasn't important. "Of course it's important," the Bush campaign replied. Any presidential election is a choice that the American people make about values and ideology. And the Bush campaign wanted that choice to be made on its terms. So they decided, as soon as it appeared that Dukakis would secure the Democratic nomination, to paint him as hopelessly liberal, preferring discredited liberal solutions to the country's problems.

MR. HORTON GOES TO WASHINGTON

In their research of Dukakis and his record, the Bush campaign did extensive focus-group sessions with registered voters. According to the Bush team, when the focus-group members heard certain things about Dukakis, such as his prison weekend-furlough program in Massachusetts and his refusal to support the Pledge of Allegiance in public schools, their response was "off the charts" negative. These focus groups helped them develop their tactical offensive for the fall campaign against Dukakis.

One of the most famous, or infamous, examples of modern attack campaigning involves the Massachusetts prisoner furlough program and the case of Willie Horton. Horton was a convicted murderer who, while out on a weekend furlough, fled, then later kidnapped a young couple, assaulting the man and raping the woman.

The Bush campaign used this case as an example of Dukakis's liberal policies toward crime and punishment issues. Bush talked about this case in stump speeches throughout the summer, railing against Dukakis as being "soft on crime" and coddling criminals instead of punishing them.

Then in September, the story became the basis of a televised political ad against Dukakis by the National Security Political Action Committee. PACs can produce and air political ads using unlimited resources if they do not coordinate their activities with a specific campaign. This is a famous political TV spot, and one that most assume was actually made by the Bush campaign rather than the PAC.

The Willie Horton ad is one of the most famous in political history. Courtesy, Julian P. Kanter Archive/University of Oklahoma.

The ad opens with photos of Bush and Dukakis, with Dukakis's photo dark and unflattering, of course. The announcer says, "Bush and Dukakis on crime: Bush supports the death penalty for first-degree murderers. Dukakis not only opposes the death penalty, he allowed first-degree murderers to have weekend passes from prison." The ad then shows a grainy, black-and-white photo of Horton, an African American. "One was Willie Horton, who murdered a boy in a robbery, stabbing him nineteen times. Despite a life sentence, Horton received ten weekend passes from prison." As an old photo of

Horton being arrested flashes up, the words "kidnapping," "stabbing," and "raping" appear on the screen. The announcer continues, "Horton fled, kidnapping a young couple (who were white), stabbing the man and repeatedly raping his girlfriend."[4]

The impact of the ad is undeniable. It was a powerful indictment of Dukakis's positions on crime and punishment, and it shocked many viewers who saw it. Most believe the ad was also intended to stir up racial fears by showing the black escaped felon harming innocent people, which was tied to the policies of Michael Dukakis.

The Bush campaign did come out with its own TV spot a few weeks later about Dukakis and the prison furlough program, but it made no mention of Willie Horton. Known as the "revolving-door" ad, it shows stark, black-and-white prison scenes, while a parade of convicted felons walk through a large, iron revolving door at the front gate of a prison, circling back toward the living rooms of the TV viewers. An announcer reports that in Massachusetts, 268 of these felons had escaped while on weekend prison furloughs. The implication is that Dukakis furloughed 268 prisoners who escaped and went on to commit violent crimes, as Horton did.

Although the Bush campaign's revolving-door ad did not mention Willie Horton by name or show his photo, the message of the two ads was clear. Dukakis routinely lets dangerous criminals out of prison that go on to commit more violent crimes. The ads gained a great deal of mention in the press, and the Bush campaign came under fire for the controversial nature of the ads. But Bush could rightfully say that his ad did not try to take advantage of Horton's race because they didn't show his picture, as the PAC ad had done. Of course, the Bush campaign didn't condemn the PAC's Willie Horton ad either.

In fact, the Horton case was atypical of the Massachusetts prison furlough program, which boasted a 99 percent success rate.[5] Dukakis's rebuttal to these ads came in the form of statistics and abstract concepts. The personal threat that Horton posed stayed with the voters and was further enhanced by the media coverage surrounding the controversy.

PATRIOTISM

There were other fronts in the campaign against Dukakis. The Bush team used a case from Massachusetts to question Governor Dukakis's patriotic commitment. He had vetoed a bill from the state legislature that mandated the recitation of the Pledge of Allegiance in Massachusetts public schools.

Dukakis had believed the bill to be unconstitutional, and made no apologies for vetoing it. But his campaign didn't realize the symbolic power the issue could have until it was too late. In a major speech to a crowd of flag-waving supporters, Bush said, "I'll never understand when it came to his desk, why he vetoed a bill that called for the Pledge of Allegiance to be said in the schools of Massachusetts. . . . I'll never understand it. We are one nation under God. Our kids should say the Pledge of Allegiance."[6]

The Bush team sought to make support for the American flag a central issue in the campaign and a major reason to vote against Dukakis. George Bush practically draped himself in the American flag. Bush was successful in pushing the issue, to a degree. Both Bush and Dukakis took pains to be photographed at rallies in front of the flag and to pass out flags to the crowds. They both literally became flag wavers.

George Herbert Walker Bush was the first sitting vice president to be elected directly to the presidency since Martin Van Buren in 1836—a span of 152 years.

To some reporters following the campaign, the high point, or low point, in the flag-waving theme came when Bush visited a flag factory in Findlay, Ohio. Findlay is also known as Flag City because of the large factory there and the number of jobs it represents. Then he visited another flag factory in New Jersey.

The traveling media could not help but make the flag front and center in the presidential campaign, but that does not mean they had to like it. Some of the media stories were critical of Bush for "trivializing" the campaign and making such an issue out of the American flag. Dukakis also consistently made the point that Bush's efforts were mainly a vehicle to question his patriotism and deflect attention away from the issues.

TANK WARFARE

Then there was the tank incident. One of the charges that the Dukakis campaign had to fight off was that he was soft on defense. He had developed a position that called for less testing and development of nuclear weaponry and missile systems, but more spending for conventional military hardware, such as tanks. To make that point, he visited a military base and was photographed taking a ride in an M-1 tank.

But it did not have the effect he intended. Instead of reporting the story in terms of Dukakis's commitment to conventional troop strength, it was reported as a shallow attempt to make up for his image problem when it came to defense issues. In other words, it was seen as nothing more than a publicity stunt and an effort to manipulate public opinion.

But the Bush campaign took it a step further. Its ad team took the video footage of Dukakis riding in a tank and put it in one of its TV spots. The image of Dukakis wearing a tank helmet, which reminded many of Snoopy from the Charlie Brown cartoons, made the governor look small and ridiculous. It reinforced the doubts many voters had that he was out of his league and not ready for the big time.

BOSTON HARBOR

Then there was the "Boston Harbor" spot, considered by many to be a classic example of strategic advertising in a political campaign. Governor Dukakis had hammered George Bush and the Republican Party on the environment all year long. The Democratic Party was the party of environmental responsibility, he warned, and Bush and the Republicans were not to be trusted with protecting the air and water.

In a policy sense, Dukakis was right. Democrats had been the party of environmental protection much more than Republicans had been. But in a political sense, he opened himself up to an act of political judo that Lee Atwater and his team performed to perfection.

The trouble was that over the years, the St. Charles River in Boston had become polluted with the by-products of industrial emissions and shipping. So the Boston Harbor was filthy, and it was in Michael Dukakis's backyard.

This gave the Bush team an opportunity to call Dukakis on one of his signature issues. Bush's advertising team shot an ad in Boston Harbor, showing the pollution-filled waters in the Massachusetts governor's capital city. The attack was meant to dent his credibility as a candidate and to sow doubt as to the veracity of his message and his leadership. Mission accomplished.

The Bush campaign's attacks on Dukakis through the summer of 1988 and into the fall drove his negatives up and helped erase the 18-point lead in the polls that Dukakis had enjoyed since early summer. By the time both parties had their national conventions, Bush had pulled ahead in most polls, and Dukakis was under pressure from Democrats and from media commentators to reverse his free fall.

One of the story lines of the 1988 campaign, in hindsight, was intense criticism of Dukakis's failure to fight back against Bush or to more aggressively refute the charges by the Bush team. It made undecided voters question Dukakis's toughness and Democrats question his commitment to winning.

This image problem is illustrated by his response to a question in one of the televised debates between him and Vice President Bush. Bernard Shaw of CNN was one of the journalists asking questions of the two candidates. Shaw asked Dukakis a question about the death penalty. "Governor, if Kitty Dukakis [the governor's wife] were raped and murdered, would you favor the death penalty for her killer?" It was a hideous question to ask someone and should have provided Dukakis with an opportunity to show some emotion and warm up his wooden image. Instead, Dukakis answered in a very low-key, matter-of-fact way—something about his commitment to human life—which sounded very political and very lawyerly. It was widely seen as a missed opportunity, to which he later admitted, "Yeah, I blew it."[7]

His presidential campaign never recovered both from Bush's attacks and from his own inability to define himself and his candidacy to the American people. On election day, Bush won a mini-landslide, taking the Electoral College vote 340 to 218.

TRICKY DICK VERSUS THE PINK LADY

Richard Nixon v. Helen Gahagan Douglas, U.S. Senate,
California, 1950

No figure in American history has a more tarnished image than Richard M. Nixon. After all, how do you come by a nickname like Tricky Dick? In his case, it was a well-earned trophy. Through years of Machiavellian-type political shenanigans, both in political campaigns and in public office, Nixon operated as though his life were at stake. Losing was just not an option.

By the time of the 1950 U.S. Senate campaign, Nixon had already gained a national reputation. As a member of the House Committee on Un-American Activities in the late 1940s, he played a leading role in the investigation of Alger Hiss, a former State Department employee accused of espionage for the Soviet Union. Hiss was convicted, and Nixon went on to become a rising star in the ranks of the anticommunist wing of the Republican Party.

Helen Gahagan Douglas was also a member of Congress from California. The wife of Hollywood actor Melvyn Douglas, she came from the world of theater and movies. Both she and her husband were politically active, cofounding a Hollywood anti-Nazi league and championing socially conscious causes. Although clearly not a communist herself, she and her husband grew close to a number of politically active Hollywood types that were active in communist circles, which formed the basis of Nixon's intensely negative campaign tactics against her.

This campaign took place near the beginning of the Red Scare of the 1950s, when the fear of communism was at its height. Communists, and potential communists, were rooted out and considered enemies of the United

States. Much of this drama played out in Hollywood and the motion picture industry. The Red Scare, or Red Menace, led to the downfall of a number of politicians. Earlier in 1950, left-leaning U.S. senator Claude Pepper, dubbed Red Pepper by his opponent, lost in the Democratic primary.

Nixon and his campaign team looked into how Pepper was defeated and borrowed some of the same tactics. Pepper's opponents had distributed a booklet called "The Red Record of Claude Pepper," which included photos of him with alleged communists and information linking him to pro-communist groups and causes. Nixon's campaign developed a similar tool to use against Douglas called "The Pink Sheet."[1] Obviously, it wanted to send the message that she was a pinko, or communist sympathizer.

In many ways, the timing could not have been better for Nixon and worse for Douglas. War fever was beginning to grip Washington, D.C., and then the nation, as North Korea invaded the south. Cold War fears were at their height, and even though Douglas supported President Truman's decision to fight, the issue worked against her and in favor of Nixon.

Young Dick Nixon was a campaign dynamo. Richard Nixon Library and Birthplace.

Helen Douglas with her husband, actor Melvyn Douglas.
Carl Albert Center Congressional Archives, University of
Oklahoma.

Nixon and his advisers worked overtime to make use of Cold War fears
to paint Douglas as a communist sympathizer, taking full advantage of the
public's anxiety about communism. Constantly referring to Douglas as the
Pink Lady was a not-so-subtle way of doing so. Nixon and his team loved to
conjure up images of "Hollywood left-wing intellectuals at pinko cocktail
parties."

STICKS AND STONES

Actually, the nickname Pink Lady was not a Nixon campaign creation but
was first used by one of Douglas's true enemies, the *Los Angeles Times*. The
Times was a staunchly Republican newspaper at the time, as were most major
media outlets in California. Kyle Palmer was the paper's political editor and,

as he and the *Times* had done sixteen years earlier in the Upton Sinclair campaign, played a significant role in the course of events. He spent considerable time building up Nixon as a statesman, all the while pretty much ignoring Douglas.[2]

The Democrats played rough, too. Nixon had appealed to Democrats to cross over and vote for him instead of Douglas. The California Democratic Committee responded by buying a full-page ad in several papers that said: "WARNING TO ALL DEMOCRATS." It featured a cartoon of Nixon coming out of a barn trying to feed hay to a Democratic donkey. The hay was labeled "Campaign Trickery." The ad is remembered because it was the first time the nickname Tricky Dick was used. "Look at Tricky Dick's Republican Record," the ad said.[3] The name stuck, and Douglas used it throughout the campaign. But calling him Tricky Dick was almost like a compliment to his cunning and skill in political maneuvering.

The name calling continued throughout the campaign. Angered by Nixon's continuous efforts to portray her as soft on communism, she referred to him as "peewee" in a major speech. When informed of this, Nixon went ballistic. "Why, I'll castrate her," he told his aides. His campaign chief, Murray Chotiner, reminded him not to engage in a name-calling contest with a woman, advice he tried to take to heart. But he also took to heart Chotiner's other advice about politics and about life: "Nice guys and sissies don't win elections."[4]

On other occasions, Nixon would refer to his opponent not as Helen Douglas but as Helen Hesselberg, which was the original last name of her actor-husband, Melvyn Douglas. Only a cynic would believe that Nixon did this intentionally, at a time and in a location where voters might not favor Jewish surnames.

Ironically, when the campaign began, Nixon called on his skills as a lawyer to make the usual disclaimers, saying, "My opponent is a woman. . . . There will be no name calling, no smears, no misrepresentation in this campaign." What a whopper! Smears dominated the campaign, dirty tricks abounded, and innuendo was everywhere.

For example, Nixon's campaign hired several companies to make anonymous phone calls to as many as a half-million voters in California asking, "Did you know Mrs. Douglas is a communist?" Of course, when confronted with this, candidate Nixon denied any knowledge. Apparently, the fact that four years earlier, voters in U.S. Congressman Jerry Voorhis's district had received the same message about him during Nixon's successful campaign to unseat him was just a coincidence.

THE HOLLYWOOD TEN

Douglas had not exactly played it safe as a member of Congress. She had cast one of only seventeen votes in the House of Representatives against citing the Hollywood Ten for contempt of Congress when they refused to testify before the Committee on Un-American Activities.

Much of the political drama of this election and others in California centered around the movie industry in Hollywood. Since the 1930s, movie executives such as Louis B. Mayer, along with a number of government officials in California and Washington, D.C., were concerned that the ranks of actors, screenwriters, and directors had been infiltrated with communist sympathizers.

There were aggressive attempts to ferret out socialists and other such "pinkos." In 1947 the House Committee on Un-American Activities issued contempt citations to a number of writers and directors who had refused to divulge whether they were members of the Communist Party. Nixon, as a member of the committee, had helped lead the fight to force suspected agents of communism to come out of hiding. Douglas had voted against such efforts, as Nixon frequently reminded voters throughout 1950.

A number of the movie employees who had been cited for contempt refused to cooperate. Known as the Hollywood Ten, they exhausted their legal appeals in an effort to fight the committee's actions. Douglas tried to explain that she did not support the Hollywood Ten but merely objected to the strong-arm tactics of the committee. But this was one of the finer points that was lost on most voters.

Douglas was among those who were accused, by Nixon as well as others, of being in the "Stalinist orbit" of communist activism. There were some prominent names in the motion picture industry who were also in this "orbit," including Orson Welles, James Cagney, Gene Kelly, Charlie Chaplin, and Gregory Peck.

Another fault line in this battle was over the forced registration of communist groups and officials. Once again, Nixon was at the forefront of congressional action to identify communist agents and infiltrators, while Douglas was seen as an opponent of those efforts.

Orginally called the Mundt-Nixon bill, the legislation was amended and called the Internal Security Act of 1950. It not only required the registration of communist organizations and members but barred them from defense or military-related jobs. Front groups would have to reveal all sources of funds; names of members would be released to the public; and all of their printed literature would be labeled "communist in origin." These actions would make it easier to arrest and deport left-wing aliens, and the United States could bar anyone from entering the country who had been a member of the Communist Party.[5]

Douglas not only voted against the bill but made an impassioned speech on the floor of the U.S. House about why she was voting against it. She said she wanted spies and traitors rooted out as much as anyone, but was not willing to sacrifice the liberty of the American people "on an altar of hysteria erected by those without vision, without faith, without courage, who cringe in fear before a handful of crackpots and their traitorous communist cronies." Nice sentiments, but all most California voters heard was that she voted against a bill that would make it easier to identify and deal with communists.

THE PINK SHEET

The Nixon campaign also went to great efforts to tie Douglas to left-wing congressman Vito Marcantonio from New York City. He was a well-known leftist, and one of the few in Congress who opposed American action in Korea. The troubling thing for Douglas was that the legislative voting record could show that she had voted with Marcantonio a very high percentage of the time, compared to most members of Congress. Nixon made full use of this.

Although most of these votes were procedural actions and routine motions, it didn't matter, because the impression that it conveyed was devastating to Douglas's campaign. After scouring the legislative record, the Nixon campaign found that Douglas had voted the same way as Marcantonio 353 times. Though Douglas tried to explain the votes, it greatly complicated her efforts to refute Nixon's charges of left-wing sympathies.

In fact, the dominant impression many California voters had of Douglas was produced by the Nixon campaign. Nixon campaign officials printed and distributed flyers on pink paper that documented his charges of "soft on communism" and her alleged ties to communist agents. Known as "The Pink Sheet," it documented her votes in Congress, her support for various left-wing causes, and her association with individuals who were pro-communist.

It featured a headline that screamed: "Douglas-Marcantonio Voting Record." It documented her votes "against national defense, national security legislation, and described her 'Communist-line votes.'" Nixon's campaign chief ordered 50,000 copies, which soon made their way around the state of California. At first, Douglas laughed it off, dismissing it as absurd

DOUGLAS-MARCANTONIO VOTING RECORD

Many persons have requested a comparison of the voting records of Congresswoman Helen Douglas and the notorious Communist party-liner, Congressman Vito Marcantonio of New York.

Mrs. Douglas and Marcantonio have been members of Congress together since January 1, 1945. During that period, Mrs. Douglas voted the same as Marcantonio 354 times. While it should not be expected that a member of the House of Representatives should always vote in opposition to Marcantonio, it is significant to note, not only the great number of times which Mrs. Douglas voted in agreement with him, but also the issues on which almost without exception they always saw eye to eye, to-wit: Un-American Activities and Internal Security.

Here is the Record!

VOTES AGAINST COMMITTEE ON UN-AMERICAN ACTIVITIES

Both Douglas and Marcantonio voted against establishing the Committee on Un-American Activities. 1/3/45. Bill passed.

Both voted on three separate occasions against contempt proceedings against persons and organizations which refused to reveal records or answer whether they were Communists. 4/16/46, 6/26/46, 11/24/47. Bills passed.

Both voted on four separate occasions against allowing funds for investigation by the Un-American Activities Committee. 5/17/46, 3/9/48, 2/9/49, 3/23/50. (The last vote was 348 to 12.) All bills passed.

COMMUNIST-LINE FOREIGN POLICY VOTES

Both voted against Greek-Turkish Aid Bill. 5/9/47. (It has been established that without this aid Greece and Turkey would long since have gone behind the Iron Curtain.) Bill passed.

Both voted on two occasions against free press amendment to UNRRA appropriation bill, providing that no funds should be furnished any country which refused to allow free access to the news of activities of the UNRRA by press and radio representatives of the United States. 11/1/45, 6/28/46. Bills passed. (This would in effect have denied American relief funds to Communist dominated countries.)

Both voted against refusing Foreign Relief to Soviet-dominated countries UNLESS supervised by Americans. 4/30/47. Bill passed 324 to 75.

VOTE AGAINST NATIONAL DEFENSE

Both voted against the Selective Service Act of 1948. 6/18/48. Bill passed.

VOTES AGAINST LOYALTY AND SECURITY LEGISLATION

Both voted on two separate occasions against bills requiring loyalty checks for Federal employees. 7/15/47, 6/29/49. Bills passed.

Both voted against the Subversive Activities Control Act of 1948, requiring registration with the Attorney General of Communist party members and communist controlled organizations. Bill passed, 319 to 58. 5/19/48. AND AFTER KOREA both again voted against it. Bill passed 8/29/50, 354 to 20.

AFTER KOREA, on July 12, 1950, Marcantonio and Douglas and 12 others voted against the Security Bill, to permit the heads of key National Defense departments, such as the Atomic Energy Commission, to discharge government workers found to be poor security risks! Bill passed, 327 to 14.

VOTE AGAINST CALIFORNIA

Both recorded against confirming title to Tidelands in California and the other states affected. 4/30/48. Bill passed 257-29.

VOTES AGAINST CONGRESSIONAL INVESTIGATION OF COMMUNIST AND OTHER ILLEGAL ACTIVITIES

Both voted against investigating the "whitewash" of the AMERASIA case. 4/18/46. Bill passed.

Both voted against investigating why the Soviet Union was buying as many as 60,000 United States patents at one time. 3/4/47. Bill passed.

Both voted against continuing investigation of numerous instances of illegal actions by OPA and the War Labor Board. 1/18/45. Bill passed.

Both voted on two occasions against allowing Congress to have access to government records necessary to the conduct of investigations by Senate and House Committees. 4/22/48, 5/13/48. Bills passed.

ON ALL OF THE ABOVE VOTES which have occurred since Congressman Nixon took office on January 1, 1947, HE has voted exactly opposite to the Douglas-Marcantonio Axis!

After studying the voting comparison between Mrs. Douglas and Marcantonio, is it any wonder that the Communist line newspaper, the Daily People's World, in its lead editorial on January 31, 1950, labeled Congressman Nixon as "The Man To Beat" in this Senate race and that the Communist newspaper, the New York Daily Worker, in the issue of July 28, 1947, selected Mrs. Douglas along with Marcantonio as "One of the Heroes of the 80th Congress."

REMEMBER! The United States Senate votes on ratifying international treaties and confirming presidential appointments. Would California send Marcantonio to the United States Senate?

NIXON FOR U. S. SENATOR CAMPAIGN COMMITTEE

NORTHERN CALIFORNIA	CENTRAL CALIFORNIA	SOUTHERN CALIFORNIA
John Walton Dinkelspiel, Chairman	B. M. Hoblick, Chairman	Bernard Brennan, Chairman
1151 Market Street	820 Van Ness Avenue	117 W. 9th St., Los Angeles
San Francisco---UNderhill 3-1416	Fresno---Phone 44116	TRinity 0661

 111

"The Pink Sheet" portrayed Douglas as a Communist crony. Carl Albert Center Congressional Archives, University of Oklahoma.

and ineffective. Others in her camp smelled trouble, but by that time it was too late to do anything about it except try to explain her way out of it—something she had spent the entire campaign doing. Douglas was always on the defensive.

THE NIXON TOUCH

Then, two weeks before the election, the campaign was brought to an even lower level. Nixon declared that as a result of the U.S. failure to aid "Free China," Asia was engulfed by communism. This brought on the communist aggression in Korea. With "great regret," he reported that six months earlier, Douglas had been one of six who had called for what he termed a "get out of China" resolution—a call for the withdrawal of American forces.

According to Nixon, the genesis of that resolution could be traced to the Kremlin and to Joseph Stalin. He explained to newspaper reporters, "This action by Mrs. Douglas came just two weeks after U.S. Communist Party leader William Z. Foster transmitted his instructions from the Kremlin to the American Communist Committee . . . which then found its way to Congress." But he didn't explain the details of how that happened or how Douglas was involved.[6]

Nixon's strategy was working; he was isolating Douglas from the political mainstream. She wasn't just a Democratic member of Congress—she was part of a small, extremist group that was endangering the security of the country.

Nixon supporters also made much of his opponent's gender. The *L.A. Times*'s Kyle Palmer referred to her as an "emotional artist," who was "emotionally attracted" to left-wing politics. In one of his earlier campaign speeches, Nixon relied on a simple rhetorical trick he used often. He would claim that his advisers had warned him to avoid certain issues, but that he was willing to "meet difficult issues straight on" and risk the politics of it.

In this case, he said, "my opponent is a woman. And my advisers have warned me not to raise questions about her qualifications." But after weighing the matter carefully, he decided he could not avoid this difficult issue because of the seriousness of the issues and the dangers facing the country. He was applauded by many for "facing a difficult issue." He also said, "there will be no name calling, no smears, no misrepresentation. We do not indulge in such tactics."[7] Right!

As the campaign went on, more and more dirty tricks appeared. In one memorable smear, a cartoon pictured Henry Wallace (former vice president and Cold War critic) courting Helen Douglas while Joseph Stalin (as the man in the moon) smiled down on them. Phone banks of Nixon supporters called voters—a half-million, according to one estimate—asking whether they were aware "that Helen Douglas is a communist." Other voters received postcards from a group calling themselves "The Communist League of Negro Women." These cards urged citizens to vote for Helen Douglas—"We are with her 100%."[8]

After at first dismissing the attacks and minimizing their impact, Douglas later realized the damage they had done and began lashing out at Nixon and his supporters. "I accuse my opponent and his spokesmen of trying to steal this election by drugging the voters with political poison concocted of misrepresentation and false charges."

She also went after pro-Nixon newspapers: "I accuse those newspapers dominated by the *Los Angeles Times* and *Oakland Tribune* axis of aiding and abetting them. I accuse those newspapers of denying their readers the facts and of twisting and distorting the news."[9] But it was too late. Plus, her outbursts seemed desperate and defensive to many voters.

> Helen Douglas completed her autobiography, *A Full Life*, only months before her death in 1980. It was published posthumously.

Considering the Cold War climate of that campaign, military action in Korea, and the Nixon campaign's successful portrayal of Douglas as a procommunist sympathizer, there was no way she could win. On election night, Chotiner and another young aide, Tracey McCluskey, brought Nixon cheerful news. He had won, 60 percent to 40 percent. This was consistent with the national electoral trend in 1950: Republicans picked up seats in the House and the Senate largely by playing on Cold War politics and accusing the opposition of either being duped by the left or actively working with them to weaken the United States.

NATIONAL PROMINENCE

Just two years later, Nixon emerged as the running mate of Republican presidential candidate Dwight Eisenhower. That 1952 campaign, and the famous Checkers speech he made on television to defend himself from charges of illegal fund-raising, put him on the national stage, where he remained for the next three decades.

As for Helen Douglas, 1950 spelled the end of her political career. Friends encouraged her to run again for Congress and some expected President Truman to appoint her to a government post, but politically, she was too hot to handle. Instead, she moved to New York to be closer to her husband. She remained active in public life, however, choosing to get involved in political and social causes as she saw fit.

The 1950 campaign was significant in that some historians believe it helped set the tone for increasingly negative and personal politics in America. In addition, it elevated a very practiced champion of political character assassination to national prominence. It also encouraged the anti-communist "witch hunt" hearings of Senator Joseph McCarthy in the 1950s.

This race helped set a divisive and rigid agenda for forty years of election campaigns. Until 1950, candidates who campaigned primarily on an anti-communist platform usually lost. In fact, the Republican presidential nominee in 1948, Thomas Dewey, criticized fellow Republicans who called for repressive new measures to control communists and other subversives. But both Republican and Democratic leaders interpreted Nixon's 1950 victory as a win for McCarthyism and a call for a dramatic surge in military spending.

GRANTISM AND MR. GREELEY

Ulysses S. Grant v. Horace Greeley, President, 1872

The choice between Grant and Greeley is like a choice between hemlock and strychnine.

—U.S. Senator Alexander Stephens, Georgia

This presidential campaign, like so many in this particular era of American history, is known as one of the nastiest, most personally vicious political campaigns ever. It deteriorated into what the *New York Sun* called "a shower of mud."[1] Indeed, President Grant's opponent, Horace Greeley, died a few short weeks after the campaign, purportedly from exhaustion and depression.

Aside from Richard Nixon, no American president was more associated with scandals than Ulysses S. Grant, president from 1869 to 1877. Actually, the sheer number of Grant's scandals probably outnumbered Nixon's, but unlike Tricky Dick, Grant himself was not personally implicated in any wrongdoing.

But apparently Grant was such a poor judge of character and so lacking in the political skills of many of his peers that he set the stage for what became known as one of the most corrupt eras in American politics. He appointed cabinet secretaries and other high-ranking officials who generated numerous political and financial scandals, dragging Grant's name through the mud in the process.

It was surprising to many—and disappointing to all—that the most distinguished military leader of the Civil War and a national hero should be so tainted by scandal and incompetence. In the post–Civil War/Reconstruction era, the word "Grantism" came to be associated with public corruption, nepotism, and the spoils system. But it did not keep him from being re-elected in 1872.

Ulysses S. Grant. Library of Congress.

Most of Grant's appointees were personal friends, or were recommended to him by close friends and family members. He appointed Congressman Elihu Washburn to the post of secretary of state, only to replace him eleven days later with Hamilton Fish. He appointed General John Schofield secretary of war, but changed his mind a week later and replaced him with General John A. Rawlins, an old Civil War confidant.[2]

His appointment of Alexander Stewart, a wealthy New York businessman, to be treasury secretary was withdrawn after Congress passed a law forbidding anyone with such strong financial ties to be the head of the federal treasury. But then he appointed a Philadelphia businessman, Adolph Borie, to be secretary of the navy even though he had no apparent qualifications for the job. This was followed by the appointment of a livery stable operator to be the ambassador to Belgium.

BLACK FRIDAY AND BAD CREDIT

One of the first scandals of Grant's administration led to the gold panic of 1869. The president's brother-in-law, Abel Corbin, assisted two gold speculators in attempting to corner the gold market. Relying on information from Corbin and from Grant himself (unwittingly), the speculators bought large quantities of gold, pushing up the price. When Grant learned he had been duped, he ordered that the government sell off some of its gold reserves.

This touched off panic selling the next day, a Friday, leading to the crash of the gold market.

But probably the most notorious scandal of the Grant administration was the Credit Mobilier fiasco. Credit Mobilier was the name of a construction company set up by the leaders of the Union Pacific Railroad to cash in on all of the building projects related to railroad expansion. Credit Mobilier officers made enormous profits for themselves by padding construction budgets and charging the Union Pacific Railroad exorbitant fees.[3]

The railroads were supported with federal government revenues, and so it was the taxpayers who were being bushwhacked. One of the officers of Credit Mobilier was a U.S. congressman from Massachusetts named Oakes Ames. When Congress learned of the scandal, Ames paid off members of Congress and other government officials with company stock.

Horace Greeley. Library of Congress.

The scandal first became public knowledge during Grant's reelection campaign in 1872. Some of Grant's key administration figures were implicated, including Vice President Schuyler Colfax, who was quickly dropped from the ticket by Grant.

ANTI-GRANTISM

Grant had been president for only a little more than a year before some Republicans became disillusioned with his leadership and began actively seeking an alternative. Thus, the Republican Party split once again, with this group of reformers—referring to themselves as the Liberal Republicans—calling for an end to the spoils system and a reform of civil service, the withdrawal of federal troops from the South (which occurred after Rutherford Hayes's victory in 1876), and a lower tariff.

A number of high-profile and distinguished Republicans were part of this reform movement, including President Lincoln's ambassador to England,

Charles Francis Adams; U.S. senators Carl Schurz and Charles Sumner; Chief Justice Salmon P. Chase; Justice David Davis; and Horace Greeley, celebrated editor of the *New York Tribune*.[4]

In a private letter to Senator Henry Wilson, a friend, Grant vents his true feelings on his critics: "Mr. Sumner has been unreasonable, cowardly, slanderous, unblushing false. He has not the manliness ever to admit an error. I feel a greater contempt for him than for any other man in the senate. . . . Schurz is an ungrateful man . . . the sooner he allies himself with our enemies, the better for us."[5]

As early as 1870, a Liberal Republican Party was established in Missouri, home of Senator Schurz. It formed an alliance with Missouri Democrats and overthrew the Republicans, a strategy they would follow nationally in 1872. In January 1872, Schurz and other Liberal Republican leaders called for a national convention to establish a platform and select a presidential candidate. They met on May 1 in Cincinnati.

But who could they nominate to take on President Grant and rally the public? Senator Schurz was born in Germany, therefore constitutionally ineligible. Senator Charles Sumner of Massachusetts took himself out of the running. Chief Justice Salmon Chase was interested, but he was too old and ill to gain much support. Former ambassador Charles Francis Adams was a possibility, but he was aloof, held very pro-British views on foreign policy, and was not committed to civil service reform.

That left Justice David Davis of Illinois, and Horace Greeley. Greeley was as unlikely a presidential candidate as could have been imagined. He was one of the best-known and most read newspapermen of his time, but he had no experience in government. In addition, he was thought to be rather odd. He was known for his eccentric, often erratic persona, and had advocated a variety of ideas that at the time were considered strange, such as vegetarianism and spiritualism. Today he might have been part of the New Age movement.

Through his newspaper columns, Greeley had also left a paper trail of controversial and often contradictory statements on issues and policies. And, "with his cherubic face, big blue eyes, pilgarlic pate, steel-rimmed glasses, and shuffling gait, he looked more like a character out of a Charles Dickens novel than a presidential hopeful, and he was an easy target for cartoonists and caricaturists."[6]

Greeley got the nomination because the campaign of Justice Davis fell apart at the convention. Leading up to the convention, Davis had been attacked by several influential Liberal Republicans on a host of issues. And the rowdy, sometimes drunken behavior of his supporters alienated many convention delegates. After four ballots, with various candidates in the lead, the convention swung to Greeley, and he was nominated on the fifth ballot. His running mate was Benjamin Gratz Brown, governor of Missouri.

The nomination of Greeley was met with shock by many. One reporter blamed the delegates' choice on "too much brains and not enough whiskey."

THE DEMOCRATIC CANDIDATE

As strange as it sounds, the Democrats, in their "anybody-but-Grant" fervor, endorsed Greeley as their candidate and adopted the Liberal Republican platform as their own. This was the only time in American history that a major party put forth no candidate of its own but endorsed the candidate of a third party.

It was ironic. Greeley was an ardent abolitionist, one of the founders of the Republican Party, and a frequent critic of the Democratic Party, yet now he was the Democratic standard-bearer. It was a marriage of convenience. The Democratic Party was in disarray and saw Greeley's candidacy as a means of getting back into political power. The Liberal Republicans, of course, thought they were taking over the Democratic Party.

Many Democrats were divided over the Greeley nomination. How could they accept a man as their nominee, many asked, who had opposed them through most of his public career? Yet many Democratic leaders, steadfast in their determination to oust Grant, defended Greeley as infinitely better for the country than the current president.

Staying with tradition, Grant did not actively campaign, instead leaving that to his organization. Greeley, on the other hand, hit the campaign trail— very unusual in those days. In late September he embarked on a grueling multistate tour that took him through New Jersey, Pennsylvania, Ohio, Kentucky, and Indiana. He delivered up to twenty-two speeches per day, for a total of almost two hundred.

However, views were mixed as to the impact of Greeley's tour. Some were impressed, but others thought it was counterproductive because he often misread his audiences and said the wrong things at the wrong time. But there was widespread agreement about the impact of the campaign efforts of his running mate, Benjamin Gratz Brown. He spoke to an audience at Yale University while drunk, then fainted before a gathering in New York City.

A SHOWER OF MUD

One critic remarked that this was a contest between a "man of no ideas" (Grant) and a "man of too many ideas" (Greeley). While that may have been true, it was also a campaign in which both candidates were savagely attacked by the opposing side.

The campaign became a public spectacle, illustrated by a blizzard of the anti-Greeley cartoons of Thomas Nast in *Harper's Weekly* and the anti-Grant cartoons of Matt Morgan in *Frank Leslie's Illustrated Newspaper*. The criticism and caricatures of Greeley were particularly biting and cruel.

President Grant's forces depicted Greeley as a traitor and a flake, while Greeley's supporters called Grant a dictator and a drunk. The cartoons of *Harper's Weekly* ridiculed Greeley at every opportunity. He was drawn as a hopelessly nearsighted and pumpkin-headed clown.

Greeley's pamphlet on food and nutrition, called "What I Know about Farming," was lampooned in a savage series of cartoons, such as "What I Know about Stooping to Conquer," "What I Know about Honesty" (in which he is shaking hands with the corrupt Boss Tweed of Tammany Hall), "What I Know about Eating My Own Words," and "What I Know about Running for the Presidency."[7]

Greeley had urged reconciliation between North and South after the Civil War, and in his acceptance of the presidential nomination, he had urged the country to "clasp their hands across the bloody chasm" and move into the future. *Harper's* ridiculed this appeal with a series of sickening cartoons of Greeley shaking hands with a rebel who had just shot a Union soldier; stretching out his hand to John Wilkes Booth across Abraham Lincoln's grave; and turning a defenseless black man over to a member of the Ku Klux

Thomas Nast of *Harper's* lampooned Greeley without mercy. Library of Congress.

Klan, who had just lynched a black man and knifed a black mother and her child.

At the end of the campaign, Greeley remarked, "I have been assailed so bitterly that I hardly knew whether I was running for the presidency or the penitentiary." Grant could probably have said much the same thing.

Greeley's supporters circulated a pamphlet called "The Grant Government: A Cage of Unclean Birds," written by Lyman DeWolf. Calling Grant's administration the "crowning point of governmental wickedness," it accuses Grant of bringing forth a "burning lava of seething corruption, a foul despotism . . . from the President down to the lowest gutter manager of small municipalities, patriotism and public virtue is a mere enterprise scheme, which awards to the victors the spoils."

The pamphlet also questions Grant's competence: "Bribery and corruption have seized all the avenues of public life; robbery, murder and assassination are of daily occurrence, and guilty perpetrators escape through the solemn mockery of law. But the wisdom of worshipping a man who says nothing (Grant), because he has nothing to say, is being questioned by the multitude."[8]

And *Frank Leslie's Illustrated Newspaper* went after Grant the same way *Harper's Weekly* went after Greeley. With each passing week, Grant was portrayed more and more besotted, incompetent, and villainous.

Grant's enemies and Greeley's supporters took to calling the president Useless Grant, a play on the name Ulysses. They even added the insult to some of the campaign songs used in street marches to deride the president:

When Useless came to Washington
He wore a jaunty plume,
The Dents and Murphys crowded in
And drove him to his doom.
His nephews and his cousins all
Came up to win the race,
And every man who gave a dog
Was sure to get his place

And therefore, so, accordingly all the people say:
Down with Grant, Useless Grant!
Up with Greeley, good old Greeley!
Down with Grant, Useless Grant!
Hurrah for Greeley! Old White Hat![9]

But the cruelest strokes were reserved for Greeley. He got the worst of it, partly because his record and his appearance made him easier to caricature than Grant, and partly because *Harper's* had a wider audience and better political touch than *Frank Leslie's*.

One particularly bitter *Harper's* issue, two days before the election, showed a prostrate, and apparently deceased, Horace Greeley being carried on a stretcher the day after the election. In a cruel twist of fate, this issue hit the newsstands on October 30, the day that Greeley's wife, who had serious health problems, died.

> Grant was a surprising and, at first, unpopular choice to lead the Union army during the Civil War. He had a reputation as a hard drinker and therefore someone of questionable reliability. To these critics, Lincoln said, "just find out, to oblige me, what brand of whiskey Grant drinks, because I want to send a barrel of it to each one of my generals."[11]

For years Mrs. Greeley had been in poor health, and in late October, she took a turn for the worse. He canceled his remaining speaking engagements to be at her side. Four days after her death, only two days before the election, he wrote a friend, "I am not dead, but I wish I were. My house is desolate, my future dark, my heart a stone. I cannot shed tears; they would bring me relief. Shed tears for me, but do not write again till a brighter day, which I fear will never come."[10] Several weeks after the election, exhausted and grief stricken, Greeley himself fell ill and died.

A Second Term for Grant

For all of the mudslinging and turmoil, Grant easily won reelection over Greeley, winning 31 out of 37 states, and 286 electoral votes to just 66 for Greeley. It was the highest winning percentage of any president elected between 1828 and 1904, although Grant did not do as well in the South.

Why did Grant win so handily? It might have had something to do with the rough-and-tumble campaign—Greeley was bloodied more than Grant. Also, most of the scandals that have come to be associated with the Grant administration were not public knowledge at the time, the Credit Mobilier scandal coming out very late in the 1872 campaign. And the most famous of all the Grant-era scandals, the Belknap scandal, did not occur until well into his second term.

The Republicans also had the advantage of Grant's war heroics, a strong economy (even with the drop in the price of gold), and a very large and motivated political party organization. The Grant organization was also supplemented by thousands of patronage appointees throughout the government who doubled as campaign workers.

Grant's supporters also took every opportunity to wave the "bloody shirt" and remind voters of the Democratic Party association with secession and the Confederate cause. The Greeley campaign, by contrast, suffered from weak, fractured, and uncoordinated organization; internal feuding; low funds; and a candidate about whom even his own supporters had doubts.

THE FIRST CAMPAIGN

Thomas Jefferson v. John Adams, President, 1800

Thomas Jefferson is a mean-spirited, low-lived fellow, the son of a half-breed Indian squaw, sired by a Virginia mulatto father . . . raised wholly on hoe-cake made of coarse-ground Southern corn, bacon and hominy, with an occasional change of fricasseed bullfrog.
—A Federalist handbill circulated in 1800

Thomas Jefferson's defeat of incumbent president John Adams in 1800 was the result of the first real political campaign in American history. This campaign is often called the Revolution of 1800 or the second American revolution because it was the first election in which power was transferred from one political party to another, and it symbolized what for many Americans was a titanic political struggle between two very different views on how to run the country.

John Adams was a Federalist. The Federalist Party galvanized around George Washington, Adams, and Alexander Hamilton, and emphasized national government power. Jefferson represented the Democratic-Republicans, who, along with James Madison, advocated more limited national power and an emphasis on state and local authority. This election tested the limits of national authority and the public's tolerance for the heavy-handed use of government power.

It was also one of the nastiest political campaigns in our nation's history. It reached a level of personal animosity that almost tore apart the young republic, and has rarely been equaled in two hundred years of presidential politics. Among other things, Thomas Jefferson was said to have financially cheated his creditors, obtained his property by fraud, robbed a widow of an estate worth ten thousand pounds, and behaved in a cowardly fashion as governor of Virginia during the revolution.[1]

One pro-Adams newspaper warned that if Jefferson were elected, "murder, robbery, rape, adultery, and incest will be openly taught and practiced, the air will be rent with the cries of the distressed, the soil will be soaked with blood, and the nation black with crimes." Jefferson's religious views were attacked as the views of an infidel who "writes aghast the truths of God's words; who makes not even a profession of Christianity; who is without Sabbaths; without the sanctuary, and without so much as a decent external respect for the faith and worship of Christians."[2]

Of course, the Jefferson Republicans did their own mudslinging. They called Adams a fool, a hypocrite, a criminal, and a tyrant, and said that his presidency was "one continued tempest of malignant passions."[3] They also

Thomas Jefferson was a champion of state power.
Library of Congress.

claimed that Adams was planning to marry one of his sons to one of King George III's daughters, start an American dynasty, and reunite America with Britain. According to some Republicans, Adams dropped his schemes only when confronted with a sword-wielding George Washington.

According to legend, President Adams had such a heavy sexual appetite that he sent his vice-presidential running-mate, Charles Pinckney, to England on a U.S. ship to procure four pretty girls as mistresses, two for Pinckney and two for the president. "I do declare upon my honor," said Adams, when informed of the story, "if this be true General Pinckney has kept them all for himself and cheated me out of my two."[4]

If anything, John Adams got even worse treatment because he faced the challenge not only from Jefferson and the Republicans, but also from within his own party. Fellow Federalist Alexander Hamilton had come to despise Adams as much as Jefferson. The two men were rivals for power within the new national government and within the Federalist Party itself.

John Adams believed in a strong central government. Library of Congress.

JEFFERSON AND THE REPUBLIC

Jefferson served as secretary of state under President George Washington. Early into his government service, he detected a significant difference between what he thought were the principles of the American Revolution, such as popular sovereignty and individual rights, and what he perceived as the "authoritarian" attitudes of many of the Federalists who were running the government.

In his diary, he wrote of his "wonder and mortification" that much of the political talk among those in power revolved around "a preference of kingly over republican government." Indeed, many of America's revolutionary leaders thought that a strong national government was necessary, and that a ruling class of elites was necessary to bring order and stability to the new government.

But to Jefferson, that was contradictory to the very heart and spirit of American democracy. After all, a republic was formed to give ordinary citizens a voice and role in government. His idea of a republic was an emphatic rejection of monarchial and aristocratic rule, which seemed to be the path preferred by most Federalists, and instead a firm belief in the sanctity of individual rights and the sovereignty of state governments. Jefferson would later refer to the Federalist machinations as "the reign of witches."

Jefferson and Madison believed that the kind of national government the Federalists were trying to build in the 1790s represented nothing less than a "counter-revolution" that would undermine the constitution and undo the gains made by the American Revolution. Jefferson and his archrival, Hamilton, who was secretary of the treasury under President Washington, disagreed on virtually every aspect of the proper balance between national and state power.

For example, Hamilton's plans for the national government to assume the country's debts and start a system of national banks threatened to build a foundation of national control over the states. To Jefferson, the Federalist game plan would destroy the constitutional balance of power and permit the central government to take on powers not delegated to it by either the constitution or the states.

Without the war hero George Washington to rally around, the election of 1796 became a contest between rival political ideologies and personalities. Although the founding fathers had not created a system of political parties, and party politics was not prevalent during Washington's two terms, rival political factions soon took the stage in America's politics. Jefferson's Democratic-Republican Party was in its infancy, and was overmatched by the better-organized and better-known Federalists. But on the sheer political strength and public notoriety of Jefferson himself, he came in second to Adams in the Electoral College vote and, thus, became vice president under Adams. (At the time, the Constitution called for the first-place finisher in the Electoral College to serve as president and for the second-place finisher to serve as vice president. This was before the Twelfth Amendment revised the process to allow parties to run a presidential candidate and vice presidential candidate as a "ticket.")

HAMILTON V. ADAMS

Foreign policy also created tensions between the two parties. Even after the American Revolution, Britain and France had competing claims on land holdings throughout North America and trade rights with the new American government. Jefferson and the Republicans thought the Federalists were too pro-British. Many Republicans favored France, whose revolutionary principles were close to that of America's, but their support for France later cooled as the French Revolution spun out of control. In fact, some of Adams's Federalist allies actively sought to involve America in Britain's naval war against the French.

The disastrous XYZ affair, in which the French foreign minister essentially tried to extort the representatives sent by President John Adams, was used by many Federalists to call for war with France. When Adams sent yet another peace mission to France, Hamilton and many of his Federalist allies derided him as "hopeless."

Hamilton's distaste for President Adams led him to work behind the scenes to deny him a second term. He hatched a scheme that would have delivered more electoral votes to the Federalist's nominee for vice president, Charles Pinckney of South Carolina, than to Adams. Hamilton wrote a scathing letter detailing Adams's shortcomings to turn other Federalist leaders against the incumbent president. Adams, he wrote, "does not possess the talents adapted to the administration of government, and there are great and intrinsic defects in his character which make him unfit for the office." He also said that Adams was petty, mean, egotistical, erratic, eccentric, jealous natured, and hot tempered.

But then for Hamilton, disaster struck. The letter became public when loyal defenders of the president turned it over to the press. Republicans had a field day, and the Federalists were in open warfare. The controversy led President Adams to ridicule Hamilton as a man "devoid of every moral principle—a Bastard!"[5]

HIGH TREASON?

As Republican criticism of Federalist policy grew in the 1790s, the Republicans organized "democratic societies," or clubs, to help them spread the word. Many Federalists considered these clubs to be revolutionary cells and therefore a threat to civil order. Some of these Republican clubs were organized and staffed by exiled British and French radicals, who opposed Federalist policy in favor of Britain.

In 1798—in an attempt to silence Republican opposition, crush their democratic clubs, and deport their foreign allies—the Congress, dominated by Federalists, passed the Alien and Sedition Acts, some of the most controversial legislation ever passed by the U.S. Congress. Its aims were overtly partisan. Republican club members, newsletter editors, writers, and others were arrested, tried, and convicted by partisan Federalist judges.

The Alien and Sedition Acts are remembered as one of the largest cases of political bungling of all time, and undoubtedly helped bring about Jefferson's victory over Adams. Public support for the Federalists and their policies decreased, as fears of national government tyranny and unconstitutional abuses of civil liberties and individual rights led many to call for action.

After leaving office in 1809, Jefferson reached out to Adams. The two began corresponding with each other, and developed a mutual admiration. They stayed in contact with each other right up to their deaths, which amazingly, came on the same day, July 4, 1826—the 50th anniversary of the Declaration of Independence.

Republican leaders, prodded by Jefferson and Madison, pushed for action by the states. Virginia and Kentucky—both of which had Republican majorities in their legislatures—passed resolutions condemning the Alien and Sedition Acts and asserting their state's rights to resist the actions of an "unlawful federal measure."

Hamilton smelled treason. He argued that the Virginia and Kentucky resolutions were an attempt to unite the state legislatures in direct resistance to the Union and served as an effort to "change the government." He warned that supporters of the national government should be ready if necessary to make its continued existence a "question of force."[6] Another Federalist writer, William Cobbett, helped bring the crisis to a fever pitch with his suspicion that "they have 50,000 men, provided with arms, in Pennsylvania alone. . . . If vigorous measures are not taken; if the provisional army is not raised without delay, a civil war, or a surrender of independence is not more than twelve months distance."[7]

THE PEN, NOT THE SWORD

But the civil war never came. Instead of taking up arms, both sides continued the political battle leading up to the presidential election of 1800. Jefferson, Madison, and other Republican writers continued to write articles and publish pamphlets pressing the case against Adams, Hamilton, and Federalist policies. Jefferson was convinced that if the people were apprised of the threat posed to their liberties, they would put out the present government by constitutional means at the earliest possible opportunity.

And ultimately they did, but not before a tumultuous and confusing presidential election. In 1800, most of the states allocated their Electoral College vote for each presidential candidate through their legislatures, which met at various times from May through December of 1800.

And Hamilton wasn't quite through. In desperation, he wrote to New York governor John Jay, a Federalist, and urged him to find a way to call the legislature back and to steer New York's electoral votes to Pinckney.[8] But Jay never acted on the request, and the Federalists' reign in government was doomed.

By late November, enough states had allocated their electoral votes to make it clear that the Democratic-Republicans were going to be victorious. Newspapers churned out stories about the changeover in power, along with the likely implications. Republicans held street festivals and banquets, and proclaimed that the "reign of terror" was past.

But it was still not over. Because the election rules made the winner of the vote the president and the runner-up the vice president, each party put forward two candidates and tried to get enough electoral votes to elect both of them. For the Federalists, it was Adams and Pinckney; and for the Republicans, it was Jefferson plus Aaron Burr of New York. It was thought that Burr might be able to help pry loose New York's twelve electoral votes, which had gone to Adams in 1796.

However, crucial to the strategy of putting forward two candidates is having at least one of the electoral votes held back, so that one of your party's candidates has more than the other. The Federalists did this, with Adams finishing with sixty-five electoral votes and Pinckney with sixty-four. But the Republicans apparently miscommunicated with each other, and both Jefferson and Burr received seventy-three electoral votes.

CONSTITUTIONAL CRISIS

This was the first "disputed" election in our country's history. According to the Constitution, when no one candidate gets a majority of electoral votes, the election is decided by the House of Representatives. So the Federalists in

Congress got an opportunity to make more trouble for the Republicans. Even though Jefferson was the Republicans' choice for president and Burr for vice president, the Federalist-controlled lame-duck Congress didn't want to make it easy for their archenemy, Thomas Jefferson.

The inauguration for the new president was to take place on March 4, 1801. On February 11, the members of Congress gathered to cast their votes. East state got one vote, which would be determined by a majority vote of each state's members. The winner would need nine states to be elected president. On the first ballot, Jefferson got eight states and Burr got six. So they voted again. And again. And again. It was a stalemate. After six more days and thirty-five more votes, they were deadlocked.

Some Federalist members of Congress then approached Aaron Burr with a deal. They would give him their votes and make him president if he would agree to carry out Federalist policies. Burr refused, but he did not drop out of the race. Hamilton had not been among those offering the deal to Burr. He certainly did not want Jefferson to be president—his choice had been Pinckney—but the very thought of a Burr presidency made him absolutely ill. He believed Burr to be an unprincipled scoundrel, and said that Burr would "employ the rogues of all parties to overrule the good men of all parties. . . . I trust the Federalists will not finally be so mad as to vote for Burr." Hamilton insisted he got along with Burr personally, but could not fathom him in executive office. Of course, several years later the two men dueled with pistols, Burr fatally wounding Hamilton in the chest.

On February 17, taking Hamilton's warnings about Burr to heart, several Federalist congressmen cast blank ballots, which threw the majority in several state congressional delegations to Jefferson, thereby ending the deadlock.

The election of 1800 was the first in which political parties played a pronounced role in the choices facing the American public. It was also the first election in which power changed hands from one political party to another, setting in motion a tradition of the peaceful transition of power that has lasted for more than two hundred years, give or take a Civil War.

During this transition of power, no troops were brought in, no legislatures were dissolved, and the previous leadership was not imprisoned or executed. In fact, the oath of office to the new president was administered by a political opponent, Chief Justice of the United States John Marshall—an ardent Federalist. These two would later tangle in the case of *Marbury v. Madison*.

The inauguration of Thomas Jefferson was the first held in the new capital city of Washington, D.C. In his inaugural address, Jefferson attempted to move beyond party distinctions and unify the country once again. "We are all Republicans; we are all Federalists," he said. "If there be any among us who would wish to dissolve this Union, or to change its Republican form, let them stand undisturbed as monuments of the safety with which error of opinion may be tolerated where reason is left free to combat it."[9]

The Alien and Sedition Acts had expired the day before President Jefferson's inauguration, March 3, 1801. The new president pardoned all those still imprisoned under the laws, and all pending trials were canceled. A new day had dawned.

A HOUSE DIVIDED

Abraham Lincoln v. George McClellan, President, 1864

It seems exceedingly probable that this administration will not be re-elected.

—Abraham Lincoln, August 1864

Abraham Lincoln was ripe for the picking. He was an unpopular president with severe political problems and significant opposition from all sides. At least, that is the way the year 1864 began. If the election had been in June or July instead of November, he would likely have lost, and the Union might have taken a different direction.

The first part of the year was spent by many Republicans trying to throw Lincoln aside and nominate someone else. Horace Greeley wrote, "Mr. Lincoln is already beaten. He cannot be elected. And we must have another ticket to save us from utter overthrow. If we had such a ticket as could be made by naming Grant, Butler, or Sherman for President, and Farragut as Vice, we could make a fight yet. And such a ticket we ought to have anyhow, with or without a convention."[1]

Lincoln faced a number of obstacles. It had been over three decades since an American president had been reelected, and many observers believed that one four-year presidential term had become the norm and a tradition. For most of his tenure in office, Lincoln was an unpopular president. There was widespread criticism of his policies and his leadership. There had been huge protests against Lincoln's military draft, which in some places erupted into riots. An antidraft protest in New York City in

July 1863 turned violent, with four days of looting, lynchings of blacks, and burning buildings.

And the war was going badly. Generals Grant, Sherman, and Sheridan were bogged down, and both the Union and Confederate armies seemed to be dug in for a war of attrition. Lincoln was under fire from both sides for his Emancipation Proclamation, with some claiming he had gone too far, and others frustrated that he had not gone far enough. The Republicans had lost seats in Congress in the elections of 1862, and with the protracted war and its uncertain outcome, there were many who believed that Lincoln was not the man for the job.

Honest Abe. Library of Congress.

Lincoln's detractors and enemies were everywhere: Confederate sympathizers, "peace" Democrats, radical Republicans, dissatisfied abolitionists. At different points throughout 1864, Lincoln was called a filthy storyteller, a despot, a liar, a thief, a braggart, a buffoon, a usurper, a monster, Ignoramus Abe, Old Scoundrel, a perjurer, a robber, a swindler, a tyrant, a fiend, and a butcher.[2] And some of those doing the name calling still ended up voting for him!

The Democrats assailed Lincoln and his administration as guilty of "ignorance, incompetence, and corruption." They believed that Lincoln's conduct of the war had been amateurish and that he was in over his head. He removed General McClellan from his position; "now we'll remove Old Abe," they cried.

The opposition press had been brutal to Lincoln ever since he emerged as a candidate for president in 1860. He was caricatured by them as a fool, an idiot, an ape, and worse. The 1864 election presented an opportunity for Lincoln's enemies because events had made him vulnerable. The *New York World* snarled its disapproval:

The age of statesmen is gone; the age of rail-splitters and tailors, of buffoons, boors, and fanatics has succeeded. . . . In a crisis of the most appalling magnitude requiring statesmanship of the highest order, the country is asked to consider the claims of two ignorant, boorish, third-rate backwoods lawyers (Lincoln, and his running mate Andrew Johnson) for the highest stations in the government. Such nominations, in such a conjuncture, are an insult to the common sense of the people. God save the republic![3]

YES, IT'S SO FUNNY WE FORGOT TO LAUGH

Not to be outdone, in February 1864, James Gordon Bennet's *New York Herald* had this to say:

His election was a very sorry joke. The idea that such a man as he should be president of such a country as this is a very ridiculous joke. His debut in Washington society was a joke; for he introduced himself and Mrs. Lincoln as "the long and short of the presidency." His inaugural address was a joke. . . . His cabinet is and always has been a standing joke. All his state papers are jokes. His letters to our generals, beginning with those to General McClellan, are

very cruel jokes. . . . His emancipation proclamation was a solemn joke. . . . His conversation is full of jokes. . . . His title of "Honest" is a satirical joke. . . . His intrigues to secure a renomination and the hopes he appears to entertain of a re-election are, however, the most laughable jokes of all.[4]

RUNNING SCARED

In an effort to broaden their appeal, Republicans invited "war" Democrats to join them in an alliance called the National Union Party. A number of worried Republicans made overtures to several national figures, trying to entice them to seek the Republican nomination.

George McClellan. Library of Congress.

Some of them believed that General Benjamin Butler, the Union commander of the regiment at New Orleans, could unite the war Democrats with the more radical wings of the Republican Party. But the general declined to enter the political fray. The *New York Herald* urged General Grant to accept the nomination, but he would hear none of it. Some radical Republican leaders even approached Vice President Hannibal Hamlin to step forward and save the party, but he insisted on loyalty to Lincoln.

But the radicals finally found their man with Salmon P. Chase, Lincoln's treasury secretary. Chase, of Ohio, agreed with the abolitionists that Lincoln's emancipation policy was inadequate. Chase quietly built his campaign with the help of treasury officials and several members of Congress, including Senator Samuel Pomeroy of Kansas.

However, early in 1864, his emerging campaign was dealt a death blow. The campaign designed a pamphlet, which became known as the Pomeroy Circular, detailing Lincoln's shortcomings and promoting Chase for the presidency.[5] It was meant to be for internal use, but it was leaked to the press. Rather than build support for his candidacy, it created a backlash that doomed it. It was seen as rash, disloyal, and self-serving. The ensuing controversy rebuilt some of Lincoln's support in the party, and Chase withdrew from consideration.

NEXT?

The next challenge to Lincoln's presidency came from the Republicans' first presidential nominee, John C. Fremont. He had become a folk hero with tales of his western exploration and adventures and, as an ardent abolitionist, had parlayed his fame into a run for the White House as the nominee of the new Republican Party in 1856.

Fremont was a Union general, and in 1861 he had issued an emancipation order in Missouri, which was rescinded by Lincoln. He had been relieved of his military command twice by the president. In the absence of any other major figures, some radical Republicans rallied around Fremont, and he resigned his military commission to take up the campaign. His support came largely from anti-slavery radicals in Missouri and Kansas, as well as some abolitionists from New England, such as Frederick Douglass and Elizabeth Cady Stanton.

Calling themselves the Radical Democracy Party, they met in Cleveland for a convention on May 31, one week before the scheduled Republican Party convention. The convention platform called for continuation of the war without compromise, a constitutional amendment banning slavery, federal protection of civil rights (later enacted in the Fourteenth Amendment), confiscation of Confederate property, and a one-term presidency.

The Lincoln White House sent spies to the proceedings in Cleveland, but was reassured when there appeared to be no groundswell of support for the Fremont ticket. It appeared that the Radical Democracy Party had hoped the Democrats would endorse its ticket and forge a unified coalition against President Lincoln. When that didn't happen, momentum for the group stalled.

> The political party system in the 1860s was a fractured mess, largely due to the divide over the Civil War and the abolition of slavery. For more information on this chaotic political era, visit AmericanPresident.org.

After the successful Republican convention in June, it became obvious that Lincoln retained the support of the main components of the Republican Party. By the fall, Fremont and a number of radicals began to fear that the Democrats could retake the White House and possibly reverse the emancipation process. Fremont was urged by Senator Zachariah Chandler and others to consider dropping out of the race, and he did so in September.[6]

THE DEMOCRATS

The Democratic Party was in just about as much turmoil as the Republicans. It was split between those who favored continuing the war and those who favored a negotiated peace. But many of the war Democrats had bolted the party and were supporting Lincoln, so it was primarily the peace Democrats who were calling the shots.

The Democrats, hoping that the pressure on Lincoln and the Republicans might result in either a breakthrough for peace or a change on the Republican ticket, delayed their convention as long as possible, finally meeting in Chicago on August 29. They adopted a peace platform calling for a ceasefire and a negotiated settlement with the Southern states. The Democrats criticized Lincoln's "four years of failure to restore the union by the experiment of war."

But politically, they had a problem. Would they be seen as a "peace-at-any-cost" movement that lacked credibility with serious Northerners, who were tired of war but believed in the reasons for fighting it? Their answer was to nominate a military man to head their ticket—General George McClellan.

McClellan and Lincoln had a history. At the beginning of the war in 1861,

McClellan was named by Lincoln to command the Union army. He was a Democrat, and opposed Lincoln's policies on slavery, but he believed in preserving the Union. He and Lincoln, however, had notorious disagreements over the conduct of the war and the use of federal troops.

The turning point in their relationship was the battle of Antietam in September 1862. It was the single most costly day of the war, with 2,100 Union troops killed and almost 10,000 wounded.[7] Lincoln was angry that McClellan had not pursued Confederate general Robert E. Lee's army across the Potomac into Virginia. The president saw it as a missed opportunity.

Lincoln wanted McClellan to launch an offensive against Lee's army, but McClellan resisted, saying he needed more horses and reinforcements. Radical Republicans now openly questioned General McClellan's loyalties and fitness for command. In November, frustrated by McClellan's hesitancy, Lincoln relieved him of his command and recalled him to Washington. "My dear McClellan," the president's message said, "If you don't want to use the army I should like to borrow it for a while."[8]

McClellan accepted the Democratic nomination in 1864, but with a twist. He believed the peace platform of the Democrats to be unrealistic and

"I KNEW HIM, HORATIO; A FELLOW OF INFINITE JEST. * * * WHERE BE YOUR GIBES NOW?—*Hamlet, Act IV, Scene 1.*

"Alas, poor Abe. I knew him well." From *The New York World*. Library of Congress.

suicidal. In his letter of acceptance he agreed with the aim of removing President Lincoln from power, but made it clear he would enter the race as a "war leader."

During the campaign, McClellan declared the war to be a "failure," and placed the blame on Lincoln. He vowed to prosecute the war in such a way as to bring about a "reunion of the states" as quickly as possible. He envisioned a convention of all the states, which would restore order to the Union. But he made it clear that the Southern states would have to negotiate their reentry into the Union.

War and Peace

With the nomination of McClellan and the continuing setbacks in fighting the war, Lincoln began to despair. The animosities hurled at him from every corner, combined with what he and his advisers saw as the dim prospects for his reelection, led him to make preparations for a defeat at the hands of the Democrats.

He wrote a brief letter and asked his cabinet to sign it sight unseen. The note was then stored in a safe and not seen again until after the election. It read, "It seems exceedingly probable that this administration will not be re-elected. Then it will be my duty to so cooperate with the President-elect as to save the union between the election and the inauguration, as he will have secured his election on such ground that he cannot possibly save it afterward."[9]

Campaign Ugliness

The fall campaign was ugly. It seemed that the Democrats thought up every lie they could think of to tell about President Lincoln, and the Republicans tried to think of as many ways to call General McClellan a miserable failure as they could.

One of the most reprehensible fibs in presidential campaign history was about Lincoln demanding a song from one of his officers after the battle of Antietam. It was duly reported in the *New York World*, the *Chicago Times*, and other anti-Lincoln newspapers.

Supposedly, after the battle, Lincoln was driving over the field in an ambulance with General McClellan and Marshal Ward Hill Lamon. As they circled through piles of dead Union soldiers, Lincoln was said to have slapped

Lamon on the knee and said, "Come, Lamon, give us that song about 'Picayune Butler,' McClellan has never heard it." "Not now, if you please," McClellan is supposed to have interjected. "I would prefer to hear it at another place and time." But Lincoln insisted, and Lamon sang the song, much to the president's delight.

The newspapers had a field day, but of course the account was completely false. The incident in question had taken place sixteen days after the battle of Antietam, far away from the battlefield, and was actually a "little sad song." Lamon pleaded with Lincoln to issue a public denial, but he refused to dignify it with a denial. "If I have not established character enough to give the lie to this charge," said Lincoln, "I can only say that I am mistaken in my own estimate of myself."[10]

The Republicans went after the Democrats pretty hard, too. They warned the voters: "Don't swap horses in the middle of the stream." They went beyond that, though, to equate opposition to Lincoln with "disloyalty." They plastered the North with pamphlets, posters, and editorial cartoons that essentially depicted Democrats as traitors.

And as for the Democratic standard-bearer, General McClellan, the Republicans had nothing but derisive comments and personal attacks. "Little Mac," as they called him, had nothing to offer but a tradition of defeat.

MISCEGENATION

But the Republicans also had to deal with the fallout from a nasty little pamphlet cooked up by two reporters at the *New York World*, who beat Richard Nixon's "dirty-tricks" squad by more than one hundred years.

Just before the election year began, the pamphlet—called "Miscegenation: The Theory of the Blending of the Races, Applied to the American White Man and Negro"—appeared in New York City. It endorsed "race mixing" as a way to invigorate the country and strengthen the society. "All that is needed to make us the finest race on earth is to engraft on our stock the Negro element," it read.

The pamphlet said the Republican Party was the party of miscegenation and that Lincoln favored it, as did most abolitionists. It contained a long section calling on the New York Irish community to overcome its hostility to blacks and "intermarry with them as Lincoln wished."

It had its desired effect. The material spread across the country as word spread of this controversial and shocking new approach to race relations. Anti-Lincoln newspapers gave the story great play and hammered away at it

Miscegenation was a theory of race mixing used to scare voters into thinking Lincoln and other Republicans had radical ideas. Library of Congress.

with editorials and cartoons. Ohio congressman Samuel Cox said the pamphlet proved that the Republicans were moving toward "perfect social equality of black and white."[11]

After the election, it was revealed that the pamphlet was the work of two *New York World* journalists—managing editor David Goodman Croly and one if his reporters, George Wakeman—who wanted to harm the Republicans' chances in the election.[12] So much for journalistic integrity.

LINCOLN'S COMEBACK

Lincoln's political fortunes, and perhaps the Union itself, were saved by a turn of events beginning on the battlefield. In September, General Sherman took Atlanta and then marched his Union troops all the way to the Atlantic Ocean. General Grant had broken the stalemate at Petersburg, Virginia, and General Farragut had captured Mobile Bay. The Confederates were on the run.

Contrary to only a month or so before, the war now appeared winnable. President Lincoln's political prospects brightened considerably. Fremont withdrew from the race, Salmon Chase went on the campaign trail for Lincoln, and even Horace Greeley came around to be a strong advocate of Lincoln's reelection.

The radical Republicans, who had been so critical of Lincoln, began supporting him. By October, it was clear that Lincoln was going to be reelected—the only question being how big a victory it was going to be.

On November 8, 1864, Lincoln won 55 percent of the popular vote, which was the third largest winning margin of the 19th century. It was an Electoral College landslide, with Lincoln winning 212 electoral votes to McClellan's 21. McClellan won only New Jersey, Delaware, and Kentucky.

The Republicans stayed in power and increased their margin in Congress to an astounding 149 to 42 in the House, and 42 to 10 in the Senate. But the Democrats did well enough to remain a viable national party. McClellan captured 48 percent of the vote in a large number of states stretching from Connecticut to Illinois. The two-party system was now well established; it had survived a Civil War, and would now provide the front lines for many battles to come.

MUD, MUGWUMPS, AND MOTHERHOOD

Grover Cleveland v. James G. Blaine, President, 1884

The 1870s and the 1880s gave us some of the most bitter and hateful political campaigns ever. America's Gilded Age was indeed a golden age for negative campaigning. The 1884 presidential contest between the Democrat, Grover Cleveland, and his Republican opponent, James G. Blaine, was one of the nastiest, most intensely personal campaigns ever.

In some ways, this campaign pitted scandal against scandal. Would voters prefer "Slippery Jim" Blaine, as his enemies called him, who was accused of financial wrong-doing and telling a boatload of lies, or Cleveland, the governor of New York, accused of every moral failure in the book by his opponents?

TIME FOR THEM TO GO?

Since the Civil War, the Republican Party had pretty much run the show, controlling the presidency and Congress for most of the 1860s and 1870s. But by the 1880s, the Democrats were staging a comeback. In the midterm elections of 1882, the Democrats took a majority in the House of Representatives and nearly did so in the Senate. The Republicans were divided and lacked effective leadership.

The economy was unstable, prone to boom periods in the industrial North followed by recession. Because they were in power, Republicans received most of the criticism. The incumbent president, Chester Arthur, was a Republican, but was seen by most as a caretaker president. Arthur had succeeded James Garfield after his assassination and was unable to rally the support of most political and economic leaders.

The Republicans were also split into two main factions. The "stalwart" Republicans, which included Blaine, had opposed the pro-Southern Reconstruction policy of President Rutherford Hayes in the late 1870s as well as reform of the civil service system, which was becoming bogged down by political patronage and corruption. The "reform" Republicans, which included the editor of the influential *Harper's Weekly*, George William Curtis, supported civil service reform, as well as a number of other social reforms, and also vigorously opposed a tariff on foreign goods, which was being pushed by Blaine and other stalwarts.

Grover Cleveland. Library of Congress.

Blaine had sought the presidency twice before, in 1876 and 1880, but failed to win the nomination. He had served in Congress for over twenty years, earning a reputation for skill and intelligence as an effective Speaker of the House and then a U.S. senator. In 1881 he was appointed secretary of state by President Garfield, but after the assassination and the ascension of Chester Arthur to the presidency, Blaine resigned and became one of Arthur's chief critics.

Blaine had accumulated a number of enemies in the Republican Party, particularly among the "reformers." He had also begun to develop a reputation for political corruption, fending off accusations of bribery and conflict of interest. He was never able to explain away the corruption charges, and remained a very controversial figure, yet he emerged as the front-runner for the Republican nomination in 1884.

Certain Republican reformers, notably George William Curtis and former secretary of the interior Carl Schurz, led a revolt within the party that invited the Democrats to nominate a presidential candidate that they could support over Blaine. So convinced of Blaine's corruption and so wary of his tariff policy, these mugwumps, as they were dubbed, committed themselves to defeating Blaine at any cost.[1]

The term "mugwump" is an Algonquin Indian name meaning "big chief." But as used here by pro-Blaine Republicans, it means a fence sitter—someone with their "mug" on one side and their "wump" on the other. Of course, Republicans loyal to Blaine used lots of other names for the pro-Cleveland Republicans, who were derided as self-righteous and effeminate—not tough enough to play in the real world of politics. Today, actor and politician Arnold Schwarzenegger might refer to them as "girly men."

James G. Blaine. Library of Congress.

A REAL REFORMER

The Democrats turned to the popular governor of New York, Grover Cleveland. Elected governor in 1882, Cleveland had gained a national reputation as a reformer. He signed into law a sweeping reform of New York's civil service system, which caught the attention of reform-minded leaders everywhere, including the mugwumps. It also helped that Cleveland was from the state that had the largest number of electoral votes in the country.

Cleveland, too, had some enemies. He had antagonized the power brokers of Tammany Hall, New York's political machine, by cutting off its system of patronage and political favors. But that decision earned him the respect of many outside New York. It also helped him establish his reformist credentials among reform-minded Republicans. During the Democratic Party Convention, General Edward Bragg, who lauded Cleveland in a convention speech, remarked that his supporters "love him most of all for the enemies he has made."

WHERE'S MY PA?

The most controversial aspect of this campaign, and the largest single part of its historical legacy, is the accusation against Cleveland of a scandalous affair with a widow named Maria Halpin. On July 21, 1884, the *Buffalo Evening Telegraph* printed an exposé entitled "A Terrible Tale." In it, the paper recounted the tale of a younger Grover Cleveland who had practiced law in Buffalo and had an illicit affair with a young widow.

The *Buffalo Evening Telegraph* was the *National Inquirer* of its day. It was a paper that tried to build readership through sensationalism, gossip, and scandals. However, when the widely respected *Boston Journal* investigated the story and printed much the same thing as the *Telegraph*, the issue gained credibility and became a national story.[2]

To make matters worse, this liaison between Cleveland and the widow Halpin was said to have produced a child, a boy, who in 1884 would have been around ten years old. According to the story published in the *Telegraph*, after the child's birth, Cleveland used his influence in Buffalo to have the child forced into an orphanage and Halpin admitted to an insane asylum to keep the whole issue quiet.

The original story was "uncovered" by a political enemy of Cleveland in New York, the Reverend George H. Ball—pastor of Hudson Street Church in Buffalo and a pro-Blaine Republican. According to Ball, this was an issue of "moral depravity such as no city in Christendom has ever witnessed." Ball and other New York Republicans claimed they had evidence of still other sexual liaisons, and that this was a pattern of Cleveland's immoral lifestyle.

The Maria Halpin scandal became a national sensation that threatened the Democrats' chances in the November elections. Republican-friendly papers, especially in the East, had a field day with it. In cartoons, in feature-length newspaper and magazine articles, and in Republican-orchestrated street demonstrations, pro-Blaine supporters shouted "Ma, Ma, Where's My Pa?" To the delight of the Blaine forces, it became a national slogan, and possibly an epitaph for Cleveland's campaign and for the Democrats' hopes in 1884. Mainstream churches and a number of religious leaders condemned Cleveland's behavior and interpreted it as a sign from on high that Cleveland was destined to lose. Women's groups, including a leading suffragette newspaper, called it an "affront to decent women."[3]

But there was a major problem with the stories and accusations about Cleveland. Most of them were not true—at least not in the way they were reported. Cleveland himself met the accusations head on and encouraged his

This famous cartoon accused Cleveland of fathering an illegitimate child.
Library of Congress.

supporters to do the same. "Tell the truth," he instructed them. He believed that if a man owned up to the circumstances and got the facts out, the falsehoods and sensational aspects of the story, for which there was no solid evidence, would quickly dissipate. And he was right.

Maria Halpin had named the child Oscar Folsom Cleveland and claimed that Cleveland was the child's father, although she had no proof. For his part, Cleveland admitted to the affair but not to fathering the child, although he had no proof either. But Cleveland had agreed to provide for the child. Why? Because, his defenders claimed, he suspected the true father was his law partner, Oscar Folsom, who had been killed in an accident in 1875. It seemed to make sense; Halpin had apparently named the child for both men. The fact that Cleveland took responsibility for care of the child was a gallant gesture, undertaken to protect his friend's memory and to spare the widow financial hardship and public humiliation.

And what about the institutionalization of mother and child? It turns out that Halpin was battling alcoholism. She was remanded by a New York judge to a mental institution, where she stayed briefly. In the meantime, Cleveland had arranged for the boy, then age one, to be cared for by a local church orphanage. The boy was eventually adopted by an upstanding western New York family, and Cleveland had no contact with the boy afterwards.

As it turns out, the timing of the scandal could not have been better for Cleveland. Had it come out a few weeks earlier, it would have likely prevented his nomination, and had it come out later in the campaign, it might have made it impossible for Cleveland to win the election. By coming out in July, it gave Cleveland and the Democrats time to get the real facts out and discredit the gossipers. Indeed, after Cleveland won the election, the Democrats answered the pro-Blaine forces' jeers of "Ma, Ma, Where's My Pa?" with "Gone to the White House, Ha, Ha, Ha!"

A VIRTUE-CHALLENGED BLAINE?

Blaine had his own scandal problem. When he first ran for the Republican nomination in 1876, it came to light that he had been involved in influence peddling and bribery. As Speaker of the House, Blaine twisted arms to guarantee passage of a land grant for a railroad. In gratitude, Warren Fisher, one of the railroad's contractors, allowed Blaine to sell financial securities in the railroad and pocket a suspiciously large commission in the form of bonds. Later, when the railroad ran into financial problems, one of its wealthy backers, Tom Scott, bought back the then worthless bonds at a price well above market value. In return, Blaine pushed legislation to benefit another financial venture of Scott's.[4]

Blaine attempted to cover it all up, but a disgruntled railroad employee, James Mulligan, obtained copies of letters from Blaine to Fisher. Although an official investigation of the matter had been dropped when Blaine was appointed to the Senate, all of the charges came roaring back during the 1884 campaign. In what came to be called the Mulligan letters, stories detailing the scandal were published widely in newspapers, tarring Blaine with corruption and charges of cover-up. In one of the letters, Blaine had written "Burn this letter!" That became a chant of Democrats at rallies throughout the campaign.

Blaine also had his own sex scandal to deal with. A rumor had been published by the *New York Times* in 1876, but when he lost the nomination, it failed to get the public's attention. But in August 1884, the *Indianapolis Sentinel* revived the allegation that as a young man, Blaine had impregnated a young woman and had married her only at the threat of her father's shotgun.[5]

Blaine quickly denied the charges and sued the *Sentinel* for libel. He was probably trying to force a public retraction, but the story only gained more attention. The paper could not prove the case of a shotgun marriage, but it did produce evidence that the Blaines had been married only three months before the birth of their first child. Not a shock in 1884, but it did lend credence to the rest of the charges against Blaine.

> Grover Cleveland is the only American president to be elected twice in nonconsecutive terms. He lost his reelection fight in 1888 to the Republican, Benjamin Harrison, but he ran again four years later and defeated President Harrison.

One might have expected Cleveland, or his supporters, to jump on the charges of Blaine's sexual impropriety, but he refused to participate. In fact, his campaign was offered evidence of the allegations against Blaine. Documentation was provided to Cleveland, who promptly dropped it in the fireplace. "The other side can have a monopoly of all the dirt in this campaign," he said to an aide.

The real political damage to Blaine was the established pattern of acting improperly, then lying to cover it up—a pattern in sharp contrast to Cleveland's efforts to come clean and get the facts out with regard to accusations against him. The stories of Blaine's involvement in a premarital sexual affair also undercut the impact of the Grover Cleveland–Maria Halpin incident.

It was a rough-and-tumble sprint to election day. The Democratic campaign focused on Blaine's corruption; the Republicans focused on Cleveland's morality. According to Democrats, Blaine's behavior was symptomatic of the greed and arrogance of a party that had been in office for too long. This strategy also helped the Democrats link Blaine to the large business corporations that were seen by many as treading over the interests of the common man in their quest for wealth and power.

In the final weeks of the campaign, the Republicans accused Cleveland of avoiding service in the Civil War. This was a volatile, inflammatory charge, intended to start rumors. They even claimed that none of his brothers had served in the war. Available documentation disproved this, and Cleveland himself explained that the family had decided that one of the brothers needed to stay and take care of the women and young children. They drew lots, and his two brothers drew the long ones, so they went to war while Cleveland stayed and kept the family together.

Rum, Romanism, and Rebellion

The turning point may have come with what is surely one of the first major gaffes in presidential politics. One of Blaine's strengths in New York was his support among Irish Americans. There were almost a half million Irish voters in New York City alone. Blaine never hesitated to tell stories about his Irish Catholic mother, rail against Great Britain's treatment of the Irish, and voice his support for the Irish in the New World.

The Irish vote would have been enough to help Blaine carry New York in the election and win its thirty-six electoral votes. But then something horrible happened—horrible, that is, if you were a Blaine supporter. On October 29, only days before the election, Blaine attended a meeting of pro-Blaine clergymen at the Fifth Avenue Hotel in New York City. One of the speakers was Reverend Samuel Burchard, a Presbyterian minister.

In his remarks, Reverend Burchard ended with this gem: "We are Republicans, and don't propose to leave our party and identify ourselves with the party whose antecedents have been Rum, Romanism, and Rebellion."[6] Now, it's bad enough when one of your supporters insults a half million of your other supporters in a crucial swing state. But Blaine's big mistake may have been to ignore Burchard's remarks instead of saying something that might have soothed Irish feelings.

Of course, it may be that Blaine didn't attach much significance to Burchard's words right away, or it may be that he didn't want to insult his patron and the hundreds of thousands of like-minded Protestants who agreed with him.

Whatever the case, the controversial remarks made their way into the newspapers and into Democratic handbills that were spread around New York, highlighting the insults. By the time Blaine got around to disavowing the controversial remarks, it was too late.

New York's thirty-six electoral votes were seen by both campaigns to be the deciding factor. In October 1884, New York City saw huge parades and demonstrations by both campaigns. There were competing brass bands, circus animals, and huge outdoor rallies. Republican supporters, dressed in medieval armor, clanked down the streets of New York shouting "Blaine! Blaine! James G. Blaine! The white-plumed knight from the state of Maine!" This was invariably met by shouts from roving groups of Democrats,

"Blaine! Blaine! James G. Blaine! The continental liar from the state of Maine!"

No Hanging Chads!

Seventy-eight percent of America's voters came out to vote in 1884. It was very close. The results were so close in the pivotal state of New York that it was several nail-biting days before the results were known. Cleveland narrowly won the state of New York and carried the election by only 23,000 votes: 4,875,971 (48.5%) to 4,852,234 (48.26%). New York's 36 electoral votes gave Cleveland a final electoral vote of 219 to Blaine's 182.[7]

Cleveland carried the entire South, which since the Civil War had become a Democratic stronghold, as well as the border states of Maryland, Delaware, West Virginia, Kentucky, and Missouri. Blaine won most of the northern states, except for New York and New Jersey, and he won all of the western states.

THE DIRTIEST CAMPAIGN IN AMERICAN HISTORY?

Andrew Jackson v. John Quincy Adams, President, 1828

There are many historians who would put this campaign in first place, as the most negative ever. This was no mere political campaign; it was a four-year-long struggle between two political factions, two different regions of the country, and two radically different views of life and of governing. This may be the only presidential campaign that led directly to someone's death.

It's hard to imagine a more negative campaign. Jackson's opponents called him a murderer, a drunkard, an adulterer, a petty thief, and a liar. The pro-Jackson forces labeled Adams a tyrant, a gambler, a spendthrift, and a pimp. And all of that was before the newspapers got involved.

Jackson and Adams faced each other twice for the presidency, in 1824 and 1828. The 1824 election descended into chaos, as Jackson actually received more electoral votes than any of his three opponents—Adams, Henry Clay, and William Crawford—but not enough to constitute a majority. As a result, the election was thrown into the House of Representatives for only the second time in the nation's young history.

THE CORRUPT BARGAIN

Before the House met to vote, Adams and Clay met in secret and concocted a deal. Clay announced his support for Adams, dismissing Jackson as a mere "military chieftain," unfit for the office of the presidency. With Clay's help, Adams received the support of thirteen states when the House of Representatives met to cast its votes. Immediately after his election, Adams named Clay his secretary of state, confirming the suspicions of Jackson and others that a deal had been made.[1] This came to be known as the corrupt bargain, and set the stage for the political warfare that followed.

Andrew Jackson of Tennessee, "Old Hickory," was a frontiersman with minimal education and an outlook on life that can best be described in the American tradition of rugged individualism. He believed in a democracy of the people, in a Jeffersonian sense. He rose to national prominence with his military victories in the War of 1812—most notably, routing the British at the battle of New Orleans.

Old Hickory. Library of Congress.

John Quincy Adams, son of the second president, was a gentleman of New England, born into a political aristocracy. He believed, as his father did, that "society's leaders" knew what was best for the people, and that the states and frontier areas should be made to yield to the more "respectable" political establishment of the East.

Although most political leaders at the time came up through the Democratic-Republican tradition cobbled together by Thomas Jefferson and James Madison, the notion of party competition had faded along with the Federalist Party. But the followers of Jackson and Adams reinvigorated party rivalries, with the Jacksonians calling themselves Democrats, and the Adams forces calling themselves National Republicans.

One of the advantages Jackson had over Adams was the enthusiasm and energy of his supporters, as well as their creativity. The Jacksonians organized early and developed political organizations in New York, Washington, and several other states. Also very important to the Jacksonian cause were a number of anti-Adams newspapers in New York, Philadelphia, and the Carolinas that assisted the Jackson campaign in waging its battle against Adams.

The Jackson forces continued to grow, as many advocates of states' rights, such as William Crawford and John C. Calhoun, became wary of Adams's focus on national government authority and flocked to Jackson's cause. And soon after, other political leaders, such as Martin Van Buren of New York and Thomas Hart Benton of Missouri, came to Jackson's side.

PERSONAL ACCUSATIONS

Much of the pro-Adams case revolved around vicious personal attacks against Jackson, his wife, and the rest of his family. According to presidential historian Paul Boller, Jackson was reduced to tears when he came across the following statement in the newspaper: "General Jackson's mother was a common prostitute, brought to this country by the British soldiers. She afterward

John Quincy Adams. Library of Congress.

married a mulatto man, with whom she had several children, of which number General Jackson is one!"[2]

When his wife, Rachel, found him sitting alone in his office and crying, she asked what was wrong. He replied, "Myself I can defend, you I can defend; but now they have assailed even the memory of my mother."

But the worst abuse was aimed squarely at Jackson's wife. Andrew Jackson and Rachel Donelson had been married since 1791, but the circumstances were suspect. It turns out that at the time of her marriage to Jackson, Rachel had not been legally granted a divorce from her first husband, Captain Lewis Robards.

She and Jackson mistakenly thought the Virginia courts had granted Captain Robards a divorce from Rachel early in 1791, but what the court had actually granted was a right for Robards to pursue his case under Virginia law. Robards did not actually finalize the divorce petition until 1793. When Jackson realized his marriage to Rachel was legally void, they were both crushed but were soon legally remarried by a justice of the peace.

So although the facts were not quite what they seemed, the mudslinging about the incident in the 1824 and 1828 elections was unforgiving. The partisan publications backing Adams screamed headlines such as "Adultress" and "Bigamist." One pro-Adams pamphlet read, "Anyone approving of Andrew Jackson must therefore declare in favor of the philosophy that any man wanting anyone else's pretty wife has nothing to do but take his pistol in one hand a horsewhip in another and possess her."[3]

Part of the criticism came from "polite" Washington society and from women's organizations about how "a person like that Jackson woman" would fit in and ever be respected. One newspaper editorial in 1824 pleaded with voters not to "place such a woman as Mrs. Jackson at the head of the female society of the United States."[4]

Jackson had at times reacted with fury to the criticism aimed at his wife. On one occasion in the 1790s, before he became a national figure, he actually challenged a man named Charles Dickinson to a duel and killed him after he admitted to slurring Mrs. Jackson as an adulterer.

Rachel Jackson. The president blamed her death on his political opponents. Library of Congress.

Between 1824 and 1828, he tried to shield Rachel, who suffered from a heart ailment, from the intense personal criticism, but to no avail. She was snubbed by most of the social leaders and society patrons. There were no tickets to balls and parties, and few invitations to dinner. And she managed to see most of the newspaper headlines and pamphlets cursing her and her "godless" marriage.

As the 1828 election campaign raged during the summer, Mrs. Jackson became withdrawn and depressed. In the fall, as her husband plotted political strategy with his advisers, she became ill. She lived long enough to see her husband elected but not long after. Her condition worsened, and with Jackson at her side, she died on December 22.

Jackson went into deep depression as he mourned the loss of his wife. She was buried back in Tennessee with a tombstone that read, "A being so gentle, so virtuous, slander might wound but could not dishonor."[5] She was buried in the satin gown she had planned to wear to the inaugural ball.

At his inauguration, Jackson wore a black armband as a symbol of his mourning. He blamed his political enemies for driving Rachel to her death, and he never forgave them.

THE HERO OF NEW ORLEANS

To the Adams forces, Jackson was a pretender to the throne. They portrayed him as ignorant and inexperienced in national affairs, and reckless in his personal behavior. One of their political pamphlets criticized him as "no jurist, no statesman, no politician. . . . he is destitute of historical, political, or statistical knowledge; that he is a man of no labor, no patience, no investigation; in short that his whole recommendation is animal fierceness and organic energy. He is wholly unqualified by education, habit, and temper for the station of president."[6]

In their zeal to tarnish Jackson, Adams's supporters knew no bounds. They said Jackson was guilty not only of adultery but of gambling, cockfighting, bigamy, slave trading, drunkenness, and theft. They even denigrated his war record, the source of his fame.

Their most outrageous attack on Old Hickory involved claims that he murdered his own soldiers during the 1813 Creek Indian war. Six of Jackson's militiamen had been executed for desertion during the conflict. One Philadelphia newspaper that supported Adams put out a leaflet called the "Coffin Handbill." This piece of propaganda portrayed the six soldiers as innocent men who had completed their service and only wanted to go home, but were murdered by Jackson in cold blood.

The "Coffin Handbill" raised a furor but was effective. At the top it read, "Some Account of the Bloody Deeds of General Jackson." It was bordered in black, showing six coffins in the middle, one for each dead militiaman. It said that one of the men, John Harris, was a "preacher of the gospel," who had patriotically volunteered his service and then was shot dead at Jackson's orders when his duty was up and he wanted to go home.

The Jacksonians hurried to limit the political damage by getting out their version of events. The facts as they gave them told of a very different John Harris than the one in the "Coffin Handbill." During the Creek Indian war, Harris and five other men plotted a mutiny among the soldiers. They broke into a military storehouse, stole supplies, burned down several adjacent buildings, and then deserted.

The militiamen were given fair trials, found guilty, then executed under the law. At no time, they insisted, were the constitutional rights of these men violated. But the Adams forces clung to their basic point, which was that Jackson in wartime had been a murderer because he "enjoyed" the killing.

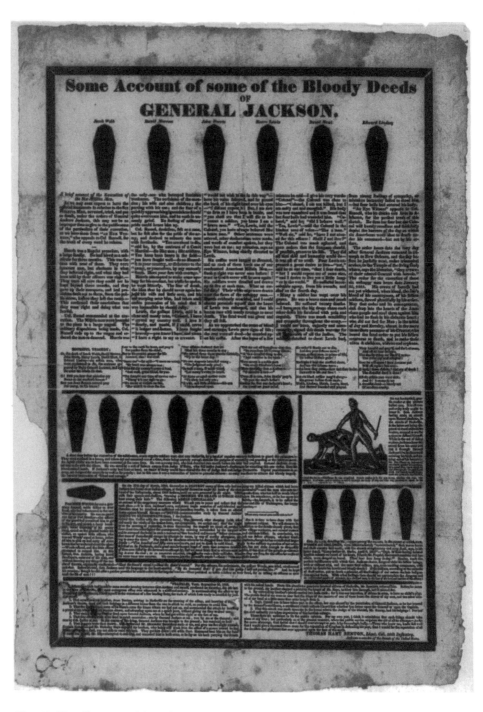

The "Coffin Bill" was a vicious slap at Jackson. Library of Congress.

KING JOHN

Of course, the Jackson people did some mudslinging of their own. Half the country thought that Adams and Clay had stolen the election in 1824. Jackson's supporters in Congress, led by Senator John Randolph, made life as miserable as they could for Adams and his administration from day one.

Congressmen and senators from the southern and western states—Jackson's main block of supporters—were particularly hostile to President Adams. They opposed his proposal to send delegates to a conference of nations in Panama, attacked his views on the tariff, and denounced his plans for improvements to the country's infrastructure.

Adams complained loud and long about the treatment he was getting from Congress, but it was hard for many to have much sympathy. Sometimes Adams was his own worst enemy. In response to the stiff resistance of his policies, he suggested that Congress not "be palsied by the will of its constituents."[7] This comment was reported widely by many newspapers, along with the rejoinder from Senator Randolph that the president's statement was an "ominous" sign for a democracy.

On another occasion, Adams was in Baltimore for a commemoration of that city's defense against the British in 1812. Asked to propose a toast, he cried, "Ebony and topaz! General Ross's posthumous coat of arms, and the republican militiamen who gave it!" The audience looked stunned. Seeing their lack of understanding, he explained. It came from Voltaire's "Le Blanc et le noir," in which ebony stood for the spirit of evil (represented by the British General Ross) and topaz stood for the spirit of virtue (represented by the American militiamen).[8]

The problem was that the Voltaire work cited by Adams was considered by most to be anti-Christian. The Jacksonians repeated the story as often as they could to as many audiences as they could. And Adams was embarrassed by the reaction of the newspapers, which ridiculed his toast as an awkward gesture. Said the *New York Evening Post*, "We supposed it to have been the production of some wicked Jacksonian wag who had undertaken to burlesque the clumsy wit and unwieldy eloquence of the ex-professor."

But the legacy of the "corrupt bargain" was the main rallying cry of the Jackson forces, and they would not let the public forget. The Tennessee legislature even called for Adams's impeachment over the issue. Jackson supporters criticized Adams as a reckless spendthrift who lived in "kingly pomp and splendor" in his "presidential palace."

As with the Adams camp, the Jacksonians were not above an occasional exaggeration. When President Adams spent his own money to buy a billiard table and some ivory chess pieces, they accused him of installing "gaming tables and gambling furniture" in the White House at public expense.

They also tried to inject religion into the campaign. Some Jackson followers noted that the puritanical Adams was not above traveling on Sunday. Some even said that he had premarital relations with his wife. But the charge that took the top prize was that when he was minister to Russia, Adams had procured a young American girl for Czar Alexander I.

Andrew Jackson is one of a handful of U.S. Army generals who went on to become national heroes and were then elected to the presidency. This distinguished list includes George Washington, Ulysses S. Grant, and Dwight Eisenhower.

At the heart of the argument from the Jackson forces was the belief that Adams was basically a "monarchist" like his father, who despised the people and favored rule by the few over the many.[9] "His habits and principles," said one critic, "are not congenial with the spirit of our institutions and notions of a democratic people."

MODERN COMMUNICATION

Jackson's 1828 campaign was the first to take advantage of a professional political organization to appeal directly to the people for support. His campaign committees organized mass rallies, parades, and barbecues to generate excitement about the campaign to oust John Adams.

One of his campaign's innovations was the formation of Hickory Clubs throughout the states. These groups were the "field soldiers" for the Jackson campaign. Called the Hurra Boys, they distributed hickory brooms, hickory canes, and hickory sticks. Hickory poles sprouted up in states across the country, as Adams's supporters wondered what all the excitement was about.

When the votes started coming in, the Adams forces soon learned what all the excitement was about. Voter participation in 1828 more than doubled from what it had been in 1824, and was four times as high as it had been in 1820.[10]

Most states by this time chose electors by direct popular vote, so many people voted for the very first time. But there was also no doubting the effect the four-year-long Jackson campaign had on the voters. Many observers felt that "democracy" had finally taken root in America, as for the first time ever, a presidential election had been a large focus of public attention and active participation.

Not surprisingly, the election results split along regional lines. Jackson won every state in the South and in the West, while Adams won every northern state except Pennsylvania. Jackson's supporters hailed his election win as a vote for victory for the "farmers and mechanics of the country" over the "rich and well born."

George Wallace and the "Negro Bloc Vote"

George Wallace v. Albert Brewer, Democratic Primary, Governor, Alabama, 1970

This was the dirtiest campaign I've ever observed. If it takes that to be governor, then I'll pass it up.

—Albert Brewer

All the powers of incumbency couldn't save Governor Albert Brewer of Alabama in 1970. He lost the Democratic primary runoff to former governor and presidential candidate George Wallace. The man who stood in the schoolhouse door at the University of Alabama in 1963 and said, "Segregation today, segregation tomorrow, segregation forever," emerged victorious in a battle between the state's racist past and its emerging moderate middle. In 1970, the past won.

George Wallace ran what turned out to be one of the last openly racist political campaigns in this country. In Alabama in 1970, you didn't need code words and double meanings to play on racial hatreds—you just said what was on your mind. "You know, 300,000 nigger voters is mighty hard to overcome," he would tell voters in small towns at campaign rallies![1] It went downhill from there.

Wallace was first elected governor in 1962 and served a four-year term. At that time, the Alabama constitution prevented serving consecutive terms as governor. Wallace and his legislative allies tried to push through an amendment to the state constitution allowing successive four-year terms, but it failed.

George Corley Wallace. Alabama Department of
Archives and History, Montgomery, Alabama.

So Wallace urged his wife, Lurleen, to run for governor in 1966. Based on her husband's popularity and political influence, she won.

Lurleen Wallace was popular. Alabamians could point with pride to the first female chief executive in state history, but everyone knew it was her husband pulling the strings and making the real decisions. Then fate intervened. Lurleen had been diagnosed with uterine cancer in 1960, but it had been treated early and apparently cured. The cancer reemerged in 1968, and this time it proved fatal. Upon her death, Lieutenant Governor Albert Brewer became Alabama's governor.

Of course, 1968 was also the year that George Wallace entered the national political stage, as a candidate for president of the United States. Wallace ran not as a Democrat—the national Democratic Party had been taken over by the hated liberal crowd, as he called them—but as an independent. Wallace's flamboyant opposition to desegregation and civil rights had made him a national figure, and he used the racial tensions of the time to propel his national candidacy into the spotlight.

In the 1968 presidential election, Wallace won 13.5 percent of the popular vote and 46 electoral votes—not enough to deny Richard Nixon the White House, but enough to solidify his national credentials and become a spur in the saddle of Nixon. Nixon had designed his presidential win largely on the basis of his "southern strategy," appealing to conservative, southern voters while maintaining his base in the Midwest and western states. But Wallace represented a threat to this strategy, and a long-term political threat to Nixon himself.

By 1969 Wallace was already plotting another run for the White House in the 1972 election, but he had a problem. Not having the Alabama governor's office or having his wife there reduced his power base and his ability to raise national money for another run at the presidency. Alabama contractors and business supporters, deprived of any quo for their quid, were suddenly uninterested in bankrolling his political ambitions.[2]

So he decided to seek the governor's mansion again, though he had another problem. After his wife died and Albert Brewer became governor, Wallace had assured him, both in private and in public, that he would not be a candidate for governor in 1970. This turned out to be a minor inconvenience. The state needed him, so he had to answer the call and give the people of Alabama the firm leadership they needed in such troubled times—at least that's what he told the Alabama newspapers.

In the fall of 1969, Wallace fired his opening salvo in his battle to win back the governor's chair. He gathered Alabama legislative leaders at his home in Montgomery, calling on them to submit a

Albert Brewer. Alabama Department of Archives and History, Montgomery, Alabama.

resolution to the legislature to ignore court-ordered desegregation orders. He admitted to them it was a long shot, but he felt that they had to try. And, he added, "that's a whole lot more than some of these sissy folks have done." Governor Brewer and his allies didn't have to guess who he meant by "sissy."

Two Very Different Candidates

Albert Brewer had an impeccable reputation. A political moderate from Decatur, Alabama, he was considered by most to be a decent person and a very capable chief executive. But most observers thought he would get his head handed to him in a confrontation with Wallace. Even among his supporters, the worry was that he was too decent, too upright. Wallace was a fighter, and Brewer was a gentleman. It was no accident that Wallace constantly referred to "sissies" too cowardly to stand up for the people of Alabama. In fact, Wallace referred to the incumbent governor on more than one occasion as "sissy-britches."

Wallace officially became a candidate in March 1970 and launched his campaign with a thirty-one-point plan for increasing state services, cutting taxes, and ridding the state of "filthy literature and narcotics." Now knowing what he was up against, Brewer hit the campaign trail. He found friendly audiences in some of Alabama's cities and suburban areas, and well as on college campuses. He also found a friendly audience in the White House. Nixon and his advisers viewed Wallace's popularity in the South as a threat to Nixon's southern base. His zeal to blunt Wallace's future presidential ambitions led Nixon to support Brewer behind the scenes.

President Nixon's people arranged for an infusion of cash into the Brewer campaign, up to $100,000 by some accounts. The Democratic governor of Alabama was accepting campaign contributions from the Republican president of the United States. Oh, the irony! But the need to stop Wallace transcended political party bonds.

Lurleen Wallace, Alabama's first female governor. Alabama Department of Archives and History, Montgomery, Alabama.

Wallace was a born campaigner. He appeared at huge outdoor rallies orchestrated by his campaign. Local speakers would warm up the crowd by warning of the dangers posed by "immoral politicians." Then Wallace would burst onto the stage, while a band played "Dixie" in the background. His speeches were pure red meat. He railed against racial integration, school busing, and federal legislators.

He also spoke of the hazard posed

by what he called "bloc voting," which, if successful, would control Alabama for the next fifty years. Some of his crowds understood this to mean black people voting in blocs for the opposition, but for some of his crowds, when he felt a need to spell it out, he would warn about the "Negro bloc vote."

In the month leading up to the Democratic primary, Wallace unleashed a blitz of TV and radio ads focused almost entirely on race and integration. Polling data commissioned by Wallace had found that although Brewer was popular personally, a significant number of voters, particularly working-class and rural voters, were concerned that he would be soft on integration.

In these ads, and in stump speeches across Alabama, Wallace denounced Brewer as a "sissy-britches" politician who "used to stand on this platform behind me and my wife . . . who rode her skirt-tails to power, and has now joined together with black militants to defeat me."[3] Pretty rough stuff—playing off the memory of his recently departed wife. He pleaded with white voters to "save Alabama as you know Alabama." He warned that if Brewer won, the state would be ruled by a "spotted alliance" of blacks and "sissy-britches from Harvard who spend most of their time in a country club drinking tea with their finger stuck up."

But when the May 5 primary came around, it at first looked as if Wallace's plan was not working. Brewer came in first, with 422,000 votes to Wallace's 414,000. The rest of the votes were split between five other candidates in the primary. Brewer didn't win a majority, which would have avoided a runoff, but history was on his side. No candidate in Alabama history had finished second in a gubernatorial runoff and come back to win.

AN EERIE CALM

The Wallace camp did not panic. Instead, his campaign seemed to display what *Newsweek* described as an "eerie calm."[4] According to one adviser, "there weren't any meetings, no brainstorming or anything like that. We all knew what he had to do—promise them the moon and holler 'nigger' as loud as he can." He did that—and much more.

Some of the dirty work was done by pro-Wallace groups and sympathizers not affiliated with the campaign. On the surface, that allowed Wallace to deny involvement, but as he did not condemn their work or ask them to stop, everyone knew he and his campaign were giving the marching orders.

Anti-Brewer circulars were printed and placed in mailboxes, on cars in parking lots, and at churches throughout the state. Some of these circulars accused Brewer of being a homosexual. This dovetailed nicely with Wallace's denunciations of him as a sissy-britches.

Other circulars and leaflets announced to voters that Brewer's two daughters had become pregnant following sexual affairs with blacks, which explained why Brewer was "soft on blacks." And still more leaflets followed, some reporting false claims that Brewer's wife, Martha, was an alcoholic, who had sought treatment at asylums. Brewer's wife was known to have collapsed in tears while shopping at a department store upon hearing the news, according to one Alabama newspaper.

Wallace himself had little to say about the rumors and accusations about Brewer's family until after the campaign was over, when he said that Brewer had a "fine family."[5]

Other ads showed doctored photos of Brewer with controversial Nation of Islam leader Elijah Muhammad and the boxer Muhammad Ali. Someone had taken a photo of Brewer meeting with two other governors at a conference and superimposed the photos of the two black Muslim leaders over their faces. The ad declared that Governor Brewer was making secret deals and would "hand Alabama over to the Muslims." A Wallace campaign worker later said, "The Klan printed that stuff, I think, but we helped them pay for it."[6]

The Wallace campaign itself ran some pretty awful stuff, too. One newspaper ad screamed, "If you want to save Alabama as we know it REMEMBER! The Bloc Vote (Negroes and their white friends) nearly nominated Gov. Brewer on May 5th. This black and white social-political alliance MUST NOT DOMINATE THE PEOPLE OF ALABAMA! This spotted alliance must be defeated! This may be your last chance. VOTE RIGHT! VOTE WALLACE!"

Another Wallace ad that ran in some Alabama newspapers showed a small blonde four-year-old girl on a beach. She was surrounded by seven grinning black boys. The headline read, "WAKE UP ALABAMA! BLACKS VOW TO TAKE OVER ALABAMA." The caption at the bottom read, "This could be Alabama four years from now! Do you want it?"

Following a call by an organization benefiting black police officers for Alabama to integrate the state patrol, Wallace ran a very controversial radio ad. Listeners heard ominous background music and a police siren, followed by an announcer saying, "Suppose your wife is driving home at 11 o'clock at night. She is stopped by a highway patrolman. He turns out to be black. Think about it. Elect George C. Wallace."

The Wallace campaign also engaged in what some might call dirty tricks. Martha Brewer actively campaigned for her husband, even more so after the attacks on the Brewer family. During the primary and runoff, she traveled around the state on behalf of her husband, speaking mostly to women's groups and garden clubs.

On several of these occasions, about fifteen minutes after she had left, a "distraught aide" would arrive looking nervous and worried, asking, "Was she okay? . . . I mean, she wasn't slurring her words or anything, was she?"

In the runoff, the Wallace campaign formed a group called Women for Wallace. These women telephoned nursing homes around the state claiming to represent Martha Brewer's office and arranged for visits from Mrs. Brewer. "You know how it is at a place like this," said the director of one nursing home in Birmingham. "The women got themselves all gussied up and were even planning to sing 'For she's a jolly good fellow.'" Of course, Martha Brewer never showed up.[7]

MR. CLEAN

By contrast, Albert Brewer ran a low-key campaign. Although he complained of the "gutter politics" of Wallace and his cronies, his strategy was to "hug the ground and pray," as he called it, while hoping for a backlash against Wallace and his harsh tactics.

He ran as an incumbent governor, heartened by his first-place showing in the Democratic primary. A moderate on racial issues, he did not openly embrace the black vote for fear of giving credence to Wallace's claims about him. And he did not directly engage Wallace in racial arguments. To do so, he said, "would only create deeper chasms and accentuate the divisiveness in this state."

To some of the Wallace campaign's more savage attacks, Brewer would respond in paid ads, through an announcer saying, "Good grief, Mr. Wallace!" To many Alabama voters, that sounded rather "sissified." He did face criticism, some from his own supporters, for not fighting back harder and instead adopting a "Mr. Clean" approach. He had ruled out attacking Wallace over race, or over ethical lapses in Wallace's first term as governor. "You can't fight Wallace with one hand tied behind your back," one aide later complained.

Brewer was content to criticize Wallace for his presidential ambitions, saying that Wallace would be only a part-time governor, while he was out seeking the presidency at the same time. On the campaign stump, Brewer characterized his opponents as "political hacks trying to defeat me because they want to get their hands back in your pockets."

In the end, the runoff election became a referendum on many white voters' fear of blacks their admiration for politicians "who fight for what they believe in," according to some observers. Harold Martin, publisher of the *Montgomery Advertiser,* said the ultimate factor that tipped the balance against Brewer was the perception that "he wouldn't fight."[8]

A PLACE IN THE SUN

Wallace won 51.5 percent of the vote, defeating Brewer by only 32,000 votes out of over one million votes cast. Brewer got more than 90 percent of the black vote, as well as large chunks of votes from the suburbs and metro areas of the state. Wallace did very well among rural voters and lower- to middle-income voters, but the decisive votes came from the state's blue-collar voters, whom Wallace had targeted through his race-based appeals.

Wallace, feeling that his aggressive campaign style and racist appeals had been vindicated by the voters, declared victory and said, "Alabama still has a place in the sun, and Alabama will continue to be heard from."

In the late 1970s, George Wallace, crippled by an assassin's bullet, repented and apologized to blacks for "all the hurt I've caused." It must have meant something, because when he was once again elected governor in 1982, he won large numbers of black votes against the Republican candidate.

Brewer was gracious in defeat, but the strain of the campaign was obvious to those around him. Months later, in an interview with CBS News about the raucous campaign, Brewer finally let some of his frustration out. "It was nigger, nigger, nigger all over again," he said in anger. "I hoped race wouldn't become an issue in the campaign, but it boiled down to a hate and smear issue. And if that is what it takes to win, the cost is too high."[9]

Of course, what happened to George Wallace is well known. While serving as governor of Alabama, he went on to run for president in 1972, this time as a Democrat. Running on a platform of "state's rights" and strict limits on the power of the federal government, he was struck down by a bullet fired from a man named Arthur Bremer, who had been stalking Wallace on the campaign trail for weeks. Wallace survived, but he was paralyzed from the waist down, and confined to a wheelchair for the rest of his life.

But that didn't stop him politically. Though denied the presidency, he stayed active in politics and was elected to a third term as Alabama's governor in 1974, and then a fourth term in 1982.

By this time, he had gone through a personal and political transition, re-nouncing racism and apologizing to all those he had "offended and hurt" over the years. In fact, his political transformation was so dramatic that in his last election, he received a significant amount of support from black vot-ers—quite an ironic twist for the old segregationist.

EPILOGUE

The characteristics of the campaigns included in this book leads to a couple of observations. First, most of the twenty-five cases cluster into one of two time periods: 1860s–1880s and 1980s–present. The years from the 1860s through the 1880s include the period historians call the Gilded Age, when American society in general was experiencing growing pains in terms of rapid business and industrial expansion, public corruption, and political gamesmanship.

Political campaigns in this era were brutal—much rougher than current standards. Name calling, character assassination, and political intrigue were commonplace and came to be an expectation on the part of most voters.

TWO GOLDEN AGES?

Similarly, the period from the 1980s to the present seems to be a time of increased vitriol when it comes to how politics is practiced in America. No one would suggest that these elements did not exist before the 1980s, but the politics of the last twenty-five years are becoming known for a particularly rough, mean-spirited, win-at-all-costs game of survival.

Can we label these two time periods the "Two Golden Ages of Negative Campaigning?" If so, what explains it? Are there commonalities in these two eras in American history? Each time period is unique, but both do have some characteristics that may help to explain their historically high levels of negativity in politics.

The raw politics of the 1860s–1880s were partly a product of the coarse nature and ill feelings surrounding public discourse of the time. Beginning

with the Civil War itself, a politically volatile period of Reconstruction, followed by its negotiated end and the ongoing disputes over emancipated
slaves, voting rights, trade policy, disagreements over banking, industry and
commerce, and westward expansion—you have the makings of quite an exciting political arena. Politicians of the era perfected the art of scapegoating
and fear mongering.

These problems were exacerbated by an extremely hostile and partisan press.
The main medium of the day—newspapers—encouraged and contributed to
the coarse political climate. There were Republican-leaning newspapers and
Democratic-leaning newspapers; there were progressive newspapers and pro-
business newspapers. The main common denominator was unbridled support
for its patron causes and open hostility to the opposing side. And, unlike today,
they did not feel constrained by notions such as objective reporting, professional standards of journalism, or community interests.

One influential and popular way to express political ideas and skewer your
adversaries was the political cartoon. For example, *Harper's Weekly* was a
widely read and influential publication that carried news, political and social
commentary, business information, and cultural happenings. One of the
most popular features of *Harper's* was the political cartoons of Thomas Nast.
Nast and other cartoonists of the time, such as those at *Frank Leslie's Illustrated News*, helped popularize that art form as a means of political discourse.
Unfortunately, they also helped sour and anger the public. Political cartoons
served as the television ads of that era.

The era from the 1980s to the present has been affected by its own share
of political and social trauma. The civil rights struggles of the 1950s and
1960s, followed by the counterculture revolution of the 1960s and 1970s,
produced a generation vastly different from the one that preceded it. Then
Vietnam and Watergate shook this country to its core. Those two experiences increased the feelings of mistrust and suspicion that the public felt
toward government in general and political figures in particular. Journalists
became more assertive and adversarial.

As news organizations increased the level of scrutiny of public officials,
their coverage became more critical. Thomas Patterson has explored the concept of the "Bad News Syndrome," in which the news media look for bad
news first and focus on it because it is more dramatic and leads to higher ratings or readership.[1]

The rise of television also raised the stakes in this drama. As TV news coverage and televised political ads took over campaigning, beginning in the
1960s, the dialogue became more intense, negative, and personal. The growing influence of political campaign consultants led to more emphasis on ag-

gressive TV advertising and increasingly hostile political attacks on opponents. The public was increasingly turned off, but experience and poll results convinced the consultants and the candidates that "going negative" works.

These changing dynamics also affected the political dialogue between politicians and political parties. In post–World War II America, there had been more of a consensus on governing and more civility on the political stage. But the divisive political dramas of the 1960s through the 1980s, aided by the growing power of the mass media and an increasingly negative political dialogue, tore that civility to bits.

This can be seen in the relationships among members of Congress, and the tone and tenor of political debate. This is not your grandmother's U.S. Congress. There is now a "gotcha" mentality. Political attack, one-upmanship, and character assassination are routine. The post–WWII political era was not Disneyland, but it seems like it when compared to the current gladiator style of politics practiced today.

The hostile environment in Congress has bled into political campaigns. Political consultants, and increasingly hostile and aggressive political parties, have aided and abetted this process for the last thirty years. The number of U.S. Senate campaigns on the list of the top twenty-five are testament to this trend. There is little doubt that many, maybe even most, campaigns for U.S. Congress of the Gilded Age in the late 19th century were also negative and nasty. But they didn't have the multi-million-dollar budgets of an Al D'Amato or a Robert Torricelli. They also did not have television.

THE POLITICS OF RACE

The final observation is the prevalence of race-based politics in many of the negative campaigns of this second golden age. Five of the campaigns in the top twenty-five, one-fifth of the total, take place between 1970 and 1993, and all of them feature intensely racial themes.

At least four of the five were campaigns in which the candidate, or a candidate's supporters, conducted outright racist campaigns. Race-baiting themes are featured prominently in the following campaigns: George Wallace v. Albert Brewer, 1970; Harold Washington v. Bernard Epton, 1983; Jesse Helms v. Harvey Gantt, 1990; and Edwin Edwards v. David Duke, 1991. The 1993 New York City mayoral campaign between Rudolph Giuliani and David Dinkins was fought largely on the grounds of race, but neither candidate was overtly racial—at least not in the league of George Wallace or David Duke.

Not too surprisingly, the George Wallace campaign against Albert Brewer was judged to be the most negative political campaign of all time. This is so largely because the openly public racist theme, and the intensely negative personal focus on the opposing candidate, make this a campaign that should have been waged in 1870 rather than 1970.

NOTES

25: From Vietnam to Iraq

1. Evan Thomas, "The Vets Attack," *Newsweek*, November 15, 2004. This was a private comment to an aide.

2. Janet Hook, "Campaigns Accentuate the Negative," *Los Angeles Times,* October 17, 2004.

3. Dana Milbank and Jim Vande Hei, "From Bush, Unprecedented Negativity," *Washington Post*, May 31, 2004, A1.

4. Milbank and Hei.

5. Hook.

6. Howard Fineman and Michael Isikoff, "Slime Time Live," *Newsweek*, September 20, 2004.

7. Thomas.

8. Transcript of Fox News broadcast, March 11, 2004.

9. Hook.

24: It's a Jungle out There

1. Social History, http://www.socialhistory.org/Biographies.

2. Greg Mitchell, *The Campaign of the Century* (New York: Random House, 1992).

3. Mitchell.

4. Mitchell.

5. Mitchell.

6. Mitchell.

7. Mitchell.

23: Senator Pothole versus "Putzhead"

1. Tim Graham, "What's Worse? Putzhead or Fascist?" Media Research Center, October 30, 1998.

2. "D'Amatoing D'Amato," *Slate.org*, October 30, 1998.

3. Michael Bailey, "Going After the Ins," *Campaigns and Elections*, June 1999.

4. Joe Conason, "The Canary," *Salon.com*, October 20, 1998.

5. Matthew Dorf, "Jewish Vote May Decide Key Senate Races," *Jewish News*, October 23, 1998.

6. Charles Kaiser, "The Best Man?" *New York Metro*, October 5, 1998.

7. BBC News, "Smear Tactics in New York Race," November 2, 1998.

8. Peg Fong and Kim Dixon, "Schumer Races to Early Win," *Third Rail*, November 4, 1998.

22: Electronic Mudslinging

1. Tony Schwartz, *The Responsive Chord* (New York: Schwartz Media, 1973).

2. Kathleen Hall-Jamieson, *Packaging the Presidency* (New York: Oxford University Press, 1984).

3. Hall-Jamieson.

4. Paul Boller, *Presidential Campaigns* (New York: Oxford University Press, 2004), 309.

5. Boller, 309.

6. Boller, 311.

21: The Art of War

1. Howard Troxler, "Jesse Helms' Legacy Is Today's Politicking," *St. Petersburg Times*, August 23, 2001.

2. Troxler.

3. *Washington Post*, August 29, 2001, A21.

4. Kathleen Hall-Jamieson, *Dirty Politics* (New York: Oxford University Press, 1992).

5. The 30-Second Candidate, *PBS.org*.

6. Hall-Jamieson.

7. Hall-Jamieson.

8. The 30-Second Candidate, *PBS.org*.

9. Claim by the Religious Freedom Coalition of the Southeast in "The Two Faces of Jesse Helms," http://www.tylwythteg.com/enemies/helms/helms.html.

10. Troxler.

20: Homo Sapiens, Thespians, and Extroverts

1. The Claude Pepper Museum.

2. The Claude Pepper Museum.

3. Tracy Danese, *Claude Pepper and Ed Ball: Politics, Purpose, and Power* (Gainesville: University of Florida Press, 2000).

4. Danese.
5. Danese.
6. Danese.
7. The Claude Pepper Museum.
8. Danese.

19: Vote for the Crook—It's Important

1. PBS Online News Hour, "Louisiana Political Profile," http://www.pbs.org/newshour/vote2002/races.la_profile.htm.
2. Martin Lee, Southern Poverty Law Center, "Detailing David Duke," 2004.
3. From Wikiquote, http://en.wikiquote.org/wiki/edwin_edwards.
4. Tyler Bridges, *The Rise of David Duke* (Jackson: University Press of Mississippi, 1994).
5. Jim Amoss, *ASNE Bulletin,* March 1992.
6. "Edwards Money from LA," *Times-Picayune*, November 25, 1991, A12.
7. Kathleen Hall-Jamieson, *Dirty Politics* (New York: Oxford University Press, 1992), 87–88.
8. Amoss.
9. Amoss.
10. Lee.

18: Who's the Boss? Richard Daley and the Chicago Political Machine

1. Adam Cohen and Elizabeth Taylor, *American Pharaoh* (Boston: Little, Brown & Company, 2000).
2. Cohen and Taylor.
3. Cohen and Taylor.
4. Mike Royko, *Boss: Richard J. Daley of Chicago* (New York: Penguin Books, 1971).
5. Royko.
6. Cohen and Taylor.
7. Cohen and Taylor.
8. Royko.

17: Polluting the Garden State

1. *Newsweek*, November 21, 1988.
2. Maurice Carroll, "And in This Corner . . . ," *Newsday*, September 6, 1988, section 2.
3. Clifford May, "Lautenberg: Well Liked but Vulnerable," *New York Times*, December 17, 1987, B1.

4. May.

5. "Polluting the Air in New Jersey," *National Journal*, November 5, 1988.

6. Carroll.

7. "Polluting the Air in New Jersey."

16: God Save the Republic, Please

1. Paul Boller, *Presidential Campaigns* (New York: Oxford University Press, 2004), 133.

2. American President Archive, *AmericanPresident.org*.

3. Boller, 134.

4. Boller, 134.

5. Boller, 135.

6. American President Archive.

7. American President Archive.

8. Boller, 137.

15: Rudy and the Jets

1. Frank Lynn, "Two Nominees Clash in Race for Mayor with Harsh Words," *New York Times*, September 14, 1989, A1.

2. Michael Cottman, "Race Politics," *Newsday*, September 23, 1992, 5.

3. Cottman, 5.

4. "Why Dinkins Lost," *Newsday*, November 4, 1993.

5. Todd Purdum, "This Time, Race Is a Murkier Issue," *New York Times*, September 19, 1993.

6. James Dao, "Dinkins Gets a Researcher on Giuliani," *New York Times*, October 8, 1993, B4.

7. Dao, B4.

8. Allison Mitchell, "Giuliani Ads Accuse Dinkins of Using Race Issue," *New York Times*, October 6, 1993.

9. Mitchell.

10. "A Victim's Mantle for Mr. Giuliani," *New York Times*, October 7, 1993, A28.

11. "Why Dinkins Lost."

14: A Jersey Street Fight

1. *CNN Inside Politics*, October 28, 1996.

2. Michelle Goldberg, *Salon.com*, August 1, 2002.

3. Jacob Weisberg, *Slate.org*, November 1, 1996.

4. Guy Gugliotta, *Washington Post*, May 18, 1997.

5. *New Jersey Capital Report*, 1996.

6. *Asbury Park Press*, October 16, 1996.

7. *Asbury Park Press*.

13: In This Corner, Little Lord Fauntleroy

1. James Sterba, "Texas Race Starts for U.S. Senate," *New York Times,* July 7, 1977.

2. Tom Wicker, "Two Against Tower," *New York Times*, September 11, 1977.

3. Kathleen Hall-Jamieson, *Dirty Politics* (New York: Oxford University Press, 1992).

4. Celia Dugger, "Pissants and Pablum," *Harvard Crimson*, October 27, 1978.

5. Hall-Jamieson.

6. Dugger.

7. Hall-Jamieson.

12: Sex, Lies, and Videotape

1. "Virginia Man Sues North over TV Ad," *Washington Post*, October 22, 1994.

2. "VA Senate Race Features Sex, Lies, God, Patriotism," *St. Petersburg Times*, October 24, 1994.

3. *New York Times*, March 14, 1994.

4. *Washington Post*, November 8, 1994.

5. "Robb Fires First Volley in War Against North," *Washington Post*, August 26, 1994.

6. *Washington Post*, August 26, 1994.

7. *Washington Post*, August 26, 1994.

8. "The GOP's Negative Force," *Washington Post*, November 1, 1994.

9. *Washington Post*, November 1, 1994.

10. "After a Summer of Cool Restraint, North, Robb Start Slinging the Mud," *Washington Post*, October 7, 1994.

11. University of Oklahoma, Julian P. Kanter Political Archive.

12. "Wilder Endorses Longtime Rival Robb, Climaxing Weeks of High-Level Talks," *Washington Post*, October 22, 1994.

13. "Robb Attacks Coleman for Abortion Shift," *Washington Post*, October 27, 1994.

11: Claytie versus the Lady

1. Bill Turque and Ginny Carroll, "Texas Rough and Tumble," *Newsweek*, February 12, 1990.

2. David Maraniss, "Letter from Texas," *Washington Post*, September 18, 1990.

3. J. Michael Kennedy, "The Cowboy and Good Old Girl," *Los Angeles Times*, October 21, 1990.

4. Maraniss.

5. "Higher Aspirations from Low Campaign," *New York Times*, April 15, 1990.

6. Roberto Suro, "Even for Texas, the Race for Governor Is Rowdy," *New York Times,* September 21, 1990.

7. Kennedy.

8. David Maraniss, "The Texas Two-Step in the Race for Governor," *Washington Post,* October 22, 1990.

9. Kennedy.

10. Maraniss, "The Texas Two-Step in the Race for Governor."

10: Richard Nixon versus the United States of America

1. Paul Boller, *Presidential Campaigns* (New York: Oxford University Press, 2004).

2. Bob Woodward and Carl Bernstein, *All the President's Men* (New York: Simon and Schuster, 1974).

3. Woodward and Bernstein.

4. Boller.

5. Woodward and Bernstein.

6. Kathleen Hall-Jamieson, *Packaging the Presidency* (New York: Oxford University Press, 1984).

7. "Election of 1972," *AmericanPresident.org.*

8. Boller.

9. Hall-Jamieson.

9: "Bye-Bye Blackbird"

1. Andrew Malcolm, "Last Debate Signals Final Stage of Chicago's Acrimonious Democratic Mayoral Race," *New York Times*, February 2, 1983, A10.

2. "Chicago History," Roosevelt University, 2003, http://www.roosevelt.edu/chicagohistory/mod3-chap5.htm.

3. "Chicago History."

4. Paul Kleppner, *Chicago Divided: The Making of a Black Mayor* (DeKalb: Northern Illinois University Press, 1984).

5. Kleppner.

6. Kleppner.

7. Kleppner.

8. Dempsey Travis, *Harold: The People's Mayor* (Chicago: Urban Research Press, 1989).

9. Kleppner.

10. Travis.

11. Travis.

12. Kleppner.

13. Kleppner.
14. Kleppner.
15. Travis.

8: America, Meet Willie Horton

1. Thomas Sweitzer, "Kill or Be Killed," *Campaigns and Elections*, September 1996, 46.
2. Kathleen Hall-Jamieson, *Dirty Politics* (New York: Oxford University Press, 1992), 16–21.
3. Hall-Jamieson, 153–55.
4. Hall-Jamieson, 153–55.
5. Jacob Lamar, *Time*, November 21, 1988.
6. Hall-Jamieson, 257–58.
7. Lamar.

7: Tricky Dick versus the Pink Lady

1. Greg Mitchell, *Tricky Dick and the Pink Lady* (New York: Random House, 1998), 6.
2. Helen Douglas, *A Full Life* (New York: Doubleday and Company, 1982).
3. Mitchell, 25.
4. Roger Morris, *Richard Milhouse Nixon: The Rise of an American Politician* (New York: Henry Holt and Company, 1989).
5. Mitchell, 101.
6. Mitchell, 101.
7. Mitchell, 101.
8. Mitchell, 161.
9. Mitchell, 233.

6: Grantism and Mr. Greeley

1. Henry Stoddard, *Horace Greeley: Printer, Editor, Crusader* (New York: G. P. Putnam's Sons, 1946), 312.
2. Shelley Ross, *Fall from Grace* (New York: Ballantine Books, 1988), 103.
3. Ross, 104.
4. Paul Boller, *Presidential Campaigns* (New York: Oxford University Press, 2004), 129.
5. Nancy Winkler, *The Election of 1872, Grant and Greeley* (Newark: Ohio Public Library).
6. Boller, 130.
7. Boller, 131.
8. Winkler.

9. Winkler.

10. Harry J. Maihafer, *The General and the Journalists: Ulysses S. Grant, Horace Greeley, and Charles Dana* (Washington, DC: Brassey's, 1998).

11. From *"Abe" Lincoln's Yarns and Stories,* 1901, Henry Neil.

5: The First Campaign

1. *American President.org/*Jefferson.

2. *Monticello Newsletter,* Thomas Jefferson Memorial Foundation, Spring 2000.

3. Paul Boller, *Presidential Campaigns* (New York: Oxford University Press, 2004), 11.

4. Boller, 11.

5. Boller, 13.

6. *Monticello Newsletter.*

7. Boller, 15.

8. Boller, 15.

9. *Monticello Newsletter.*

4: A House Divided

1. *Harpweek,* http://elections.harpweek.com/1864.

2. Paul Boller, *Presidential Campaigns* (New York: Oxford University Press, 2004), 116.

3. Stefan Lorant, *The Glorious Burden: The American Presidency* (New York: Harper and Row, 1968), 262.

4. J. G. Randall, "The Unpopular Mr. Lincoln," *Abraham Lincoln Quarterly* 2 (June 1943): 275.

5. *Harpweek.*

6. *Harpweek.*

7. *Harpweek.*

8. John Waugh, *Reelecting Lincoln* (New York: Crown Publishing, 1998).

9. Boller, 121.

10. Ward Hill Lamon, *Recollections of Abraham Lincoln, 1847–1865* (Lincoln: University of Nebraska Press, 1994), 141–46.

11. Boller, 122.

12. Boller, 122.

3: Mud, Mugwumps, and Motherhood

1. Mark D. Hirsch, "Election of 1884," in Arthur Schlesinger Jr., *History of Presidential Elections.*

2. *Harper's Weekly,* http://elections.harpweek.com.

3. Mark W. Summers, *Rum, Romanism, and Rebellion: The Making of a President, 1884* (Chapel Hill: University of North Carolina Press, 2000).

4. *Harpweek*, http://www.harpweek.com.

5. Hirsch.

6. Summers.

7. *Harpweek.*

2: The Dirtiest Campaign in American History?

1. "Presidential History," *AmericanPresident.org.*

2. Paul Boller, *Presidential Campaigns* (New York: Oxford University Press, 2004), 44.

3. Shelly Ross, *Fall from Grace* (New York: Ballantine Books, 1988), 53.

4. Ross, 55.

5. Ross, 55.

6. Boller, 46.

7. Boller, 49.

8. Boller, 49.

9. Boller, 49.

10. Digital History, "The Presidency of Andrew Jackson," http://www.digital history.uh.edu.

1: George Wallace and the "Negro Bloc Vote"

1. "How George Did It," *Newsweek*, June 15, 1970.

2. Dan Carter, *The Politics of Rage* (New York: Simon and Schuster, 1976), 221.

3. Carter, 221.

4. "How George Did It."

5. Phillip Crass, *The Wallace Factor* (New York: Mason Charter, 1976), 81.

6. Crass, 168.

7. Carter, 357.

8. Carter, 357.

9. Carter, 357.

Epilogue

1. Thomas Patterson, *Out of Order* (New York: Random House, 1994), 20.

BIBLIOGRAPHY

"After a Summer of Cool Restraint, North, Robb Start Slinging the Mud." *Washington Post*, October 7, 1994.

Amoss, Jim. *ASNE Bulletin*, March 1992.

Bailey, Michael. "Going After the Ins." *Campaigns and Elections*, June 1999.

BBC News. "Smear Tactics in New York Race," November 2, 1998.

Boller, Paul. *Presidential Campaigns*. New York: Oxford University Press, 2004.

Carroll, Maurice. *Newsday*, September 6, 1988, section 2, 4.

———. "And in This Corner . . . ." *Newsday*, September 6, 1988.

Carter, Dan. *The Politics of Rage*. New York: Simon and Schuster, 1976.

"Chicago History." Roosevelt University, 2003.

Cohen, Adam, and Elizabeth Taylor. *American Pharaoh*. Boston: Little, Brown & Company, 2000.

Conason, Joe. "The Canary." *Salon.com*, October 20, 1998.

Cottman, Michael. "Race Politics." *Newsday*, September 23, 1992, 5.

Crass, Phillip. *The Wallace Factor*. New York: Mason Charter, 1976.

Danese, Tracy. *Claude Pepper and Ed Ball: Politics, Purpose, and Power*. Gainesville: University of Florida Press, 2000.

Dao, James. "Dinkins Gets a Researcher on Giuliani." *New York Times*, October 8, 1993, B4.

Dempsey, Travis. *Harold: The People's Mayor*. Chicago: Urban Research Press, 1989.

Digital History. "The Presidency of Andrew Jackson," http://www.digitalhistory.uh.edu.

Dorf, Matthew. "Jewish Vote May Decide Key Senate Races." *Jewish News*, October 23, 1998.

Douglas, Helen. *A Full Life*. New York: Doubleday and Company, 1982.

Dugger, Celia. "Pissants and Pablum." *Harvard Crimson*, October 27, 1978.

"Edwards Money from LA." *Times-Picayune*, November 25, 1991, A12.

Eisele, John. "Polluting the Air in New Jersey." *National Journal*, November 5, 1988.

"Election of 1972." AmericanPresident.org.

Fineman, Howard, and Michael Isikoff. "Slime Time Live." *Newsweek*, September 20, 2004.

Fong, Peg, and Kim Dixon. "Schumer Races to Early Win." *Third Rail*, November 4, 1998.

Goldberg, Michelle. *Salon.com*, August 1, 2002.

"The GOP's Negative Force." *Washington Post*, November 1, 1994.

Graham, Tim. "What's Worse? Putzhead or Fascist?" Media Research Center, October 30, 1998.

Gugliotta, Guy. *Washington Post*, May 18, 1997.

Hall-Jamieson, Kathleen. *Dirty Politics*. New York: Oxford University Press, 1992.

———. *Packaging the Presidency*. New York: Oxford University Press, 1984.

Harpweek, http://elections.harpweek.com/1864.

"Higher Aspirations from Low Campaign." *New York Times*, April 15, 1990.

Hirsch, Mark D. "Election of 1884." In Arthur Schlesinger Jr., *History of Presidential Elections*.

Hook, Janet. "Campaigns Accentuate the Negative." *Los Angeles Times*, October 17, 2004.

"How George Did It." *Newsweek*, June 15, 1970.

Kaiser, Charles. "The Best Man?" *New York Metro*, October 5, 1998.

Kennedy, J. Michael. "The Cowboy and Good Old Girl." *Los Angeles Times*, October 21, 1990.

Kleppner, Paul. *Chicago Divided: The Making of a Black Mayor*. DeKalb: Northern Illinois University Press, 1984.

Lamar, Jacob. *Time*, November 21, 1988.

Lamon, Ward Hill. *Recollections of Abraham Lincoln, 1847–1865*. Lincoln: University of Nebraska Press, 1994.

Lee, Martin. "Detailing David Duke." Southern Poverty Law Center, 2004.

Lorant, Stefan. *The Glorious Burden: The American Presidency*. New York: Harper and Row, 1968.

Lynn, Frank. "Two Nominees Clash in Race for Mayor with Harsh Words." *New York Times*, September 14, 1989, A1.

Maihafer, Harry J. *The General and the Journalists: Ulysses S. Grant, Horace Greeley, and Charles Dana*. Washington, DC: Brassey's, 1998.

Malcolm, Andrew. "Last Debate Signals Final Stage of Chicago's Acrimonious Democratic Mayoral Race." *New York Times*, February 2, 1983, A10.

Maraniss, David. "Letter from Texas." *Washington Post*, September 18, 1990.

———. "The Texas Two-Step in the Race for Governor." *Washington Post*, October 22, 1990.

May, Clifford. "Lautenberg: Well Liked but Vulnerable." *New York Times,* December 17, 1987, B1.

Milbank, Dana, and Jim Vande Hei. "From Bush, Unprecedented Negativity." *Washington Post*, May 31, 2004, A1.

Mitchell, Allison. "Giuliani Ads Accuse Dinkins of Using Race Issue." *New York Times*, October 6, 1993.

Mitchell, Greg. *The Campaign of the Century*. New York: Random House, 1992.

———. *Tricky Dick and the Pink Lady*. New York: Random House, 1998.

Monticello Newsletter. Thomas Jefferson Memorial Foundation, Spring 2000.

Morris, Roger. *Richard Milhouse Nixon: The Rise of an American Politician*. New York: Henry Holt and Company, 1989.

New York Times. "A Victim's Mantle for Mr. Giuliani," October 7, 1993, A28.

Patterson, Thomas. *Out of Order*. New York: Random House, 1994.

PBS. "The 30-Second Candidate," PBS.org.

PBS Online News Hour. "Louisiana Political Profile," Presidential History, AmericanPresident.org.

Plotz, David. "D'Amatoing D'Amato." Slate.org, October 30, 1998.

Purdum, Todd. "This Time, Race Is a Murkier Issue." *New York Times*, September 19, 1993.

Randall, J. G. "The Unpopular Mr. Lincoln." *Abraham Lincoln Quarterly* 2 (June 1943): 275.

Religious Freedom Coalition of the Southeast. "The Two Faces of Jesse Helms, http://www.tylwythteg.com/enemies/helms/helms.html."

"Robb Attacks Coleman for Abortion Shift." *Washington Post*, October 27, 1994.

"Robb Fires First Volley in War Against North." *Washington Post*, August 26, 1994.

Ross, Shelley. *Fall from Grace*. New York: Ballantine Books, 1988.

Royko, Mike. *Boss: Richard J. Daley of Chicago*. New York: Penguin Books, 1971.

Schwartz, Tony. *The Responsive Chord*. New York: Schwartz Media, 1973.

Social History, http://www.socialhistory.org/Biographies.

Sterba, James. "Texas Race Starts for U.S. Senate." *New York Times*, July 7, 1977.

Stoddard, Henry. *Horace Greeley: Printer, Editor, Crusader*. New York: G. P. Putnam's Sons, 1946.

Summers, Mark W. *Rum, Romanism, and Rebellion: The Making of a President, 1884*. Chapel Hill: University of North Carolina Press, 2000.

Suro, Roberto. "Even for Texas, the Race for Governor Is Rowdy." *New York Times*, September 21, 1990.

Sweitzer, Thomas. "Kill or Be Killed." *Campaigns and Elections*, September 1996, 46.

Thomas, Evan. "The Vets Attack." *Newsweek*, November 15, 2004.

Troxler, Howard. "Jesse Helms' Legacy Is Today's Politicking." *St. Petersburg Times*, August 23, 2001.

Turque, Bill, and Ginny Carroll. "Texas Rough and Tumble." *Newsweek*, February 12, 1990.

"VA Senate Race Features Sex, Lies, God, Patriotism." *St. Petersburg Times*, October 24, 1994.

"Virginia Man Sues North over TV Ad." *Washington Post*, October 22, 1994.

———. August 29, 2001, A21.

Waugh, John. *Reelecting Lincoln*. New York: Crown Publishing, 1998.

Weisberg, Jacob. Slate.org, November 1, 1996.

"Why Dinkins Lost." *Newsday*, November 4, 1993.

Wicker, Tom. "Two Against Tower." *New York Times*, September 11, 1977.

Wikiquote, http://en.wikiquote.org/wiki/edwin_edwards.

"Wilder Endorses Longtime Rival Robb, Climaxing Weeks of High-Level Talks." *Washington Post*, October 22, 1994.

Winkler, Nancy. *The Election of 1872, Grant and Greeley*. Newark: Ohio Public Library.

Woodward, Bob, and Carl Bernstein. *All the President's Men*. New York: Simon and Schuster, 1974.

INDEX

About the Author

KERWIN C. SWINT is Associate Professor of Political Science at Kennesaw State University in Georgia, a campaign consultant, and a political commentator for local and national media. He is the author of *Political Consultants and Negative Campaigning: The Secrets of the Pros* (1998).